CHEESE

A Connoisseur's Guide to the World's Best

CHEESE

*A Connoisseur's Guide
to the World's Best*

MAX McCALMAN &
DAVID GIBBONS

Photographs by David Gibbons

Clarkson Potter/Publishers

New York

Published in the United States by Clarkson Potter/
Publishers, an imprint of the Crown Publishing
Group, a division of Random House, Inc., New York.
www.crownpublishing.com
www.clarksonpotter.com

CLARKSON N. POTTER is a trademark and POTTER
and colophon are registered trademarks of Random
House, Inc.

Library of Congress Cataloging-in-Publication Data
McCalman, Max.
    Cheese: a connoisseur's guide to the world's best /
Max McCalman and David Gibbons.—1st ed.
Includes index.
(hardcover)
    1. Cheese.   2. Cheese—Varieties.   I. Gibbons, David,
1957–   II. Title.
TX382.M354   2005
641.3'73—dc22   2004018932

ISBN: 1-4000-5034-0

Printed in China

Design by Skouras Design Inc.

10   9   8   7   6   5   4   3   2   1

First Edition

CONTENTS

INTRODUCTION

Since I embarked on my career as a full-time cheese man at New York City's Picholine Restaurant over a decade ago, there has been a remarkable explosion in gourmet cheese production and interest. Call it the Great Cheese Revolution. People everywhere have come to realize that cheese can be not only indescribably delicious but also extremely nutritious and satisfying. They've discovered that real cheese—the only kind I care to discuss—is a gourmet artifact to rival any dish concocted by the world's greatest chefs. They've acknowledged that cheese is a great food value, with a far better safety record than the vast majority of other foods.

One impetus driving this revolution is cheese's complementary partnership with that other salubrious fermented delicacy—wine. Cognoscenti increasingly recognize the importance of cheese in providing the gustatory euphoria that wine, by itself, can only suggest. Another important factor is political correctness: on a planet whose resources are growing scarce and whose population is increasingly hungry, cheese remains an amazingly efficient source of nutrition. Furthermore, dairying remains one of the last agricultural enterprises able to sustain the family farm. In our U.S. market, the discovery of fine wines has proceeded at a steady pace over the past quarter century. Now it's cheese's turn. Cheese is finally being lauded as the near-perfect food that it is.

I was lucky enough to be given a role in helping to spearhead America's cheese revolution. Picholine was the first restaurant with a full-time *maître fromager* (me), and it was the first with its own temperature- and humidity-controlled cheese *cave*. The cheese program at Picholine expanded tremendously to the point that it spawned a second restaurant, Artisanal, with cheese as its driving force. This new establishment became the temple of cheese while Picholine remained its shrine. Now, there is a third location—a splendid cathedral—called the Artisanal Cheese Center. The ACC is a depot for the gourmet cheese trade in North America: a full-service importer, *affineur*, and wholesaler as well as a training facility for future *fromagers*. All this is due to the passion, vision, and marketing savvy of our chef, Terrance Brennan, who deserves a medal for the boost he's given to real cheeses.

I'm overjoyed that the past several years have seen so many exciting developments all over the cheese world. In America, with our ever-increasing appreciation of real cheeses, there is a wider range and higher quality of fine table cheeses available every day. Importers and distributors are working hard to move more exceptional product into the country, and we're seeing plenty of authentic European cheeses that were rarely if ever seen in this country four or five years ago. Artisanal cheese production on the domestic front has also improved dramatically. Although European cheeses still set the standards by which all are judged, our "local" cheesemakers have come a long way. Because local demand is smaller and because they don't receive the government encouragement—mostly in the form of price subsidies and marketing assistance—they face greater burdens and challenges in their quest to match the highest European standards. Fortunately, quite a few of them are up to the task.

Much of this is due to the tireless efforts of proponents of real cheeses—organizations such as the Cheese of Choice Coalition, which is an offshoot of the American Cheese Society; Oldways Preservation and Exchange Trust; the Slow Food Movement; and people like the cheese purveyor Debra Dickerson, Dun Gifford of Oldways, the *affineur* Daphne Zepos (currently one of my colleagues at the Artisanal Cheese Center), Roberto Rubino, publisher of the journal *Caseus International*, and Dr. Kathy Donnelly, microbiologist at the University of Vermont, who intervened with the USDA to help prevent the extension of the aging minimum for raw-milk cheeses from 60 to 120 days. Along with the artisanal manufacturers, it is cheese heroes like these who are sustaining the new wave of gourmet indulgence.

The encouraging signs are everywhere—from most of Europe as well as North America. Over the next five to ten years, I expect to see many more improvements in cheesemaking and cheese handling around the globe. From the "just-came-on-board" to the "get-it-while-you-can" to the "please-don't-make-me" varieties, cheese is hot! And we're not just talking fondue here, though there seems to be quite a craze currently in the crock as well, as evidenced by the presence of a fondue pot on just

about every table at Artisanal at high noon one day last August (that's right—*August*). Cheese is here and it's here to stay.

But even with all these fine cheeses coming in to the United States and now being produced on home soil, there is still a lot of mishandling—not to mention erroneous pairing recommendations. I am strongly compelled to speak out against these crimes against cheese. Fine cheeses are still misrepresented by poor examples of their kind—where restaurants serve precut cheese plates straight from the fridge, for example, or private citizens serve their cheeses equally cold (and tasteless), or stores smother their cheeses in shrink-wrapping for days on end till they suffocate. Cheeses that may have had top-tier potential are often improperly ripened or stored, incorrectly aged, poorly wrapped, haphazardly shipped, and/or mishandled in some other way. Cheese has suffered enough. It's time to set things straight!

The final chapter of our first book, *The Cheese Plate,* included detailed listings of some of my favorite cheeses that I expected to be reasonably easy to acquire in the United States. But by the time the book came off the presses, the cheese menu at Artisanal had around 100 new selections that did not fit into the format of the first book; there were also many more for sale at the restaurant's retail counter. We have about 200 cheeses listed in this new book; there are hundreds more worthy of consideration that didn't make the final cut. Not that they didn't uphold high standards—there were some tough decisions. Cheeses are always on the move. If we were to start revising this book tomorrow, its index of cheeses would already have several added and others deleted.

If our first book was a useful introduction to the world's finest cheeses, this one aims to be a standard-bearer. It is not intended to be encyclopedic, but rather a Hall of Fame. (We must admit to the probability that we have missed a great cheese that should have been included.) The selections in this book are determined by my own views, opinions, prejudices, wisdom, and—most important—my palate. As such, they are informed, fact-filled, fun, and useful but, alas, not quite perfect.

What do I look for and what are the basic criteria that might qualify a cheese for inclusion in my Pantheon of Real Cheeses? First, I look for a cheese that is artisanal, ecological, and organic, or comes as close to these qualities as possible. (And unfortunately, too few are strictly organic.) I look for cheeses of outstanding individual character, ones that express the beautiful natural flavors of the milk from which they're made and the pastures in which the animals graze. I look for unique expressions of *terroir* and of local cheesemaking traditions.

By artisanal, I mean a cheese that is handmade, primarily by small independent cheesemakers using traditional methods and employing no shortcuts or adaptations in the name of "modern efficiency." (The only deviations from traditional methods should be ones that preserve the unique character of a cheese and further emphasize its individual qualities.) The makers of real cheese are artisans in the true sense of the word. Their goals are quality as opposed to quantity, individuality and character rather than uniformity.

The classic artisanal cheese is made with unpasteurized milk from a single source, preferably a local herd. It comes from a farm or a small dairy and its rind is not made out of plastic or wax. This doesn't mean that a superior cheese can't be made in a factory and/or from pasteurized milk. Likewise, it doesn't mean that artisanal methods are guarantees of greatness.

If a cheese satisfies the following criteria, I'll at least give it consideration: it's made artisanally and from raw milk (preferably); it's manufactured in a farmhouse (ideally); it is consistently very good or great but not necessarily always the same (I have no problem with variation in a given type, but if the cheese is inconsistent it won't make my final cut).

Availability—or the lack thereof—is much less of a consideration now than it was when *The Cheese Plate* was published. At that time, I was reluctant to include a lot of cheeses that I knew were simply impossible to obtain in this country. Why frustrate our readers by tempting them with what they couldn't have? Another important consideration, as mentioned, is consistency over time. Some of the cheeses selected herein are made by more than one producer. Some of them are spin-offs or imitations of other cheeses that may have longer histories or more impressive pedigrees; yet these "imitators" are made to high enough standards that they're worth singling out. On the other hand, a few of these cheeses are unique—in a class by themselves—which makes them almost impossible *not* to mention. Another consideration is that I'm looking to tap a wide variety of cheese types. And, last but not least, a quality I especially value in a cheese is its affinity for wine pairings.

These considerations have been supported by and large by the feedback I receive from the people to whom I've served cheese over the years. Their opinions and values have certainly influenced my selections and ratings. It thrills me to see a person smile and hear them exclaim "wow!" when they taste a cheese I've recommended. To them it's a great cheese, and I'm taking their assessment into account. The thrill is all the greater when they experience one of those amazing pairings of cheese and wine.

For this book, I've taken a cue from others in assigning each selected cheese a rating on a 100-point scale. Since this is an elite selection, you won't find any cheeses herein that are rated less than a 70. You also won't find any cheeses that score a perfect 100. I hesitate to tackle the philosophical question of whether there is such a thing as a perfect cheese. Nevertheless, you may encounter a few 99s—cheeses that, on a given day, may be pretty close to perfect in my estimation. (Cheeses of character—like human beings, with all their individual quirks—have their good days and bad ones.) I encourage you to enjoy all of my selections, be inspired to seek your own, and remember that the quest for cheese perfection is a rewarding, delicious, and infinite journey.

May the cheese be with us!

—Max McCalman, New York City, January 2005

TASTING CHEESE

If you asked me to name the single most important factor in becoming a true cheese connoisseur, my answer would be tasting as many different cheeses as possible. In my ongoing quest for cheese knowledge, I read a lot and speak to many cheese people. I live and breathe, eat and sleep cheese. I've discovered that not only the opinions but also the purported facts about cheeses are wide-ranging, disparate, and sometimes contradictory. I often find myself disagreeing with conventional wisdom, with what many established experts have written. Therefore, I've come to one resounding conclusion: the best way to learn about a cheese is to examine it carefully and then put it in your mouth. The real experts, it turns out, are the palates of people who taste cheese on a daily basis.

PRINCIPLES OF CHEESE TASTING

Each and every fine piece of cheese has a story to tell. Here are a few basic principles to help you enjoy the full spectrum of what the world's great cheeses have to offer:

- ✦ Almost all fine cheeses have interesting aromas that can be very closely aligned with their flavors—or indeed very different. Many excellent cheeses really stink. Others have aromas so subtle you might not notice them. There may be a surprising lack of correlation between a cheese's aroma and its flavor, both quantitatively and qualitatively. Some of the worst-smelling cheeses taste the best. By the same token, it is not necessarily true that the stinkier the cheese, the stronger its flavor.

✦ Aroma is crucial to our sense of taste. The taste buds, located on the tongue, can only detect four basic flavors—sweet, sour, bitter, and salty (or five, if you subscribe to the Japanese notion of *umami*—the elusive "fifth flavor," which is often described as "savory"). The olfactory system—our smelling apparatus—can sort out something closer to 10,000 different odors. The physiological reason we're able to detect so many flavors is that the nose is connected to the throat at the back of the mouth by a small canal called the retronasal passage. Much of our ability to taste foods is due to "retronasal aroma"—the smells detected through that passage once the food is in our mouths. This is why flavor scientists also frequently refer to taste as "flavor by mouth."

✦ America is a culture that has been out of touch with its nose. Many artisanal cheeses have funky odors, the type we've been conditioned by the personal hygiene, cosmetics, and home-products industries to shun. To enjoy the world's great cheeses, it's important to be receptive to a lot of "funny smells."

✦ Tasting a lot of cheeses and staying attuned to your palate is crucial to developing cheese connoisseurship. There is no substitute for experience and practice.

✦ Among true cheese connoisseurs, patience is a particularly useful virtue. Cheese moves at its own pace. Take your time studying, selecting, buying, and tasting cheeses; you will eventually become an expert.

✦ Fine cheeses can offer a multiplicity of aromas and flavors adding up to a level of complexity comparable to what you'll encounter among fine wines. This interplay of flavors often evolves from the initial impression (the "attack") to a lingering or lasting picture (the "finish"). Allow plenty of time to perceive and contemplate this phenomenon.

HOW TO TASTE CHEESE

The best advice I can give about tasting a cheese is to slow down and pay attention to your nose, mouth, and tongue. Make sure your palate and nose are clear, and be prepared to concentrate. You can taste cheese casually and informally—that is, strictly for pleasure. Or you can take a more formal, "professional," step-by-step, checklist-type approach. Either way is valid. Here are the basic steps in tasting a cheese.

LOOK

Examine the cheese closely. Take a careful look at the rind and note all its textures and colors. Do the same for the interior. Compare it with the standards listed in the corresponding entry in this book. Note any potential faults. Then give the cheese the benefit of the doubt; some cheeses that look bad taste great.

TOUCH

Tap the cheese lightly and/or press on its surface. Give it a firm but gentle poke and try to note its consistency. Also take note of how the blade of the knife or cutting wire slices through it. Is it hard, brittle, meaty, springy, soft, or mushy? Another way of gauging a cheese's consistency is to roll a small piece of it between a thumb and forefinger.

SMELL

To get a good whiff, it's necessary to hold the cut surface of a cheese right up to your nose. You can pick it up with your fingers or use a fork. Before touching any cheese with your hands, however, be sure they are clean and completely odor-free. Even the faintest hint of hand soap, perfume, or cologne can interfere with your ability to appreciate a cheese's smell.

TASTE

Always take a small, very thin slice and let it luxuriate on your tongue, stimulating your mouth and getting all the juices flowing in there. Be sure to note the "attack," the evolution of flavors, and finally the "finish." When tasting, take a small specimen of no more than a teaspoonful—especially if you're unfamiliar with a cheese. (A tablespoon is roughly equivalent to half an ounce; a teaspoon is a third of this.) I find it helps me to concentrate if I close my eyes when I'm tasting a cheese. This is no mere affectation; it really does help me shut out distractions and focus on the cheese. In addition to the taste (sweet, sour, salty, bitter) and "flavor by mouth" (sea breeze, mountain air, piney woods, and hundreds if not thousands of other possible flavors), it's important to take note of the texture or mouthfeel. Is it astringent or drying, mouthwatering, buttery (rich), smooth, crumbly, heavy or light, gooey or runny?

DESCRIBING CHEESE

As is the case with wine descriptions, the language of cheese relies almost exclusively on analogy; that is, "it tastes like caramel" or "it tastes grassy or floral." Many naturally occurring and manufactured smells are evoked to describe wines; the same is true of fine table cheeses. Fruity and nutty, for example, are common descriptions of cheese; yet we know there are no fruits or nuts in cheeses (or at least there shouldn't be).

Physical descriptions of cheeses are much more objective than any attempts to delineate even their most basic flavors. A cheese that tastes salty to me may seem relatively bland to you. My "tangy" may be the next guy's "sour," although we'd probably both agree that the cheese in question possessed a component of acidity. Composite descriptions, qualitative terms, and the most interesting adjectives are all quite subjective. A cheese that is "lush and luxurious" to one interpreter may be a dull blob of butterfat to another. (Of course, in real life, there will be differences of opinion over much finer points.)

I firmly believe it's a mistake to put words in people's mouths when their own perceptions and descriptions can be so much more telling and valid. A strong connection between the nose and taste buds via the brain to the linguistic apparatus is not necessarily an innate human attribute. So here is a "cheese thesaurus" to help you match some descriptors to your cheeses. All of these—and many more—have been conjured at some time or other to describe cheeses.

✦ COLOR: aquamarine, blue, brown, golden, gray, green, greenish, ocher (aka ochre, which is darkish yellow or reddish brown), ivory, orange, orangish, pink, pinkish, purple, purplish, red, reddish, rusty or rust colored, white (chalky, off-white, pure), yellow, yellowish.

✦ COLOR MODIFIERS: bright, bleached, deep, dirty, dull, uneven, uniform, pale, shiny, smudged.

✦ FIRMNESS OR DENSITY: compact, dense, firm, hard, liquid, runny, semihard, semisoft, soft, tight.

✦ TEXTURE: cracking or cracked, crumbling or crumbly, chalky, drying or dry, elastic, fissured, flaky, grainy or granular, greasy, leathery, pasty, resinous, ropey, smooth (satiny), spongy, spreadable, springy, rough, waterless, with holes.

✦ FLAVOR AND AROMA: acidic, ammoniacal, barnyardy, beefy, bitter, bland, burnt, buttery, chalky, cooked, cloves, farmy, floral, fruity, funky, garlicky, goaty, grassy, herbal, meaty, metallic, lactic, moldy, musty, nutty, oily, oniony, rancid, salty, savory (or savoury, using the British spelling), sour (sour milk), spicy, sweaty, sweet, tangy, weedy, woodsy, yeasty.

✦ FLAVOR MODIFIERS (at least partly subjective): harsh, mild, persistent, pronounced, rich, strong, weak.

✦ SUBJECTIVE, QUALITATIVE, OR INTERPRETIVE: bite (or biting), complex, concentrated, elaborate, gentle, insipid, luxurious, loud, obstreperous, opulent, powerful, rich, robust, sharp, simple, sonorous, stout, timid, unctuous, zesty.

PROGRESSION OR SEQUENCE

If you don't have a lot of reference points and haven't mastered the vocabulary, it can be difficult to come up with a compelling description of a single cheese; you're practicing your fledgling connoisseurship in a vacuum. Once you've got two cheeses to compare, however, you can begin to say "A is smoother and milder than B," or "X is drier and saltier than Y." Your pronouncements become more assertive and authoritative. Next you move on to a sequence of three or more cheeses, which is where the real fun begins.

In determining the proper sequence in which to taste cheeses, several factors come into play: the first is strength of flavor, followed by density or firmness and then consistency or texture. You want flavors to progress from mild to strong. For firmness and texture, you want alternation; for example, soft-hard-soft-hard, or smooth-rough-smooth-rough. A plate of all soft cheeses might spell monotony (unless you're guaranteed a tremendous variety and range of flavors); ditto all hard. The main goal is to mix things up, to emphasize variety and alternation. Variety generates excitement; alternation helps highlight and separate different flavors on the palate.

In planning a sequence for a plate or tasting, create a tentative order based on what you know about your roster of cheeses. But don't forget to try the cheeses before finalizing the order. Very often a cheese's stage of ripeness will affect its place in a sequence and necessitate some shuffling.

BUYING AND STORING CHEESE: SOME PRACTICAL ADVICE

KNOW YOUR SOURCES

Staying close to your sources, literally and figuratively, is the most important principle in the food business. If you can't be physically close to your cheese sources, you need to be completely and utterly confident in their shipping, handling, and storage procedures. Due to the logistics of importation, it's not possible to buy all foreign cheeses directly from their *affineurs* or producers. So we deal with importers, brokers, and wholesalers, insisting, to the extent possible, they do the right thing by the cheeses. With the American cheeses we order, however, we deal directly with the farmhouse producers. A lot of valuable information flows both ways.

As a consumer, you can "stay close to your sources" by learning as much as possible about your cheeses and their producers. Just ask your favorite cheesemongers; if they don't have the information handy, they ought to be able to obtain it for you (or at least point you in the right direction). Whether you're at a restaurant, cheese shop, or gourmet deli, try to speak with the person responsible for selecting and obtaining the cheeses. Pick his or her brain for all the facts, opinions, and recommendations they're willing to offer.

CHEESE SERVICE IN RESTAURANTS

Some people first encounter fine cheeses at a gourmet shop, others discover them at a restaurant. Over the past decade, there has been a tremendous upswing in the American market for fine cheeses. In any major metropolitan area, as well as other well-distributed pockets of food and wine connoisseurship, you're likely to find at least one or two retail purveyors of the world's finest cheeses. But true European-style cheese service in American restaurants is still relatively hard to come by. Here are its criteria:

✦ A cheese board with a variety of properly ripened fine cheeses across a broad spectrum of types.

✦ Plates of fresh-cut cheeses served at room temperature with appropriate food and beverage accompaniments.

✦ Pleasant, informative, unobtrusive service. Recommendations—for cheeses, for their progression, and for wine pairings—that fulfill your requests and (hopefully) exceed your expectations.

✦ Accurate, interesting, and relevant information. A *maître fromager* and/or cheese-savvy staff members who know their cheeses and can add a personal touch—with humor—as appropriate.

I'd like to say that at Picholine we set the standard in U.S. cheese service: with fifty or more cheeses on the board *every* day, careful selection and *affinage,* a representative sampling of various cheese types from all of the world's important cheesemaking regions—in a presentation that is well laid out and assiduously maintained. (If a restaurant or shop doesn't take good care of its cheeses, it shows, and that's a shame.)

As a cheese server, I always welcome feedback. As a consumer, you should be encouraged to share your tastes and opinions. When I make recommendations, I want to know whether they were successful. Each palate is different; a young Roquefort may taste strong and salty to one person but relatively bland to the next. (I also strive to add the personal touch by remembering my regulars' preferences.) If I see an opening, I'll inject an anecdote. It's always easier to remember the details—a cheese's name, provenance, and specifications—when there's a story behind it.

CHOOSING A CHEESEMONGER

The first step toward becoming a cheese connoisseur is to pick out a good source of fine cheeses. Find the best cheesemonger convenient to your location and visit regularly. For cheese gourmets, finding a retailer that takes proper care of its cheeses and provides good service is crucial. A good retailer, like a *maître fromager*, realizes that an artisanal cheese is a living thing and treats it accordingly. Thoroughbred cheeses require attention commensurate to their status. I hate to see fine cheeses mishandled, ignored, suffocated, clumsily merchandised, poorly cut, haphazardly served, or badly stored to the point where they misrepresent themselves.

For your cheesemonger of choice, look for the following:

✦ Cheese should be cut to order. A taste should be offered or readily given upon request. If it's refused, leave and go shop elsewhere. The only instance where tasting is impossible is with small to medium-sized cheeses meant to be sold whole, say buttons or small rounds of chèvre; washed-rind delicacies such as Époisses, Livarot, and Munster; or *torta*-style cheeses such as Serra da Estrela, Queso de la Serena, and so forth.

✦ A good selection—broad and wide-ranging, comprising various and diverse types of cheeses from all the cheesemaking regions of the world. That said, I prefer a shop that carries 50 to 100 superb cheeses, caring for them well, to one that carries 500 cheeses and behaves like a supermarket or department store.

✦ The cheeses are well cared for, all prominently displayed and clearly labeled so they are easy to locate and examine.

✦ A well-informed staff, offering advice on selection and storage (as necessary).

✦ The cheeses are sold *à point*—that is, at peak ripeness or in their window of maximum delectability. As a consumer, you certainly shouldn't have to worry about *affinage* (bringing a cheese to its peak) or even storage. Ideally, fine cheeses should be consumed on the day or the evening of their purchase.

✦ The store sells our books. Seriously, though, as I've said before, information is key, and the more cheese literature you read, the smarter you'll be.

HOW MUCH TO BUY

My first piece of advice in this respect is to buy less but buy often. How much to buy is largely a matter of common sense and a function of how you're going to serve your cheeses. For a plate of five to ten cheeses, I recommend between 1 and 1½ ounces of each per person. With a more extensive lineup of, say, fifteen to twenty cheeses—typical for the larger, more formal tastings I conduct—the ration should be no more than ¾ ounce. (With a full ounce of each of sixteen cheeses, each taster could consume a pound of cheese, which is too much.) To determine how much cheese to buy, choose an appropriate serving size according to the occasion, then multiply its weight by the number of people being served and buy that total weight. When it's time to serve, simply divide the cheese up into equal-sized slices or chunks.

PER-PERSON SERVINGS

Always remember that a little bit of real cheese goes a long way! All weights below are per person per cheese so simply multiply by the number of people you expect to serve. For denser cheeses, reduce the portions by as much as $1/2$ ounce. It's better to err on the side of caution and serve smaller pieces.

TASTINGS

5–10 cheeses: $1/2$ ounce

15–20 cheeses: $1/3$ ounce

APPETIZER PLATES

3–5 cheeses: $3/4$ ounce

MAIN COURSES

3–5 cheeses: $1^{1}/4$ ounces

5–10 cheeses: $2/3$ ounce

AFTER-DINNER PLATES

3-5 cheeses: $3/4$ ounce

5–10 cheeses: $1/2$ to ounce

More than 10 cheeses: $1/3$ ounce

ASSESSING A CHEESE

If you're going to spend a considerable number of your hard-earned dollars for a piece of gourmet cheese, you need to able to judge its worthiness. When you buy from a good cheesemonger, the selection process should have already have been performed. Nevertheless, for your own edification, you'll want to examine the cheeses and their labels, wrappers, boxes, and/or rind markings and note the following:

✦ Name, origin, and producer (where exactly is it from and who makes it?)

✦ Type of producer (e.g., is it farmhouse, local dairy or co-op, factory or industrial?)

✦ Status of cheese: is it protected or defined by laws or regulations such as the French A.O.C. or Italian D.O.C. standards? Are there any official seals or symbols on the label, wrapper, or box or stamped onto the cheese itself?

✦ Type of milk (cow, sheep, goat)

✦ Fat content (expressed as "fat in dry matter")

✦ Pasteurized or unpasteurized (I prefer the term "uncompromised") milk

✦ Type of rind (natural/hard, bloomy, washed)

Then, most important, note a cheese's condition. Take a careful look at its outward appearance and check it against the standards in this book. No cheese should appear brittle, bruised, or bumped. With few exceptions—notably the soft-ripened cheeses that will ooze out of their skins when unctuously ripe—it should not have cracks or major indentations. Nor should it be bulging or bloated from lack of air exchange. Soft-ripened, bloomy-rind, or washed-rind cheeses should be moist and radiant on the exterior. Their rinds should be intact. They shouldn't be hardened or dried up; however, they may have some funny-looking, even downright weird, molds growing on them. (Among them is the furry mucor, aka *poil du chat*, "cat's fur" in French.) Molds—unless they're very dark brown or black—are no cause for alarm.

If you spot cheeses in a shop whose wrappers haven't been properly unstuck or that aren't being allowed to breathe, think twice before buying. Some cheeses suffer on the journey from their makers or *affineurs* to their retail outlets. Soft-ripened cheeses are sometimes suffocated in thick plastic wraps. They're thrown in freezers or left unturned for weeks (another sure route to suffocation). Most conscientious producers of soft-ripened and washed-rind cheeses provide packaging that both protects and aerates their product in transit. They pack their smaller, more delicate cheeses in crates for cushioning and breathability. Several makers package their washed-rind cheeses individually in laminated wooden boxes. The cheeses themselves are covered with perforated thin plastic shrink-wrapping—protected but also able to breathe. Plus, the consumer can open the box, take a look at the cheese, and have a whiff without breaking the wrapping.

Thick plastic shrink-wrapping is a red flag for almost any cheese. Hard cheeses are meant to be protected by their rinds. Precut chunks of hard cheeses can take some shrink-wrapping for a limited period before they're sold. I prefer not to see it, though, and certainly softer cheeses can be ruined by it.

CHEESE AND AMMONIA

If a cheese smells of ammonia when you first unwrap it, don't give up on it immediately. Let it air out for a few minutes and up to half an hour. In many cases, the ammonia will simply dissipate. If a cheese remains hard, bitter, and full of ammonia even after it's aired out, then it's dead. So do the decent thing and give it a proper burial.

RIPENESS

Every real cheese is in a constant state of change; it continues to ripen and evolve due to the effects of many different bacteria and enzymes. There is a period, often referred to as a window, when each cheese is at its peak or, in French, *à point*. As a *maître fromager*, I aim to serve each cheese at its peak so it represents itself in the best way possible. A given cheese may pass through as many as six or seven stages of ripeness. Many cheeses have a distinct peak where one would prefer to eat them, but they can also be good to eat at several stages. Certain cheeses seem to undergo miraculous transformations in a short time. (Likewise, they can go bad overnight if they're ignored.) A blue cheese can turn much bluer in a matter of minutes when its molds are suddenly exposed to air after a long hibernation in the cave. A ripening soft or semisoft cheese can melt to a smooth, spoonable, and irresistibly delicious consistency after less than an hour at room temperature.

The softer, fresher, more moist cheeses have narrower windows, usually about a week. They should be supple and creamy, but not runny. Soft and semisoft mold-ripened cheeses ferment from the outside in; if they're nearly as soft in the middle as they are around their outside edges, they're most likely at or close to peak.

The harder, drier, longer-aged cheeses undergo a more gradual ripening process and have broader windows. Young goat cheeses, soft and moist, can be transformed to hard, sharp, and flinty within a matter of weeks or even days. The common denominator of aging is that the aromas and flavors of any cheese become more concentrated.

THE SEVEN DEGREES OF RIPENESS

Degrees of ripeness apply to soft cheeses but are not particularly relevant for the harder, longer-aged ones such as Parmesan, Gruyère, and Romano. You won't ever see those cheeses at Stages 1 and 2, which occurred months ago in the cave, long before they were ready for release. The peak ripeness for fresh goat's milk cheeses, on the other hand, lasts just a few days: you'll see them mostly at Stages 3 to 5—and only occasionally at Stages 2 or 6, when they're underripe and overripe, respectively.

Whenever the question of storage comes up, my first advice is always to eat whatever you buy the same day or the day after. This applies especially to the softer cheeses, and I hope your cheesemonger will offer those only when at peak—that is, Stage 4. Rarely will you find a cheese in a retail store at Stage 1, when it isn't "set." Any cheese should have at least passed its infancy before it left the creamery. But often cheeses do arrive a little too young. And better too young than too old, because once a cheese has passed its peak there is no reversing the ripening. Cheeses shouldn't be sold (or bought) at Stage 2 either, unless you feel sufficiently expert and you have the proper cave to complete the ripening yourself. Ripening is most successful when it's carried out close to where the cheese was manufactured. The ripening phase, however, can only proceed so far before a cheese is released to the retailer or restaurateur. This is the challenge for the *affineur* or ripener: to determine when cheeses are ready for release, that is, *almost* at peak.

Here are the stages:

1. Too young: the cheese is fully formed but not ready to eat—like taking your bread out of the oven when it's still doughy. At this stage of infancy, the cheese won't be close to its ideal consistency when ripe. Many cheeses will be almost still liquid; others will be too firm. Although some cheeses are meant to become very soft, none should be watery; they will require some drying before they can offer anything close to their full flavors. A Taleggio will be very light pink on the outside and firm, with square edges that show no signs of softening. A Banon will feel as if it could spill out of its leaf wrapping if squeezed.

2. Beginning to show character, some flavors starting to emerge. This is as early as we'll see many cheeses, especially any pressed ones, which do pass through a Stage 1 but aren't released until at least this second stage. Some people prefer to eat some cheeses at this stage, before they acquire the round, mouth-filling flavors that make them remarkable and distinct. It's a "nice," tender stage where they can be eaten, but you're better off waiting. Goat cheeses are very moist. Many soft cheeses are spongy or a bit too firm and resistant. The "rind-ripened" cheeses—the ones that ripen outside in—are not soft yet. A Reblochon, for example, is still a bit tight. The *tomme*-style cheeses would seem a little "green" and just a bit wet, although they're not supposed to be released from the dairies until they're closer to peak. In general, the flavors of cheeses at Stage 2 will be one-dimensional or flat.

3. This is the prelude to the symphony; the melody has been introduced, but the deeper, richer harmonies and complexity is still to come. Cheeses at this stage may appear more attractive and tempting than their taste bears out; they have acquired some character but they still look a little too perfect and tight. Texture-wise, a goat cheese such as Sainte-Maure has too much give at this stage; it is still a little too melting or moist to cut properly. A Camembert will have a nearly perfect cylindrical shape; the rind will be completely white and there will be very little if any give when it's pressed lightly.

4. Peak, memorable, exemplary. Get it while you can! The Sainte-Maure would be firm yet still moist. Washed-rind cheeses such as Taleggio and Munster start to smell funky, signaling the glorious flavors that lie within. The triple crèmes will have some gold flecks in their rinds and should feel supple and yielding to light pressure. The farmhouse Cheddars should feel hard but not be bone-dry; a fresh-cut piece should have fruity aromas over a grassy backdrop. A Torta del Casar should have the distinct feel of a firm rind encasing a much softer interior. The smell of the rind of a Torta—and other thistle-renneted sheep's milk cheeses—may be a little sheepy or barnyardy, a little off-putting, but the aroma of the paste should be pleasing and yeasty.

5. Still tasty but past peak. You start to hear some of the minor keys, a hint of sadness in the melody. The Sainte-Maure is hardening. The Lancashire is becoming a bit brittle. At room temperature, the Camembert oozes too easily. The blue in the blue cheese has begun

to dominate the milk flavor. The hard Pyrénées sheep's milk cheeses are becoming harder and drier, and their rinds are becoming a bit dusty. An Époisses has attached itself firmly to the interior of its little wooden box; the top of the cheese is a darker red and its smell is funky. At this stage, the "blush," "smear," or washed-rind varieties tend to liquefy significantly. But in some cases they may remain too firm, which means they unfortunately bypassed Stage 4—their peak—probably due to careless *affinage*.

6. Still barely edible, but definitely fading. An Époisses or other "stinky cheese" may show some putrescence. The Sainte-Maure is chalky with some harshness. At this stage, the appearance of most types suggests overripeness, and whatever faults may have been contained in the milk will come to the fore. A Morbier may be edible in its interior, but its exterior will begin to crack. A Gouda has lost most of its sweetness and become quite salty. Once a cheese progresses past its peak, with the loss of moisture and the continuing breakdown of sugars and proteins, it loses the balance in its flavor profile, and one or another feature becomes dominant.

7. Too far gone, dead, *fuhgedaboudit*! The Sainte-Maure is calcified; the stinkers are unbearable. They collapse, liquefy, and give off ammonia.

Many fine cheeses are sold at different stages of ripeness and are labeled with as many as five age gradations. Some of them—aged Gouda (Goudse Boerenkaas) is a good example—are not at all exciting until they acquire some maturity; all their more interesting flavors and aromas arise as a result of slow, careful aging.

SEASONALITY

Cheeses also vary by season. Traditionally, the best cheeses have been made during summer when the herds graze on fresh outdoor greenery. Nowadays, due to staggered breeding and other so-called modern advances—yes, I'm always a bit wary of "progress" in the cheese world—many fine cheeses are available year-round. Bottom line: the best ones are still dependent on the ancient natural rhythms of the animals and their herders. You can determine a cheese's peak season with a simple calculation taking into account the animals' grazing season and the

amount of time it takes to age. If you know the cows go up to their mountain pastures from May to September and the cheese needs four months to mature, then you can be sure the best cheeses will be shipped from September till January. In this book's entries listing the world's finest cheeses, we provide seasonal notes whenever relevant.

OVERRIPENESS

Telltale signs of overripeness include:

+ Sharpness, rancidity, persistent aromas or flavors of ammonia, "saponified" (soapy) textures and flavors.

+ Excessive aromas and flavors, especially ones that are putrid or decaying and noxious beyond mere barnyard or animal aromas; strong is one thing, rotten is another.

+ Washed-rind cheeses such as Époisses, Munster, and Livarot exhibit excessive bulging, misshapenness, or runniness; they collapse and get completely stuck to their wrappers.

+ Older aged goat cheeses may become too hard, too dry, or too "goaty" in flavor and aroma.

✦ Dryness or graininess, except in a Parmesan or Grana-type cheese; excessive hardness, softness, or saltiness, beyond the standards listed in this book.

✦ Black exterior mold; and blue, green, or gray interior mold except in a blue cheese.

STORAGE

My first piece of advice regarding storage of fine cheeses is —*don't!* Ideally, they should be purchased at or near their peak and eaten while they're still at their best. Otherwise, the ripening process continues and, even under perfect cave conditions, which can be difficult to duplicate at home, they will eventually deteriorate. Why risk it?

There are two atmospheric conditions crucial to cheese storage: temperature and humidity. Cheeses are generally happiest at temperatures of 45 to 60 degrees Fahrenheit, relative humidity of at least 80 percent, and moderate air circulation. If the environment is too cold, they will dry out and crack (cold air holds less moisture); if it's too warm, they'll begin to ooze butterfat, smell bad, and turn mushy.

Cheeses can be stored almost anyplace as long as the temperature is moderate, the humidity is high enough, there is no direct exposure to sunlight, and there is some air exchange without excessive drafts. With about 30 percent humidity and a temperature of around 38 degrees Fahrenheit, your fridge is a harsh and inhospitable environment for cheeses. Any cool, clean, dark, fairly humid place in your house—a corner of the basement, for example—is probably better than the refrigerator. (Suggestion: use a hanging basket for air circulation and to keep the goodies out of reach of household pets and other vermin.) If you do store cheese in the fridge, the best place is in the vegetable drawer, which contains more moisture, especially when there are vegetables or other cheeses in there.

Avoid wrapping any cheese entirely in heavy, impermeable plastic for a significant period of time. This can cause suffocation or spoilage. But to protect exposed paste for short periods, you will need some kind of wrapping. If the cheese is sold in a good semipermeable two-ply-type paper (one side like thin wax paper, the other like thin parchment paper), this is probably the best solution for rewrapping. Otherwise, for short-term storage of larger chunks of hard or semihard cheeses, I recommend covering the cut surfaces with a lightweight plastic cling wrap, yet leaving the rind exposed so the cheese can breathe. Smaller pieces and softer, washed- and bloomy-rind cheeses should be wrapped snugly but not too tightly first in some type of lightly waxed, greaseproof paper such as butcher paper or pastry paper (or even unwaxed parchment paper). On top of that, add a layer of light plastic cling wrap. This protects the cheese, holding in moisture but also creating enough of an air pocket so it won't suffocate, slowing down degradation of the cheese, giving it its own little microcosm. Be sure to change these wrappings every day so the cheese can catch its breath. And finish the piece as soon as possible.

Many washed-rind cheeses such as Livarot, Pont l'Évêque, Époisses, Pavé d'Auge, and Maroilles come in individual boxes wherein they enjoy their own personal biospheres. If a cheese comes in a box, whenever possible it should be kept in it. Open the box first, however, unwrap the cheese, separate it from its wrapper carefully, and replace the wrapper with a clean piece of butcher or pastry paper. Tidiness ensures longevity of cheeses. Used paper that has rubbed up against moist pastes or smeared rinds may bring undesirable molds or bacteria into play. In this case, it's much better to use a fresh, clean piece of paper.

If a moist cheese appears to be wetter on the bottom, always turn it over and store it wet side up to redistribute the moisture. When cutting a cheese that may be stored afterward, always try to minimize the surface area that is exposed, especially with softer cheeses. Even if they're properly covered, cut surfaces will eventually dry out. Whenever you unwrap a cut cheese, be sure to trim off any dried-out surfaces.

IDEAL STORAGE CONDITIONS

Blues: 42–46 degrees; 85–95 percent humidity

Soft ripened: 50–52 degrees; 80–90 percent humidity

Washed rind: 50–55 degrees; 90+ percent humidity

Hard, aged: 55–60 degrees; 80+ percent humidity

STORING BLUE CHEESES

The blues are a separate category unto themselves. To protect them from excessive molding, they're stored at lower temperatures—usually below 42 degrees Fahrenheit. With exposure to air, blues turn progressively bluer and there's no turning back. They generally hold more water and can suffer from drying out—in cold storage or with increased air exposure. This is why they should be wrapped snugly in plastic and/or foil before being put in the fridge. Again, the two-ply paper used by the better wholesalers and retailers is an excellent wrap. If the cheese arrived in it, reuse it, but also cover the entire package with some plastic cling wrap.

EQUIPMENT AND ACCESSORIES

My recommendation is to keep it simple, avoid any fancy accessories or gimmicks, and spend your discretionary income on the cheeses themselves. For equipment, all you really need is several sturdy, sharp steak knives or paring knives for the smaller cheeses and several large chef's, chopping, or carving knives for the larger ones. You'll also need a few cloth napkins for wiping your knives and cutting surfaces.

Other optional accessories include a large wooden cutting board or boards, serving trays, marble slabs, baskets, and an apron. If you're dealing with cheese on a more frequent basis, you'll find that wire-cutters make nice smooth, clean cuts, especially for the moist blues. If you're handling big chunks or wheels of the larger, harder cheeses, you might want to invest in a double-handled "guillotine" knife. But you need to be pretty serious to make this worthwhile.

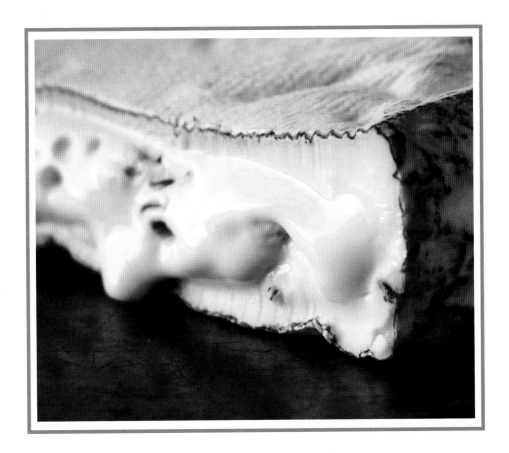

SERVING CHEESE

GENERAL GUIDELINES

- Cheese should always be cut fresh. Exposure to air immediately begins to diminish its charms through oxidation and/or dispersion of its aromas—not to mention drying. The longer you wait, the more you lose. There is simply no substitute for fresh-cut cheeses.

- If you choose to serve leftovers (not recommended), trim them carefully.

- Always serve cheese at room temperature—in the range of 65 to 75 degrees Fahrenheit. Cold diminishes aroma and flavor. Serving cheeses too cold is the most common and worst mistake people make. Take them out of the fridge *at least an hour* before serving.

- Use a separate knife for each cheese or at least for each of the following categories: hard cheeses; fresh white goat's milks; blues; bloomy rinds; and washed rinds, especially the stinkier varieties. Or at least wipe your knife clean after each cut. Here, cleanliness is not simply a matter of appearances; it helps avoid muddling of flavors.

- Slice cheeses into small evenly sized wedges with some of the rind still attached. This may be impossible with crumbly or soft, runny cheeses, so simply try to keep the portions as intact and discreet as possible. This is partly for identification but it also serves as a potential "handle": leaving some rind helps distinguish similar-looking cheeses as well as providing an aesthetic touch—borders and contrasts.

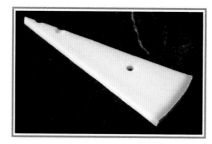

✦ To cut: (1) slice hard cheeses into thin wedges or strips; (2) serve crumbly, hard cheeses in small wedges or chunks; (3) cut soft-ripened cheeses of larger diameter into long, thin wedges; (4) cut smaller soft cheeses and washed-rind ones into small wedges, about $^1/_2$- to $^3/_4$-inch wide at the outer edge.

✦ For a cheese course, use a regular dinner plate unless the course consists of three or fewer cheeses, in which case you can employ salad plates.

✦ Utensils: provide the smaller version of a regular dinner knife or a butter knife. Salad-sized forks may also be offered, especially for eating accompaniments. They're strictly optional for cheese; eating it by hand is *de riguer.*

✦ If a cheese is melting, use a spoon and a separate small crock, bowl, or ramekin, as necessary.

THE CHEESE PLATE

As mentioned previously, the classic progression in any tasting is from simpler to more complex, younger to older, lighter to heavier, milder to stronger. I almost always organize a plate this way, beginning at the bottom—in the six o'clock position—and proceeding clockwise.

ACCOMPANIMENTS

Fine table cheeses should always be capable of standing alone with very minimal accompaniments. This is especially true for a tasting or the cheese plate at the end of a multicourse meal. For lunch or supper, just a handful of cheeses with a few well-chosen accompaniments is enough.

BREAD

This is cheese's oldest and most reliable friend. Down through history, a piece of hearty bread, a chunk of nutritious cheese, and a glass of the local wine, beer, or ale has remained the quintessential meal. For cheese gourmets, a good piece of crusty bread is the ideal complement to fine cheeses and also the perfect scooping device for an unctuous, soft, ripe portion. Also, bread in small quantities is useful as a palate cleanser during serious cheese tasting.

Here are some good bread options:

+ Classic baguettes, sourdough, whole wheat, rye, or olive breads

+ Tuscan rounds or other peasant-style breads

+ Focaccia (plain or with onions, herbs, tomatoes, grapes)

+ Wheat or rye crackers, flatbreads, or thin slices of toast, which provide nice texture contrasts—but they should be fairly neutral in flavor so as not to mask the flavors of the cheeses.

Think in terms of the food-matching principles above, particularly compatibility and balance. Robust cheeses such as Cheddar, Gruyère, or Cantal call for a more flavorful, multigrain, coarser-textured bread. Mild white breads go best with the subtler, more delicately flavored cheeses. Raisin walnut bread goes well with blue cheeses as well as some of the other stronger, saltier types.

FRUIT

The sweet juiciness of fresh fruit provides a fundamental contrast with the dry saltiness of many fine cheeses; try matching figs, apples, grapes, peaches, pears, or melon. Other possible fruit preparations to accompany cheese include dried figs, Catalonian fig tart, plum cake, dates, or quince paste (*membrillo* in Spain), dried apricots, apricot preserve, chutneys, and relishes.

If you're serving a special accompaniment such as a small slice or chunk of quince paste, a ripe fig, dates, a small bunch of grapes, or a dollop of chutney, it can be arranged on the plate alongside the cheeses or, on a more crowded plate of five to ten cheeses, placed ceremoniously in the center. Otherwise, accompaniments should be served separately on the side.

VEGETABLES

Vegetables offer some excellent contrasts with cheeses: crunchy/smooth, raw/fermented, sweet/sour, sweet/salty, juicy/dry, hard/soft, dense/aerated. Here are a few suggestions for cheese-vegetable matchups:

✦ For a large appetizer plate at a luncheon or supper, try fresh vegetables such as carrots, celery, radishes, zucchini, red bell peppers, and green beans (blanched or lightly steamed).

✦ For a snack or light meal, try an old Tuscan favorite—Pecorino and freshly shelled fava beans.

✦ For lunch, try a pickled-vegetable salad or marinated roasted red peppers with cheese and bread.

✦ For an appetizer plate, serve green or black olives with fine cheeses; just check to be sure the stronger-tasting ones don't overwhelm your milder cheeses.

MEATS

Try Italian prosciutto, sorpressata, capicola, or salami; Spanish jamon serrano or chorizo; German Speck; or Virginia ham. But beware of their tendency to overwhelm the more delicate, milder types of cheese.

NUTS

Try almonds, Brazil nuts, cashews, hazelnuts, pecans, walnuts—raw or toasted.

CHEESE AND WINE

As wine experts will tell you, the essential character and personality of a wine is due mostly to two key factors: *terroir* (provenance, or where the wine comes from, including all the details that make up the specific microclimate in which the grapes were grown) and grape variety. Any wine is the expression of its grape variety (or blend of varieties) as grown in a specific place. Great wines reflect their places of origin and have individual character; mediocre or bad wines—often undistinguished blends—have little character and could be from anywhere. Great winemakers are facilitators who bring out the best in grape variety and *terroir* rather than call attention to whatever it is their "art" may add to the wine. Fine cheeses are governed by a similar set of principles, and they have just as many wonderful idiosyncrasies.

Most of the time, people want rules and generalizations that apply broadly and yield foolproof results. Unfortunately, as I've discovered through my research, it doesn't work that way with cheese-wine pairings. I've pursued a detailed inquiry into pairings methodically for several years now and it has turned into a crusade. As I proceed, I've become increasingly convinced that pairings are actually quite specific.

Fine wines tend to retain their essential character traits from vintage to vintage. Yet, for the aforementioned reasons, no two are exactly alike. There are variations, and each subtle difference has the potential to tip the balance from a great match—a "marriage made in heaven"—to a so-so one. Ah, you might say, Max is obsessing; this is splitting hairs. Or maybe he's afraid of exposing his pairings to the second-guessers. On the contrary: I welcome challenges to my pairing advice—keep those cards and letters coming, folks! I also recognize the important role played by another crucial factor: individual preference. My marriage made in heaven may be your honeymoon in hell (or some such variation of a nightmare).

Under the entry for each cheese in the main body of this book, we've listed successful wine pairings, providing the wine's grape variety (or blend) and a reference to its place of origin or appellation. Where it's relevant, we've also listed additional qualities or categorization of a wine; for example Chianti Classico Riserva as opposed to regular Chianti; Vouvray sec versus Vouvray demi-sec; vintage Port as opposed to LBV, ruby, non-vintage, and so forth. In cases where the wine is lesser known, we offer a short phrase of explanation or definition. If you come across a wine called Minervois, for example, you might be stumped. So we add "Syrah-Grenache blend from the Languedoc-Roussillon region of southernmost France" and everything is once again crystal clear.

Our goal is to provide simple, accessible guidelines for purchasing the wines that go best with a given cheese. We strive to be as specific as possible, but we also want to generalize enough to ensure the advice is thoroughly practical and applicable. When you go to the wine shop, it helps to be able to ask for a certain wine category rather than a specific producer and vintage, which may not be so readily available. For example, we might list a wine as "Côtes-du-Rhône red" and in parentheses state the grape varieties, "Syrah-Grenache-Mourvèdre blend." If your wine shop doesn't carry a Côtes-du-Rhône red, there might be a similar or comparable wine from a different region. If there aren't any Syrah-Grenache-Mourvèdre blends from anywhere, then maybe a 100 percent Syrah-based wine would be worth a try.

Don't be alarmed if there aren't more than a few wines listed as potential partners for a given cheese. It doesn't mean I didn't try a lot of wines with the cheese; only that the cheese had limited pairing potential. Some cheeses are naturally wine-friendly, easily finding twenty or twenty-five wine partners; others simply aren't so congenial.

The pairing recommendations contained in this book's cheese-by-cheese listings are all based on tastings I've done either on my own, with colleagues at work, or with students in my cheese seminars. I also sometimes rely on feedback from diners I've served. I record and rank each pairing in my notebook. Many times, I revisit them and revise or reconfirm them. The recommendations are, admittedly, subjective, and conflicts occasionally do arise from one person's palate to the next. Comparing my notes with those of other tasters, however, I've also observed another interesting phenomenon regarding the mystery and miracle of cheese-wine pairings: there seems to be a lot more consensus than there is disagreement.

We encourage you to view these recommendations as guidelines rather than prescriptions, and to experiment with your own pairings. Take them as your starting point for an adventure (or maybe a grand experiment) involving your nose and palate.

CHEESE-WINE PAIRING PRINCIPLES

Although the science of matching wines with cheeses is still in its infancy, I've been able to investigate many potential pairings since we wrote our first book. The caveats and admonishments I voiced in that first effort, however, all hold true:

✦ Cheese-wine pairings can be a tricky, inexact, and, at times, confusing calculus.

✦ Generalizations don't always work (except this one).

✦ Beware of advice from experts; many of them haven't tried the pairings they're recommending and/or are basing them on faulty principles.

✦ Be skeptical of conventional wisdom (e.g., "Red wines go better with cheeses" or "The stronger the cheese, the more complex and robust the wine should be").

◆ My first instinct is to get away from traditional notions about pairings. I like to promote pairings of lesser-known, less "serious" or ponderous but nonetheless delightful wines with cheeses. Savennières, Pinot Blanc, and Albariño are good examples.

◆ Cheese knowledge is gained empirically. Apply the principles that follow, try as many pairings as possible, be bold and experiment, then decide which ones work best for you.

I approach a pairing with an open, inquisitive mind, always bearing in mind, however, that it's often a matter of style and compatibility—or hidden chemistry—that can't be easily explained by simple rules and easy generalizations. Sometimes it seems to me that for every cheese there is a best wine partner, just as for every wine there is a best cheese partner; some cheeses, on the other hand, find many fine partners, while others just don't.

SENSORY RELATIONSHIPS

The primary considerations for successful marriages between cheeses and wines are based on their respective organoleptic profiles, by which I mean the array of sensory impressions they leave in our brains. These impressions include flavors; aromas; textures; sapidities, a fancy word for the depth, length, and persistence of flavor found in a given delicacy (as an example, a well-aged complex-tasting Gruyère has more sapidity than a light, fresh Wabash Cannonball); retronasal tastes, the magical and multifaceted mix of flavors and aromas that occurs at the back of your throat; and temperatures (of course, we assume the temperatures of the cheese and wine will maximize their attractive qualities, but if they aren't right, it can ruin a pairing).

The first relationship we notice in the mouth—and the one that makes cheeses and wines probable partners to begin with—is the one between sweet (fruit/wine) and savory (salty/cheese). To forge a successful partnership, these two elements should be more or less in balance.

The saltier the cheese, the sweeter the wine should be. Again, a classic example of this is the pairing between Roquefort and Sauternes.

The next key factor is the relative acidities or pH levels of the wine and cheese. More often than not, we're looking for a harmonious or complementary interplay there. The more puckering a wine, the better it seems to work with the more acidic cheeses. For example, a tart Crottin de Chavignol melds well with a crisp white Sancerre.

Texture comprises the next important aspect of the dance between cheeses and wines. It can be contrasting or harmonious. For example, a velvety soft-textured cheese may blend more successfully with a lighter, more effervescent wine. Or a more granular cheese may blend best with a more toothsome wine possessing some backbone. Here are two examples of harmony or similarity in texture: a soft, buttery Queso de la Serena blends well with a Blanc de Noir Champagne; and an aged crystalline Appenzeller dissolves nicely into a well-structured red Bordeaux. On the other hand, consider the following two contrasting textural partnerships: an aged granular farmhouse Cheddar will dissolve pleasantly into a smooth-textured pinot noir; and a soft, unctuous washed-rind cheese such as Durrus fits beautifully into the multilayered finery of an Alsatian Riesling.

These first three relationships—salty/sweet balance, harmony of pH levels, and texture—are the ones we most easily recognize. Another potentially important consideration regards the potential presence of umami in the cheese and/or the wine. Regardless of what other qualities they may be lacking, some cheeses seem to be chock-full of umami, to the point where they seem to indicate limitless pairing possibilities. Umami can be described as pungent, meaty, warm flavored, or simply delicious. A number of cheeses

come to mind in connection with this quality: Vermont Shepherd, Époisses, Ardrahan, Queso de la Serena, and Ibores. (And, if you check their respective entries in the pages that follow, you'll find they offer an impressive range of wine-pairing possibilities.) Many wines can be said to possess umami, too—among them well-made, fruity Zinfandels; the finer cru Beaujolais; vintage Champagnes; and well-cellared white Burgundies. This is not to say these wines necessarily afford a huge breadth of potential pairings with cheeses, but that when you do find matchups they will likely be glorious.

What seals the deal for a great match between a cheese and wine, after all the other considerations have been addressed, is the "finish." Just as a wine or cheese alone has a lingering aspect to its flavors and aromas, so does the pairing itself. At times, all other factors may spell synergy but the finish is lousy. A pairing may start out well—or at least inoffensively—but it may deteriorate fast. The wine may have been lovely

and the cheese may have been excellent, but they are simply not meant for each other. The relationship gets off on the right foot but then it becomes muddled, begins to signal off flavors, and eventually becomes distasteful—sometimes even disastrous. If all the other pairing considerations are in place, then it's in the finish where the thrills occur. Often an entirely new and different flavor/aroma sensation than what was apparent in the initial combination can emerge. And if the cheese and wine do meld all the way to the finish—and especially well *at* the finish—then you have a chance for a cheese-wine epiphany. For this reason, it pays to take time to savor and contemplate a pairing so you're able to judge its true measure.

VARIETALS

I've noted an interesting tendency for a given grape varietal—across different appellations and vinification methods—to marry consistently well with a given cheese. After ease of identification, this is the main reason we clearly indicate grape varieties alongside wine names in the pairings recommendations throughout the book.

BALANCE

Neither partner should overwhelm the other. Certain wines—as well as certain cheeses—are simply too complex and overpowering, their flavors are simply too hefty and voluminous to be enjoyed any way but on their own. Strong, salty cheeses such as blues most likely require a concentrated wine with a generous dose of sweetness—either inherent in the fruit of the wine or in what is known in the wine trade as "residual sugar," left over from the fermentation process—to achieve a balance. Perfect balance can be difficult to achieve. When you find it, you'll know it.

KEEP IT SIMPLE

If you've got a complex cheese, try to pair it with a simpler wine, and vice versa. Two multifaceted partners probably won't go together and may even clash. A cru red Burgundy—complex, subtle, and sublime—for example, would probably pair best with a good, straightforward, British farmhouse traditional such as a Cheddar, Lancashire, or Caerphilly. Likewise, a first-growth Bordeaux would call for a full, buttery Vacherin Fribourgeois or a Pyrénées cow's milk cheese such as Le Moulis. Washed-rind delicacies such as Munster or Époisses should work well with a brighter white wine such as the Viognier-based Château-Grillet, Alsatian Riesling, dryish Muscats, or spicy Gewürztraminers.

SIMILARITY AND CONTRAST OR COMPLEMENT

Successful pairings consist of partners that not only balance each other but also provide mutual complement. This blissful, harmonious, balanced state of affairs can be achieved either through compatibility (similarity) or difference (contrast). Choose wines and cheeses that are similar *or* different—for example, spicy cheeses and spicy wines, fruity-tasting cheeses and fruity wines *or* salty cheeses and sweet wines, fatty

cheeses and acidic wines. (And with contrast, always be mindful of balance.) Under this category fall many traditional pairings that continue to make a lot of sense. Blue cheeses are often paired with sweet, thick dessert-type wines for contrast and balance; two classic examples are Sauternes with Roquefort or tawny Port. Buttery cheeses such as triple crèmes can pair well with tannic or acidic wines; the acids and/or tannins of the wines balance the creaminess of the cheeses, allowing the wines' fruitiness to shine. Reblochon, for example, a mild creamy mountain cheese with a satiny smooth paste and refreshing fruity flavors, pairs well with a bright, fruity young wine such as Beaujolais.

REGIONAL PAIRINGS

Pairings of local wines with local foods frequently yield harmonious marriages. In searching for successful matches, they would often be the first ones I might attempt—the ones I'd expect might yield interesting synergies. In theory, regional pairings should work well with cheese, but it's not always the case; it pays to investigate. The best matches often occur between "lesser" (i.e., not world-class) regional wines and local cheeses. Here are some successful "local pairings" that can delight the palate:

 ✦ Hard apple cider with the cheeses of Normandy such as Pavé d'Auge and Livarot.

- Fine hand-crafted Belgian or northern French beers and ales with the northern French, Belgian, and Dutch cheeses.

- Loire Valley goat cheeses such as the classic Selles-sur-Cher or Crottin de Chavignol pair extremely well with the famous local white wine Sancerre.

- Munster with Alsatian wines: Gewurztraminer, Pinot Blanc, Riesling, and Pinot Gris.

- Champagne and Langres; the Ossau-Iraty family of cheeses and Madiran; Fontina D'Aosta and a fine northern Italian Chardonnay; Serra da Estrela and Port.

DON'T BE AFRAID TO EXPERIMENT

My cheese-tasting and pairing advice always contains recommendations to explore new and different avenues whenever possible. Don't fall into the proverbial "I'll have a glass of Chardonnay" rut. A tip on pairings: try the "variation on a theme" approach—think of a pairing you've enjoyed in the past or one recommended by a trusted expert, then find a similar or related wine to substitute. For example, if you're looking for a pairing with Queso de la Garrotxa, the rustic Catalonian goat's milk cheese, and you know from experience that it marries well

with a Meursault, the superior white Burgundy, why not try it with another classic Chardonnay-based wine—an elegant, sparkling, dry Blanc de Blancs Champagne? Take this approach and you're sure to discover some unconventional yet highly successful marriages.

MISMATCHES

Some pairings simply fall flat or create "off" flavors. You'll recognize this right away—like the clang of a wrong note in a beautiful Mozart sonata. Failed pairings often manifest themselves with that pronounced metallic taste you've probably experienced if you've ever tried to combine red wine with a mouthful of spinach or asparagus. Other times, either the wine or the cheese will bring out some unattractive characteristic of its partner or amplify a trait that doesn't need it. As you explore different pairings, some of them unconventional, you're bound to come across a few real clunkers. Pairing theory doesn't always account for all of the successful—nor unsuccessful—matches.

What is important in all this cheese-and-wine chatter is that when cheese-wine combinations are pleasing, which they are in many cases, everybody is happy. But when they aren't so good, people tend to blame the cheese for the mismatch. If the cheese and wine are not meant for each other, as indicated either right out of the gate or at the finish, then so be it. It may have been a very fine wine and an equally fine cheese, but they're simply incompatible. (So please don't blame the cheese, because cheese has suffered enough.)

TASTING WINES WITH CHEESES

First, you should try each partner separately to get a sense of their individual traits. I generally recommend tasting the wine first since the cheese most often leaves the strongest impression on your sensory receptors. Once you have a sense of each partner on its own, take a moderate-sized bite of cheese and, as soon as its flavors fill your mouth, crumble some of it up against the back of your front teeth and take a sip of wine, creating a nice little sauce or stew in there. Savor the combination, take some time to consider it, then swallow and reflect.

One important additional point: be sure to present both the cheese and the wine at their optimal temperatures. Cheese, as previously mentioned, should always be served at room temperature. And wines should be offered at their recommended serving temperatures: reds at a bit below room temperature (around 65 degrees Fahrenheit); whites at somewhere between 45 and 60 degrees Fahrenheit (the sweeter wines cooler, the drier ones a bit warmer); and Champagne chilled to around 45 degrees Fahrenheit.

VERSATILE WINE PAIRINGS

Two of the more versatile red wines for matching with cheeses are the zinfandels and those made from the gamay grape. Cabernet Sauvignons and Amarone della Valpolicellas are close runners-up. My top whites in terms of versatility are Chenin Blancs, various styles of Muscat, Rieslings, and Sauvignon Blancs. Dessert wines are an old standby; their sweetness works nicely to contrast and balance the saltiness of cheeses, particularly the stronger types.

In general, the red wines with the most versatility for pairings are the fruitier, less dry ones. You'll find many more pairings in the "simple wine" category; the famous, *grand cru*, high-pedigree wines are generally more complex, potentially finicky and therefore more difficult to match. For example, a Dão wine from Portugal is a very satisfying red, a good value, nothing to be scoffed at, and an excellent potential partner for many cheeses. Beaujolais is another example; it is up front, a little fruity, and very versatile. In choosing any one of these "nonpedigree" wines, however, make sure you select the top of its category—for Beaujolais, choose a Moulin-à-Vent or a Morgon. Generally, the better quality the wine, even if it's a humble or rustic type, the more likely the success of pairings. (Remember, we're talking about quality as opposed to subtlety or complexity.) I've actually discovered more of those elusive "marriages made in heaven" with white wines than with reds. That is not to say many cheeses don't work better with reds, only that the truly thrilling pairings occur more with whites than reds.

As a general rule, white wines seem to be more successful partners for cheeses than reds. This is not to say there aren't plenty of cheeses that do favor red wines. In those cases, I usually find at least one or two good pairings. But overall I've been more impressed with the quality and

quantity of white wine matchups.

The relative pairing success of whites is partly due to the presence of tannins in the reds that can clash with the fermented milk in the cheese. (Think about it: fermented grape juice and soured milk . . . you have to figure it would be a dicey combination.) The whites generally tolerate complexities in the sensory profiles of cheeses more gracefully than reds. Whites can offer the fruitiness, sweetness, the relative acidity, the texture, some umami perhaps, and sufficient "presence" to complement their cheese partners. And they can do it without the potential for conflicts inherent in the "stronger" or more "aggressive" reds. In most cases, we drink white wines before reds. This is because they are usually less complex or "strong" than reds. To start with stronger, more complex wines—with their larger organoleptic profiles— would diminish the enjoyment or appreciation of the milder wines. The same principle applies to cheeses: you may miss the subtleties and nuances in the milder ones if you start with a big bang.

One potential advantage of cheese-wine pairings—and in particular of the compatibility of white wines with cheeses—is that a cheese course can allow diners to "go back" to a white wine after drinking a red with their main course. Furthermore, the fact that cheeses and white wines are often so compatible may encourage the large percentage of wine drinkers who much prefer reds (there are many people—wonderful people—who will *only* drink reds) to take a chance and try a white wine with some cheese.

An interesting corollary of this discussion is that pasteurized cheeses seem to find better pairing success across a broader spectrum of wine types than raw-milk cheeses. (It seems the raw-milk cheeses have a narrower tolerance for inappropriate wine partners.) Pasteurized cheeses have less depth and complexity of flavors and aromas due to the destruction of many of the aromatic esters in the milk, and this actually seems to enhance their pairing potential. They still have the salt to balance the sweet fruit in the wine; and they still have acidity that offers potential harmony with the wine's acidity. Their textures, though somewhat plasticized through heat treatment, can still correspond

appropriately with a wine's mouthfeel. Their simpler retronasal profiles are less likely to muddle the finish with the wine.

On the five-point scale I employ to rate cheese and wine pairings, from a "plus two" (the top rating) to a "negative two" (the worst rating), I find the pasteurized-milk varieties afford many "plus ones," few "negative twos," and many "zeroes," which means the pairing is fairly neutral—that is, "only okay" or possibly "not bad" if it's the only cheese and wine I have to work with. The "plus two" pairings do happen, if infrequently. When you find them, they're worth noting and remembering for the next time you want to impress your date. Pasteurized cheeses offer some "plus twos." There are more "plus twos" to be found with white wines than reds, and there are plenty among the wines that have more fruit and/or residual sugar, particularly the dessert wines. (Note: This five-point scale is the one I use in recording my own tasting notes for pairings; it does not relate to the six-point strength ratings or one-hundred-point quality ratings applied to the cheeses alone.)

MARRIAGES MADE IN HEAVEN

Here is a selection of what we believe to be the finest wine pairings for the cheeses in this book:

AFUEGA'L PITU
Ribera del Duero

AMARELO DA BEIRA BAIXA
Dulce de Monastrell

L'AMI DU CHAMBERTIN
Sauternes

APPENZELLER
Late-harvest California
Chardonnay
Grüner Veltliner

ARDRAHAN
California Chardonnay
Muscat de Rivesaltes
German Muskateller Kabinett

AZEITÃO
Barbera d'Asti
Bonnezeaux or Quarts de
Chaume
LBV Port

BANON
White Burgundy

BEAUFORT
White Burgundy
California Pinot Noir
Northern Rhône red

BEENLEIGH BLUE
Beaujolais cru
Muscat de Rivesaltes
Sauternes
Hungarian Tokaji
California Zinfandel

BERKSWELL
Red Burgundy
Malvasia Delle Lipari
Ribera del Duero
German Riesling Spätlese
Sauternes
California Syrah-Mourvedre-
Grenache blend

(QUESO DE LOS) BEYOS
New Zealand Sauvignon Blanc
Sherry (Oloroso)

BLEU DES CAUSSES
Beaujolais

BLEU DE GEX
Sauternes

BLEU DE TERMIGNON
California Zinfandel

BONDE DE GÂTINE
Pouilly-Fumé
California Sauvignon Blanc
Vouvray sec or demi-sec

BOULETTE DES AVESNES
White Burgundy

BRIN D'AMOUR
White Burgundy
Alsatian Riesling

CAERPHILLY
Northern Rhône Syrah
Vouvray sec

CASHEL BLUE
   Late-harvest California
      Chardonnay

CENTOVALLI TICINO
   Australian Shiraz

CHABICHOU DU POITOU
   Alsatian Pinot Blanc
   Tawny Port
   New Zealand Sauvignon Blanc

CHAOURCE
   Champagne (Blanc de Noirs)

CHEDDAR
   Red Bordeaux
   Rhône reds (Syrah)
   LBV Port

CHESHIRE
   Moscato d'Asti
   Pouilly-Fumé

CHEVROTIN DES ARAVIS
   Moscato d'Asti
   Sauternes
   Vouvray demi-sec

COOLEA
   California Zinfandel

DODDINGTON
   California Chardonnay
   California Merlot

DURRUS
   German Riesling Auslese
   Sauternes

ÉPOISSES
   Sauternes

(QUEIJO) EVORA
   Chianti Classico

FIUMORBU BRÉBIS
   Sauternes

FONTINA D'AOSTA
   Minervois

GAMONEDO
   California late-harvest Pinot Gris
   Sherry (Pedro Ximénez)

(QUESO DE LA) GARROTXA
   White Burgundy
   Ribera del Duero
   Alsatian Riesling

GORGONZOLA
   Dulce de Monastrell

HARBOURNE BLUE
   Bonnezeaux
   German Gewürztraminer Spätlese
   Moscato d'Asti
   Hungarian Tokaji

HOCH YBRIG
   German Riesling Auslese

IBORES
   German Riesling Spätlese
   Alsatian Riesling

KRÜMMENSWILER
FÖRSTERKÄSE
Amarone della Valpolicella
Tokay Pinot Gris

LANCASHIRE
Grüner Veltliner

LIVAROT
Alsatian Gewurztraminer

LLANGLOFFAN
Rhône Syrah

MAHÓN
Tawny Port

MIMOLETTE
Carignan

MONT ST. FRANCIS
Pouilly-Fumé

MONTASIO
Barbaresco

MONTE ENEBRO
Dulce de Monastrell
Muscat de Rivesaltes
Sauternes

LE MOULIS (CHÈVRE)
Beaujolais cru
Moscato d'Asti

OSSAU-IRATY BRÉBIS
Pouilly-Fumé

PAVÉ D'AUGE
Red Bordeaux
California red Bordeaux-style
blend
Champagne (Blanc de Blancs)

PECORINO TOSCANO
California Merlot

PÉRAIL
Beaujolais cru
Red Bordeaux
Northern Rhône red (Syrah)

PERSILLÉ DE TIGNES
Beaujolais cru

PIAVE
Amarone de Valpolicella
Sauternes

PIERRE-ROBERT
Red Bordeaux

PRÄTTIGAUER
Muscat de Rivesaltes

REBLOCHON
German Riesling Kabinett

RED HAWK
Syrah (from the Languedoc)

ROBIOLA DI LOMBARDIA
Alsatian Riesling

ROBIOLA A TRE LATTI
Amarone della Valpolicella
Periquita-Tempranillo blend

RONCAL
California Sauvignon Blanc
Ruby Port

ROOMANO
Red Bordeaux

ROQUEFORT
Sauternes

ROUCOULONS
Grüner Veltliner

SAINT-FÉLICIEN
Vouvray sec or demi-sec

SAINTE-MAURE DE TOURAINE
Pouilly-Fumé
Savennières

SBRINZ
Barbera d'Alba
Champagne (Blanc de Noirs)

SELLES-SUR-CHER
White Bordeaux
White Burgundy
California Sauvignon Blanc

(QUESO DE LA) SERENA
California Cabernet Sauvignon
    blend
Tawny Port
Ribera del Duero
German Riesling Kabinett

SERPA
White Bordeaux
Rioja

(QUEIJO) SERRA DA ESTRELA
Vintage Port
Vouvray sec

SPENWOOD
Red Burgundy
Northern Rhône red
Rioja

STANSER RÖTELI (AKA
INNERSCHWEIZER WEICHER)
Moscato d'Asti

STANSER SCHAF REBLOCHON
(AKA INNERSCHWEIZER
SCHAFKÄSE)
Alsatian Gewurztraminer
Sauternes

STANSER SCHAFKÄSE
Moscato d'Asti
Late-harvest Muscat from the
    Languedoc

TALEGGIO
Barbaresco or Barolo
Muscat de Rivesaltes

TAUPINIÈRE
Sauvignon Blanc from the
    Languedoc

TORTA DEL CASAR
Rhône Valley reds (Syrah blend)
Sauternes

TUMALO TOMME
  Alsatian Pinot Blanc

URNER ALPKÄSE
  Tawny Port

VACHERIN FRIBOURGEOIS
  Red Bordeaux
  California Merlot
  Moscato d'Asti
  German Muskateller Kabinett
  Alsatian Riesling

VACHERIN MONT D'OR
  Champagne (Blanc de Blancs)
  Southern French Syrah

VAL BAGNER
  Moscato d'Asti
  Alsatian Riesling

VALDEÓN
  Beaujolais cru
  Late-harvest California Chardonnay

VERMONT SHEPHERD
  Red Burgundy
  Champagne (Blanc de Noirs)
  California Pinot Noir
  California Syrah
  California Zinfandel

WILDMANNLI
  California Chardonnay

ZAMORANO
  California Zinfandel

THE CHEESES

AARAUER BIERDECKEL

(ah-rauw-er BEER-deckle) This cheese, also known as Kuentener (alternate spelling Küntener), has a distinctive musty aroma somewhat similar to other washed-rind cheeses, the differences I'm sure being accounted for by the fact that it's washed in unfermented wheat beer and not marc or some more commonly used solution. The taste is moderately sour, sturdy, and substantial, with a pleasing tinge of bitterness—again very likely due at least in part to the beer washings. Texture-wise, this cheese is akin to a Taleggio: semi-soft, creamy, and supple. In terms of its expansive flavors and pleasant lingering finish, it has been compared with Epoisses; it can be quite salty and rich yet it maintains admirable balance. All this said, the Aarauer is really a unique cheese that, interestingly, seems to tolerate few wine partners. A *bierdeckel,* by the way, is Swiss parlance for one of those coasters (usually made from cheap cardboard) you get underneath your beer glass in traditional taverns and restaurants.

TYPE: Raw cow's milk.

PROVENANCE: The village of Kuenten, Canton Aargau, north-central Switzerland.

PRODUCER: Made and ripened by Sepp Brulisauer.

PRODUCTION: From the milk of several local herds of Red Swiss cows. Traditional artisanal production; the cheeses receive a salt bath and are lightly pressed before being placed in a ripening cellar for 4 weeks where they are washed regularly in unfermented wheat beer.

APPEARANCE: A smallish drum with rounded edges 4$\frac{1}{2}$ inches in diameter and 2$\frac{1}{4}$ inches high. The rind is beige to light reddish brown, thin, smooth, moist, and sticky. The paste is more yellow and firm with occasional very small irregularly shaped holes.

SIMILAR CHEESES: Bergues, Fiumorbu; also original Belgian abbey cheeses such as Chimay.

SEASONAL NOTE: Spring and summer cheeses are the tastiest.

WINE PAIRINGS: A difficult partner for reds, the Aarauer Bierdeckel tolerates several whites and some sweeter wines.
WHITE: Alsatian Pinot Blanc; California Sauvignon Blanc; Vouvray sec (Chenin Blanc).
RED: Beaujolais (Gamay).

SPARKLING: California Champagne-style cuvée (Chardonnay).
DESSERT/FORTIFIED: Moscadello di Montalcino (late-harvest Moscatel from Tuscany); Tawny Port.

RATINGS

QUALITY

90

STRENGTH

5

ABBAYE DE BELLOC

(ah-BAY duh Bell-OCK) Never a braggart, this ancient cheese is smooth, reliable, and endlessly satisfying. It is abbey-made and belongs to the Ossau-Iraty Brébis A.O.C. category of cheeses. They are the Pyrénées region's answer to the great Alpine cheeses Beaufort and Comté. Abbaye de Belloc features a semihard paste with a fairly dense, concentrated consistency. Its flavors are deliciously smooth, buttery, and nutty with sweet, fruity, lactic tones and a graceful finish.

TYPE: Pasteurized sheep's milk.

PROVENANCE: Ossau-Iraty Brébis Pyrénées A.O.C., southwestern France, along the Spanish border.

PRODUCER: Farmhouse-style cheese from the Abbaye de Belloc, a Benedictine abbey that has made and matured this cheese for centuries.

PRODUCTION: The great Pyrénées sheep's milk cheeses are all made by essentially the same recipe, one that is more than 3,000 years old; therefore, their differences reflect *terroir* and ripening conditions.

APPEARANCE: 8-pound millstones, 8$\frac{1}{2}$ inches in diameter and 3 inches high with rounded edges. The rind is mottled with spots of brown, gray, and white, and it displays a cross-hatch pattern. The paste is smooth, semihard, and bone-colored.

SIMILAR CHEESES: Berkswell, Le Moulis (sheep version), Spenwood, Vermont Shepherd, Zamorano.

SEASONAL NOTE: Best eaten August through May.

WINE PAIRINGS: A versatile partner for a broad range of wine types, a quality which is typical of fine aged sheep's milk cheeses.
WHITE: White Bordeaux (Sémillon-Sauvignon Blanc blend); white Burgundy (Chardonnay); German Riesling Kabinett; California Sauvignon Blanc.
RED: Carignan; Sancerre Rouge (Pinot Noir); California Zinfandel.
DESSERT/FORTIFIED: Sherry (Pedro Ximenez).

RATINGS

QUALITY

79

STRENGTH

2

ABONDANCE

(ah-bohn-DAHNCE) One of the medium-sized A.O.C. cheeses of the French Alps and a great example of artisanal skill. Abondance dates back nearly 700 years and originated in the abbey of the same name. Since it's in the middle of so much superlative cheese production (the Rhône-Alpes region east of Lyons), Abondance is easy to overlook; but that would be a mistake. You can almost smell the clean, crisp mountain air, and you can certainly taste the fresh milk. With proper aging, the Abondance is simply an amazing cheese. Its flavors are delightfully fruity and sweet, mildly sour, and reminiscent of wildflowers. While similar to Comté, the farmhouse versions of Abondance are richer and deeper in flavor.

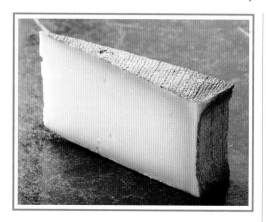

TYPE: Raw cow's milk.

PROVENANCE: The Abbey of Abondance in the Haute-Savoie region of the Rhône-Alpes, east of Lyons, France, and west of Lake Geneva.

PRODUCERS: There are approximately 70 farmhouses, 18 dairies (*laitiers*), and eight *affineurs* that produce genuine A.O.C. Abondance. The farmhouse versions are the ones to buy. Recommended raw-milk producers are as follows. *Fermiers:* GAEC Mont Chauffé; L'Alpage; SCEA Barbossine; SCEA Grillet Aubert. *Laitiers:* Fromagerie Chabert; Fromagerie Seignemartin; Lactalis; SCA Les producteurs de reblochon de Thônes; Societé Laitière des Hauts de Savoie. *Affineur:* Fromagerie Joseph Paccard.

PRODUCTION: Made from the milk of the Abondance, Montbéliarde, and Tarine breeds of cows. The curds are scalded and pressed. The cheeses are ripened for a minimum of 4 months with regular washings and rubbings of salt. The blue casein label is a sign of authenticity—oval for *fermiers* (farmhouse) cheeses and square for *laitiers* (creamery) ones.

APPEARANCE: Medium to large wheels about 15 to 17 inches in diameter and up to 3¼ inches thick that weigh from about 15 up to 26 pounds (the farmhouse cheeses tend to be the smaller ones). The wheels are very smooth and even on the surface with a beautiful concave curvature to their rounded edges. The rind is hard and orangish beige or amber in color with dustings of white mold. The paste is yellowish ivory in color, dense, smooth, and semihard with occasional holes and/or small fissures.

SIMILAR CHEESES: Beaufort, Comté, Vacherin Fribourgeois.

SEASONAL NOTE: Best September through January.

WINE PAIRINGS: Stands up well to reds that aren't too stout.
RED: Aglianico del Vulture (concentrated, complex, tannic, and fruity red of southern Italy); California Merlot; Periquita blend (Portuguese red with Tempranillo, Syrah, and Merlot); Super Tuscan blend (Sangiovese and Merlot).

RATINGS

QUALITY

90

STRENGTH

3

AFUEGA'L PITU

(ah-FWAY-ghael pee-too) The name means "fire in the throat" in the Asturian dialect and refers to the fact that due to its concentrated paste, it feels as if it might stick to the back of your throat. (According to legend, it was given to hens as a test: if it stuck in their craw it was deemed mature and ready to eat.) Young Afuega has a milky and mildly acidic flavor. It is semisoft, smooth, delicate, quite dense, and has a stimulating, slightly granular mouthfeel. A ripe Afuega certainly lights a fire in you—not to mention its raunchy smell—and I recommend it for people who like a powerful cheese with a lot of character. With age, it becomes piquant and astringent on the palate and may even taste a bit musty. Its paste should always feel slightly firm; once it starts to go soft, it's probably overripe. Ditto if the rind starts to turn distinctly reddish. Afuegas can be variable, which makes for the "love-hate" disclaimer. The red version (see "Appearance" below) is one that can be loved; the white, merely liked. The red Afuegas must be set—that is, firm and moist. If they're very wet, beware, because it may turn out to be more than you bargained for. This cheese is unusual enough without that extra challenge!

TYPE: Raw or pasteurized cow's milk.

PROVENANCE: Central Asturias, in the region around the town of Grado, near Oviedo, on the north coast of Spain.

PRODUCERS: Small local farmhouse and artisanal manufacturers.

PRODUCTION: Made year-round from uncut, unpressed curds formed by lactic coagulation, the gentlest, least "intrusive" treatment of the milk. Some of the cheeses are shaped the old-fashioned way—that is, by hand inside a piece of cloth that clearly leaves its mark on the rind. Aged from 2 weeks to 50 days.

APPEARANCE: There are two principal forms of Afuega: one a truncated cone and the other an irregular, somewhat asymmetrical globe shape. The former is shaped in molds; the latter in cloth bundles. There is also a version that is treated with paprika (*pimentón*) and turns orangish red as a result; it is also known as Rojo del Áramo (ROH-hoh del AH-rah-moh) after the mountain range where it's produced). Most Afuegas are about 4½ inches in diameter and 1½ inches high and weigh about 1 pound. I prefer the more rustic, traditional or artisanal globe-shaped Afuegas. The Picos de Europa, my favorite brand, weighs less (10½ ounces). Regular Afuegas have an ivory white paste that turns to orangish yellow with age.

RATINGS

QUALITY

79

STRENGTH

5

(continued)

SIMILAR CHEESE: Queso de los Beyos is somewhat similar, but really there's nothing quite like Afuega.

SEASONAL NOTE: Spring through fall.

WINE PAIRINGS: Afuega is primarily a red-wine cheese; it shatters most whites.

WHITE: Alsatian Riesling.

RED: Barbaresco (Nebbiolo); Côtes-du-Rhône red (Syrah-Grenache-Mourvèdre blend); red Bordeaux (and other predominantly Cabernet Sauvignon blends); Pinot Noir (red Burgundy or California); California Merlot; Beaujolais cru (Gamay); Ribera del Duero (Tempranillo blend).

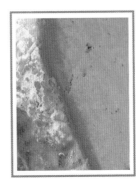

AISY CENDRÉ

(ay-SEE son-DRAY) Aisy Cendré is a delectable, rustic, washed-rind cheese from Burgundy. Its ash-covered rind may be unattractive to some, and it's usually more appealing to the taste with most of the ash shaken or lightly brushed off. Appearance does count: this cheese's orange-yellow, soft, glowing paste offers a pronounced visual contrast to its brownish gray rind. Aisy Cendré is similar to Époisses—a good specimen is equally delicious and it provides comparable wine-pairing potential. The ash covering, which gives the cheese a rustic appearance, is supposed to soak up some of the slime you'll find on your typical Époisses-type cheese, but I've encountered some Aisys whose rinds are quite muddy. (They definitely call for a napkin vis-à-vis handling them!) A ripe Aisy features a delightfully smooth, creamy interior; its flavors can be quite powerful and salty.

TYPE: Cow's milk.

PROVENANCE: Burgundy, the Auxois region to the northwest of Dijon.

PRODUCER: Berthaut.

PRODUCTION: Soft ripened, washed rind. The ash is applied after the washings have allowed the *B. linens* bacteria to work its magic and is designed to help control and mellow the ripening process.

APPEARANCE: A disk or shallow drum, up to 4³/₄ inches in diameter and 1¹/₂ to 2¹/₂ inches high, weighing about 9 ounces. It has a slimy orangish washed rind (à la Époisses) that is covered with grayish brown ash. The paste is very smooth and cream-colored.

SIMILAR CHEESES: Époisses, Affidélice, Soumaintrain.

SEASONAL NOTE: Best from May to September.

WINE PAIRINGS: Shows an affinity for Chardonnays and Claret-type wines.
- **WHITE**: White Burgundy (Chardonnay); Italian Chardonnnay (Grechetto blend); Argentinian Torrontés (full-bodied, aromatic white).
- **RED**: Barbaresco (Nebbiolo); California Cabernet Sauvignon; California Merlot.

RATINGS

QUALITY

78

STRENGTH

2

AMARELO DA BEIRA BAIXA, QUEIJO

(ah-mah-REL-loh dah BAY-ruh BUY-shah, KAY-zho) I love this cheese! It's a *torta*-style artifact from Portugal along the lines of Serpa, Serra, and also their Spanish cousins Serena and Torta del Casar. The Amarelo can be fairly soft if acquired young, but compared to similar Iberian cheeses made from 100 percent sheep's milk it tends to firm up more rapidly. A good Amarelo offers milky, slightly musty (yet pleasantly sheepy) aromas and a rich bitter-sweet lactic earthy flavor profile with a long, satisfying finish. The addition of goat's milk gives it a lighter, more yellow color rather than straw or golden, hence its name, which means "yellow" in Portuguese. Amarelo, by the way, represents a category of mixed-milk types that come from small-scale farmhouse producers, especially in southern Europe but also increasingly in the United States. They're atypical in flavor and tend to be quaint, picturesque representatives of traditional cheesemaking with quite a bit of variation in a given cheese from one producer to the next—a fascinating, albeit at times confusing, phenomenon. The softer, younger Amarelos are more gentle; with age, they become a bit aggressive, a quality I appreciate but one for which you should be prepared.

TYPE: Raw goat's and sheep's milk.

PROVENANCE: Idanha-a-Nova, east-central Portugal.

PRODUCERS: The local cheese producers' cooperative as well as local farmhouse producers, including Quinta da Serra du Gardunha.

PRODUCTION: A mix of goat's and sheep's milk—and not necessarily 50-50—is used to produce this unusual cheese. Production is small enough that the proportions of milk are not mandated by law. The curds are coagulated with animal rennet as opposed to the thistle rennet typical of other Portuguese sheep's milk cheeses. D.O.P.-protected.

APPEARANCE: A small flattish drum approximately $5^1/_2$ inches in diameter and $1^3/_4$ to 2 inches high, weighing from $1^3/_4$ to just over 2 pounds. The rind is thin and light brown to beige with occasional pinkish orange tinges and sometimes dustings of white mold. The paste is cream- to ivory-colored with small irregularly shaped and spaced holes and fissures. It often comes wrapped in a cloth bandage around its waist to keep its shape.

SIMILAR CHEESES: Serpa, Serra da Estrela, Torta del Casar, Queso de la Serena.

SEASONAL NOTE: Available year-round but best between spring and fall.

RATINGS

QUALITY

86

STRENGTH

4

WINE PAIRINGS: Amarelo prefers softer reds and dessert wines.

WHITE: Southern French Sauvignon Blanc.

RED: Red Burgundy (Pinot Noir); Argentinian Malbec; Provençal Mourvèdre–Cinsault–Grenache blend (full-bodied, spicy red from southern France); Periquita blend (Portuguese red with Tempranillo, Syrah, and Merlot); California Pinot Noir.

SPARKLING: Moscato d'Asti.

DESSERT/FORTIFIED: Dulce de Monastrell (from Jumilla, southeastern Spain).

L'AMI DU CHAMBERTIN

(lah-MEE doo shahm-behr-TAN) This cheese was introduced in the early 1950s by cheesemaker Raymond Gaudry in the village of Gevrey-Chambertain, which is probably better known for its superb red Burgundy wines. It's smooth and creamy with an excellent balance of salty and milky flavors, its subtlety and allure belied by its strong funky aroma. Call it a younger and potentially more ornery cousin of Époisses. L'Ami du Chambertin can be relatively rare; when you do encounter a good one, it's a particular thrill.

TYPE: Raw cow's milk.

PROVENANCE: Gevrey-Chambertain, Burgundy, near Dijon, central eastern France.

PRODUCER: Laiterie de la Côte, Brochon, France.

PRODUCTION: Ripened with washings of Marc de Bourgogne (brandy made from the grape solids left after wine-pressing).

APPEARANCE: A smallish drum approximately 3½ inches in diameter and 1½ inches tall weighing about 9 ounces. It has a characteristic pinkish orange rind that transforms to reddish or brownish; it is moist, as a result of repeated washings with a mixture of brine and marc during its aging period (minimum 1 month), and exhibits the cross-hatch pattern of its draining mold. The paste is ivory colored and it ripens from the outside in, from a semisoft almost chalky consistency to a deliciously smooth one.

SIMILAR CHEESE: Époisses.

SEASONAL NOTE: Best spring through fall.

WINE PAIRINGS: Simple reds and sparkling Chardonnay-based wines work best with L'Ami du Chambertin (the Sauternes pairing is an exception).
RED: Beaujolais cru (Gamay); Barolo or Barbaresco (Nebbiolo).
SPARKLING: Brut Champagne.

DESSERT/FORTIFIED: Sauternes (late-harvest Sémillon).

RATINGS

QUALITY

89

STRENGTH

4

APPENZELLER

(AH-pen-tsell-er) When properly manufactured and patiently washed during its maturation period, Appenzeller is a treasure—a beautiful and delicious artifact, an exemplar of traditional Swiss mountain cheeses. A traditional semihard mountain cheese, Appenzeller seems to explode with bursts of complex sour-milk and flowery pasture flavors on your palate. It balances sweetness with stout, smoky, deep flavors. With age, it develops a crystalline structure yet it is also smooth and not too fatty or buttery. It has a close-textured, homogenous paste that is fairly dense with well-rounded flavors, fruity overtones, and a creamy mouthfeel as compared with its more strident cousin, the Prättigauer. The great Swiss cheese importer Caroline Hostettler said, "There is no 'Swiss Cheese' but there are 'Swiss cheeses'"; it was this type of cheese to which she was referring.

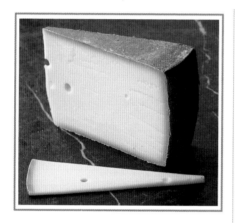

TYPE: Cow's milk.

PROVENANCE: Appenzell, northeastern Switzerland, near the border with Austria—a small town surrounded by steep yet lush mountains.

PRODUCERS: Only three local cooperative dairies still produce raw-milk Appenzeller; some of the best of them are made by Alois Pfister in the village of Goldingen, near Appenzell, and selected and ripened by Rolf Beeler.

PRODUCTION: Made from the milk of the Simmentaler breed of cows. Traditionally, it's made from all raw milk, but standards are being relaxed and, alas, there is some pasteurization. The curds are cooked and pressed. Aged 7 to 12 months, Appenzeller generally peaks around 9 months. The rinds are formed with washings of a special marinade containing herbs, white wine, and sometimes herb brandy. There is talk, as of this writing, of giving this traditional artifact "name protection" that may involve a relaxation of the raw-milk requirement—an unfortunate development if it occurs.

APPEARANCE: Small wheels 3 to 3½ inches tall, 12 to 14 inches in diameter, weighing about 15 pounds with occasional pea-sized holes.

SIMILAR CHEESES: Prättigauer, Torgenburger (a very similar cheese made nearby whose producers are holding the line regarding raw milk).

SEASONAL NOTE: Cheeses made in the warmer months, when the vegetation is full and varied, are better.

RATINGS

QUALITY

97

STRENGTH

5

WINE PAIRINGS: Sides best with Claret-style reds and spicier whites.
- **WHITE:** Alsatian Gewurztraminer; Grüner Veltliner; Tokay Pinot Gris (Alsace).
- **RED:** Barbera del Monferrato (similar to Barbera d'Alba); red Bordeaux; California Cabernet Sauvignon; California Merlot.
- **SPARKLING:** Blanc de Noirs Champagne (Pinot Noir).

- **DESSERT/FORTIFIED:** Late-harvest Chardonnay.

ARDRAHAN

When I think of this cheese, one word comes to mind: *deliciousness!* Ardrahan was a well-regarded cheese for years that seems to have come into its prime recently as an unprepossessing delight. On first tasting, it may seem simply "cheesy"—nothing more. On later encounters, though, this masterfully crafted cheese will be appreciated for its lovely balance. A pungent, monastery-type expression of western Irish *terroir*, its paste is sticky, rich, soft to semisoft, and curdy. Its flavors are savory, warm, nutty, and toasty; it has a judicious measure of salt. The overall impression is full and satisfying. The Friesian cow's milk from the full, rich grazing lands of County Cork gives breadth and warmth to this cheese. Although the milk is pasteurized, it's hard to find fault with the lovely flavors and many wine-pairing options afforded by Ardrahan.

TYPE: Pasteurized cow's milk

PROVENANCE: County Cork, southwestern Ireland.

PRODUCER: Members of the Burns family have been dairy farmers at Ardrahan for generations. Eugene and his wife, Mary, began making cheese in the early 1990s; he passed away in the year 2000 but Mary continues the cheesemaking. (Thank you, Mary, for sustaining this great tradition.)

PRODUCTION: Washed rind. All handmade by artisanal methods from milk produced on the farm.

APPEARANCE: 2-pound wheels 8 inches across and 1½ inches high. The rind is moist and pinkish beige; the paste is yellowish cream-colored.

SIMILAR CHEESES: Durrus, Gubbeen, Milleens.

SEASONAL NOTE: Good year-round but at their best spring through early fall.

WINE PAIRINGS: You name the grape! Ardrahan is a wine-lover's cheese and a very versatile partner. It pairs well with a broad range of red wine types, many whites, and quite a few dessert wines. Interestingly, it shows an affinity with a range of wines made from the Muscat grape, including German Muskateller Kabinett; the Italian sparkler Moscato d'Asti; and Muscat de Rivesaltes, a dessert wine from the Languedoc of southern France.

WHITE: California Chardonnay; Alsatian Riesling; Tokay Pinot Gris (Alsace).

RED: California Cabernet Sauvignon blend; southern Rhône (Syrah blend); Nebbiolo; California Pinot Noir; California Zinfandel.

RATINGS

QUALITY

91

STRENGTH

2

AZEITÃO

(ah-zay-DONH) Azeitão has a thick, soft, smooth, shiny paste that begins to ooze when ripe at room temperature. Its aroma is strong, earthy, and barnyardy; it offers rich, creamy flavors with a flowery finish, and a pronounced sour-milk taste when ripe. Like many fine artisanal sheep's milk cheeses, it offers a very pleasant bittersweet quality, which comes from the thistle renneting. As it continues to mature, the Azeitão's paste gradually gets harder and drier; its flavors intensify and become more "sheepy." Buy it plump and full—not flat—and not too sheepy smelling. Otherwise, it may be past its prime, although still intriguing and potentially very satisfying. This cheese is a descendant of the better-known Serra da Estrela. Serra-makers, from northern Portugal, brought their mountain sheep's milk cheesemaking techniques and traditions to the area where Azeitão is made, and thus the similarities. No doubt many of their differences are attributable to *terroir*.

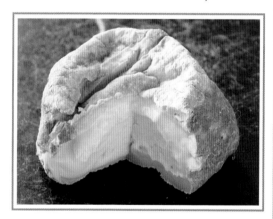

TYPE: Raw sheep's milk.

PROVENANCE: Azeitão and the environs of Setúbal, Palmela, and Sesimbra in the foothills of the Arrábida Mountains, south of Lisbon, Portugal.

PRODUCERS: Artisanal farmhouse dairies; among them Quinta do Viso Grande (Pedro Fontes, cheesemaker) and Quinta do Anjo (Fernando de Oliveira Simões, cheesemaker).

PRODUCTION: Handcrafted by traditional methods. Coagulated with thistle rennet; aged a minimum of 90 days. D.O.P. protected.

APPEARANCE: 8- to 9-ounce rounds, $2^{1}/_{2}$ to $3^{1}/_{2}$ inches wide and 1 to 2 inches high. The rind is beige and mottled with greenish and pinkish molds; a ripe Azeitão has a rough, undulating rind that may show signs of cracking and collapsing. The paste is off-white, soft, creamy, smooth, and verging on unctuous.

SIMILAR CHEESES: Queso de la Serena, Queijo Serra da Estrela; Serpa; Torta del Casar (although much smaller).

SEASONAL NOTE: Available year-round but best April through September.

WINE PAIRINGS: Azeitão tends to favor reds, from light-bodied to robust, but also some of the finer sweet whites.
- **WHITE:** Alsatian Pinot Blanc; Vouvray sec (Chenin Blanc).
- **RED:** Barbera d'Asti; California Pinot Noir; red Rhône wines (Syrah blends); Ribera del Duero (Tempranillo blend); California Zinfandel.
- **DESSERT/FORTIFIED:** Bonnezeaux or Quarts de Chaume (from the Chenin Blanc Grape, grown in the Loire Valley); LBV Port.

RATINGS

QUALITY

92

STRENGTH

2

BANON

(bah-NOHN) A rustic, Provençal cheese that reflects its rugged *terroir* and local character. When too young and too soft, a Banon hasn't yet had a chance to acquire that pleasantly tart, tangy quality that comes from slow acidification. With proper ripening, its texture will become smoother and it will develop richer flavor and mouthfeel. In addition to the expected chalky, lactic, creamy goat-milk textures and flavors, a good ripe Banon can offer pleasant woodsy and fruity notes. It has a small window of peak ripeness and, for an innocent-looking chèvre in a pretty little package, it can make a strong impression. In addition, its dip in *eau de vie*, intended to protect it from bad molds, can give it a distinct aftertaste.

TYPE: Cow's, sheep's, and goat's milk, depending on season and availability (but the goat's milk version is by far the most prevalent).

PROVENANCE: The rugged mountains of northern Provence (Alpes-de-Haute-Provence) in the environs of the town of Banon.

PRODUCERS: There are about 100 artisanal farmhouse and dairy producers in the proposed A.O.C. zone. Recommended raw-milk producers are as follows. *Fermiers:* Alexis and Marie-Christine Pellegrin; Ferme les Billardes; Gérard Loup; Joël and Brigitte Corbon; Marc Debaiseux. *Laitiers:* Capitelles; Fromagerie de Montéglin; Fromagerie de Banon.

PRODUCTION: Soft, unpressed, and uncooked. As a rule of thumb, it is made with sheep's milk in winter, goat's in spring, and cow's year-round. It takes 1 quart of milk to make each 3-ounce cheese. Bathed in *eau de vie* (*marc*) and aged for a minimum of 15 and up to 40 days. A.O.C. pending.

APPEARANCE: Smallish disks about 3 to 3½ inches in diameter and up to 1¼ inches high, weighing about 3⅓ ounces, wrapped in chestnut leaves and bound by four strips of raffia. Some versions are made flecked with herbs and called Banon Herbes de Provence or Tomme à L'Ancienne; others are studded with peppercorns. Underneath the leaves, the rind ranges from white to pale or brownish. The paste is soft and white.

SIMILAR CHEESE: Hoja Santa.

SEASONAL NOTE: Available spring through fall.

WINE PAIRINGS: Pairs best with dry whites.
WHITE: Chardonnay (white Burgundy or Italian); South African Chenin Blanc; Sauvignon Blanc (Sancerre or California).
RED: Chianti Classico (Sangiovese); Beaujolais cru (Gamay).

SPARKLING: Moscato d'Asti.

RATINGS

QUALITY

81

STRENGTH

2

BAYLEY HAZEN

A lovely shade of blue against a backdrop of a light cream-colored paste makes an elegant invitation to taste this particularly buttery cow's milk blue cheese. The sting of its *Pencillium roquefortii* is held in check by masterful cheesemaking using some of the finest cow's milk available in North America. A blue that seems to be made not for the sake of making a blue but rather to deliver a hearty welcome to any cheese lover who is hesistant to embrace this category. (An interesting historical aside: The cheese got its name from two Revolutionary War–era generals, Bayley and Hazen, who built the Hazen Military Road in anticipation of battling the English on a Canadian Front, which never developed. The road, however, did lead to settlement of the area by colonists in the 1780s and 1790s. Constant Bliss, another cheese made by the Kehler brothers, is named after a settler who was killed by local natives while guarding the road in 1781.)

TYPE: Raw cow's milk blue.

PROVENANCE: Greensboro, northeastern Vermont, USA.

PRODUCER: Mateo and Andy Kehler, Jasper Hill Farm.

PRODUCTION: Farmhouse, using the milk of their own small herd of Ayrshire cows who are intensively grazed from late spring to early fall. After each milking, the cows are turned out onto a fresh patch of grass on the 225-acre farm. During the remainder of the year, the cows are fed dry hay—no silage. The cheese is made with predominately morning milk (evening milk being used to make the Constant Bliss). The curds are uncooked, cut, and stirred by hand. The cheeses are dry salted with fine-grain sea salt. A natural rind develops after 30 days, beginning with an array of different colored strains of *Brevi linens* bacterium and yielding to a diversity of molds, which become inert and form a stable rind by 90 days. The cheeses are matured for $3\frac{1}{2}$ to 4 months at the farm.

APPEARANCE: Produced in two different sizes: 6- to 7-pound wheels and 12- to 14-pound ones. The small wheels are 6 inches in diameter and approximately 9 inches tall while the larger ones are 8 inches in diameter and 9 inches tall. The rind is beige to light brown with a cross-hatch pattern on top and a dusting of white mold all around. The ivory- to cream-colored paste has deep striations of blue-gray mold and plenty of cavities and cracks.

SEASONAL NOTE: Produced year-round but look for variations in flavor from early summer and fall cheeses; a recent batch of July cheeses, for example, had distinct herbal and licorice tones.

WINE PAIRING:
🍷 **DESSERT/FORTIFIED**: Tawny Port.

RATINGS

QUALITY

84

STRENGTH

2

BEAUFORT

(bow-FOR) Famous since Roman times, Beaufort, along with Abondance, Tomme de Savoie, and Reblochon, is one of the noble cheeses of the French Alps. It is frequently referred to as the Prince of Gruyères, a term applied by the great gastronome Jean-Anthelme Brillat-Savarin. The best Beauforts are arrestingly satisfying—that is, they give you all you need or desire when hungry. Nothing else is required—no bread, no accompaniment, not even any wine. Beaufort's curds are cooked, but they're not subject to as much heat as other classic Gruyère-type cheeses (Emmental, for one). So the cheese is solid but retains its melt-in-the-mouth character and avoids the firmer consistency and "cooked" flavors of its Gruyère cousins. Beaufort features a fairly dense, concentrated, buttery consistency, a fruity aroma, and rich, nutty flavors with a hint of sweetness. (The summer cheeses feature additional herbal and flowery tastes.) As Beaufort ages, it takes on a pronounced, delicious flavor of spoiled milk that most people find mouthwatering if not utterly irresistible. The best Beauforts are aged over a year and a half, yet they have no fissures, blemishes, or holes. Avoid Beauforts with cracked rinds, traces of mold on the interior, any discoloration of the paste, or airholes.

TYPE: Raw cow's milk.

PROVENANCE: Haute-Savoie, in the mountains of east-central France, south of Lake Geneva, Switzerland.

PRODUCERS: There are about a dozen cooperative dairies and many more farmhouse producers of genuine Beaufort A.O.C. Recommended raw-milk producers: Coopérative de Val Cenis Vanoise; Coopérative Laitière de la Chambre; Fromagerie Chabert; Fromagerie Mouchelet; Fromagerie Seignemartin; SCA Les producteurs de reblochon de Thônes; Societé coopérative laitière de Haute-Tarantaise; Societé coopérative laitière Unicopa-Rippoz; Societé coopérative laitière du Beaufortain; Verdannet SA.

PRODUCTION: The best Beaufort, labeled Haute-Montagne, is made from the milk of the Tarentaise and Abondance breeds of cows that graze in the high-mountain pastures during the summertime (mid-June to mid-September). The summer mountain cheeses have a green oval casein label embedded in them while the regular ones have a blue label. Under Beaufort's A.O.C. rules, cheeses may be labeled *alpage* only if they are made in a chalet in the summer from the milk of a single herd. *Eté* (summer) cheeses are made in a dairy, June to October. The curds are cooked and pressed; all Beauforts are cured in cellars for at least 6 months and up to 18 months with potential to age for as long as 3 years; generally, the longer the better.

RATINGS

QUALITY

93

STRENGTH

5

APPEARANCE: Large wheels with distinctive concave sides, about 2 feet in diameter, 5 inches thick and weighing from 85 to 130 pounds. The rind, formed by regular saltings and rubbings during the maturing period, is beige to reddish brown. The paste is creamy off-white to light yellow, very smooth with the occasional hole and/or grainy thread.

SIMILAR CHEESES: Gruyère is a more general term encompassing the hard cheeses of the provinces of Franche-Comté and Haute-Savoie, which include Emmental, Comté (aka Gruyère de Comte) and also Beaufort. Swiss Gruyère and Emmental (aka Emmentaler) are also related; Beaufort is also like an aged Fontina d'Aosta.

SEASONAL NOTE: See "Production" above.

WINE PAIRINGS: Works well with Champagnes, white Burgundies and Rhône reds.
- **WHITE**: Chardonnay (California or Burgundy); German Riesling Spätlese.
- **RED**: Madiran (tannic, traditionally rustic wine from southwestern France; made primarily from the Tannat grape); Pinot Noir (California or Oregon); various Syrah and Syrah-Grenache blends from southern France (northern Rhône or Languedoc).
- **SPARKLING**: Champagne (Blanc de Noirs or rosé).

- **DESSERT/FORTIFIED**: Sauternes (late-harvest Sémillon).

BEENLEIGH BLUE

(BEEN-lee) Beenleigh Blue wraps the caramelish, mildly herbaceous depth of flavor of artisanal sheep's cheeses with the salty bite of a blue into a truly impressive and alluring package. It's been among the most successful blue-veined sheep's milk cheeses to date, including Roquefort. For one, it has never exhibited the detrimental oversalting problem encountered even among the best Roqueforts. Although it's now made with "compromised" (pasteurized) milk, Beenleigh is still a fine cheese. (It seems that the Beenleighs have been fading more quickly than when made with raw milk; also, there are not as many eye-popping thrills from so many different wine pairings.) Beenleigh's remarkable aromas suggest the sweetness of nectar and perhaps honeysuckle. Within the range of blue cheeses, I place Beenleigh on the mild side. That a moldy cheese can also be tantalizingly sweet is yet another miracle. Its consistency is semisoft and fudgy yet it can also tend toward flaky.

TYPE: Sheep's milk blue.

PROVENANCE: Sharpham Barton, South Devon, southwestern England.

PRODUCER: Robin Congdon and his cheesemaker, Nick Trant.

PRODUCTION: Artisanal, all local milk; aged 4 to 8 months.

APPEARANCE: Comes in 6- to 8-pound cylinders with naturally moist rinds. The interior is also moist, light ivory in color, and full of striations of grayish blue mold with some cavities.

SIMILAR CHEESES: Harbourne Blue, Roquefort.

SEASONAL NOTE: Fall to spring.

WINE PAIRINGS: Beenleigh Blue is partial to dessert wines and also fruitier reds.
WHITE: German Muskateller Kabinett.

RED: Beaujolais cru (Gamay); California Cabernet Sauvignon; Zinfandel (California).

DESSERT/FORTIFIED: Coteaux de Layon (late-harvest Chenin Blanc from the Loire Valley); Muscat de Rivesaltes (from the Languedoc); Tawny Port; Sauternes (late-harvest Sémillon); Hungarian Tokaji.

RATINGS

QUALITY

92

STRENGTH

2

BERKSHIRE BLUE

This is an award-winning one-man cheese, made by painstakingly careful, traditional artisan methods that create outstanding character. Berkshire Blue was developed over 12 years by Dr. Alan Duffield in Somerset, England. Since the year 2000 it has been made by Michael G. Miller in the Berkshires under a licensing agreement and with the supervision of Dr. Duffield. Berkshire Blue has a big, wide, warm flavor. The blue zing is present but it doesn't eclipse the buttery flavor of the Jersey cow's milk. Restrained salting further enhances the full, sweet flavor of the milk. It can be inconsistent, depending on its draining and drying, but it rarely disappoints. I prefer my Berkshire Blues a little drier—not too wet.

TYPE: Raw cow's milk.

PROVENANCE: Great Barrington, Berkshire County, western Massachusetts, USA.

PRODUCER: Michael G. Miller.

PRODUCTION: Made entirely by hand from 200-gallon batches of Jersey cow milk, picked up by the cheesemaker each day during the morning milking. The only machinery used in the manufacturing process is Mr. Miller's truck, pump, and heating-and-refrigeration equipment. The curds are stirred, cut, and ladled into molds all by hand. The cheeses are brine-soaked overnight, then drained for two days before hand-needling. They spend 12 to 15 days in the maturing room, where they are turned on a regular basis, and an additional 45 days in a cold room. The recipe calls for two starter cultures, two blue molds, one white mold, and vegetable rennet. The incubation is low-temperature and long-duration; salt and acid contents are deliberately kept low, well below industry averages for other blue cheeses.

APPEARANCE: Comes in two sizes of cylindrical wheels: 5 inches in diameter, weighing about 3 pounds; and 7 inches in diameter, weighing about 7 pounds. The exterior—referred to by the maker as a "skin" rather than a rind—is entirely edible and contains shades of blue, light brown, and white. The interior is ivory with veins of light and dark blue.

SIMILAR CHEESES: Cashel Blue, Fourme D'Ambert.

SEASONAL NOTE: Due to the variation in the Jersey cows' diets, the cheeses tend to be harder during the grazing months and softer in winter; the taste remains pretty much the same.

WINE PAIRINGS: Berkshire Blue likes fruity reds and toasty Ports, but it also blends well with California Chardonnay.

🍷 **WHITE:** California Chardonnay.

🍷 **RED:** Beaujolais cru (Gamay); California Cabernet Sauvignon.

🍷 **DESSERT/FORTIFIED:** Tawny Port.

RATINGS

QUALITY

91

STRENGTH

4

BERKSWELL

This award-winning cheese boasts remarkable density, concentration, and myriad flavors. Its paste is firm but slightly pliant. Its flavors are somewhat reminiscent of a fine Tuscan Pecorino—some say it's akin to a sheep's milk version of Parmesan—but with a marvelous long-lasting caramel-like sweetness, both fruity and savory. Berkswell is often perceived to speak eloquently of the fresh, rich grasses and herbs of a pristine English meadow, hence its enduring sweetness. Even its stronger-tasting, more mature examples never quite assume the sharp smokiness or saltiness of comparable cheeses (e.g., an aged Pecorino). I've often thought of Berkswell as the cheese that Manchego wishes it was. I've also referred to it as a "boss cheese," and it is certainly one that won't be easily forgotten. When properly stored and aged, a fresh-cut Berkswell will give you a rush of pineapple-like aromas. You might be tempted to buy an entire wheel of it, hoping you can hold on to it for a long while, until you've fondly (and sadly) devoured the last morsel. But it would be best to take only what you can consume within a day or two. Note that Berskwell's makers seem to have overcome a few problems with inconsistency of its flavor profile.

TYPE: Raw sheep's milk.

PROVENANCE: Berkswell, Forest of Arden, Warwickshire, a little enclave of charming English countryside sandwiched between the sprawling urban industrial areas of Birmingham and Coventry, in the western Midlands, northwest of London.

PRODUCER: Stephen Fletcher and family.

PRODUCTION: Made in the style of the sheep's milk cheeses of the Pyrenees (e.g., French A.O.C. Ossau-Iraty Brébis). Pressed; aged 6 to 12 months. Berkswell has a plasticote rind. This is a synthetic material that is painted on young cheeses. It does not crack but at the same time allows the cheeses to breathe. In Berkswell's case, the plasticote eventually wears off, leaving a natural rind. In this sense, it is the equivalent of the lard applied to Cheddars to protect their developing rinds early on.

APPEARANCE: A "basket" or compressed sphere, weighing 5 to 9 pounds.

SIMILAR CHEESES: Pecorino Toscano, Spenwood, Trade Lake Cedar, Vermont Shepherd.

SEASONAL NOTE: Fall to spring, but at times available sporadically.

RATINGS

QUALITY

94

STRENGTH

3

WINE PAIRINGS: Berkswell is a solid and reliable cheese partner for many reds as well as crisp, fruity whites.

WHITE: German Gewürztraminer Spätlese; German Riesling Spätlese.

RED: Barbaresco or Barolo (Nebbiolo); red Burgundy (and other fuller-flavored expressions of Pinot Noir); Chianti Classico (Sangiovese); Rhône Valley reds and other Syrah blends; Ribera del Duero (Tempranillo blend).

SPARKLING: Moscato d'Asti.

DESSERT/FORTIFIED: Malvasia delle Lipari (from Sicily); Sauternes (late-harvest Sémillon).

BEYOS, QUESO DE LOS

(BAY-ohs, KAY-soh day lohs) This is a traditional rustic or peasant-style cheese also sometimes referred to as Beyusco. In mature cheeses, the paste is semihard—firm but not rock hard—dense, and compact, tending toward crumbly with a dryish texture and mouthfeel that quickly turns deliciously buttery as it melts in your mouth. Its flavors should be lactic and creamy with a moderate acidity and delightful tang. It also features an intriguing yeasty taste and earthy hints of mushrooms (chanterelles, trumpets). The creamy flavor that a Beyos yields after just a brief presence on the palate is thrilling. Although it offers a wide window of peak ripeness—even to the moldier, grayer, harder stages—Beyos is best consumed when younger, more yellow, and somewhat pliant in the paste. In its advanced maturity, it turns hard and begins to taste chalky, but it may still be delicious. If you're seeking a cheese partner for a martini or some other drier, more alcoholic beverage than wine or beer, the first cheese that comes to mind is a Beyos.

TYPE: Pasteurized cow's or goat's milk, but not a mix.

PROVENANCE: The townships of Amieva and Pinga in the Los Beyos Gorge in the western foothills of the Picos de Europa on the edge of Asturias, central northern coast of Spain.

PRODUCERS: Farmhouse made; four producers only.

PRODUCTION: Cured for 40 days at high humidity. Traditionally, the cheeses were made from raw milk and were lightly smoked.

APPEARANCE: Small, slightly irregular cylinders weighing 1 pound or less that have a somewhat bloomy, straw-colored rind, which may display cracks and often turns mottled with brown, gray, and green spots and patches of fuzzy white mold as it ages. The paste is off-white to light yellow and chalky textured.

SIMILAR CHEESE: Afuega'l Pitu, but the Beyos is more lactic and claylike.

WINE PAIRINGS: Beyos's chalky claylike texture dissolves into a wide range of wines. Try it with light, crisp whites and fruitier reds. (It even works with a martini.)
WHITE: Albariño; Alsatian Pinot Blanc; Sauvignon Blanc (California, New Zealand, or Pouilly-Fumé); Tokay Pinot Gris (Alsace).
RED: Barbaresco (Nebbiolo); Barbera d'Alba; Beaujolais cru (Gamay); Zinfandel (California).
DESSERT/FORTIFIED: Ruby Port.

RATINGS

QUALITY

84

STRENGTH

2

BIG HOLMES

One of LoveTree Farmstead's impressive array of artisanal cheeses (see also Trade Lake Cedar, page 271), reflecting the *terroir* of the wild woods of northern Wisconsin and the skill of its proprietor/cheesemakers, Mary and David Falk. They like to say you can taste the wild woods and fresh autumn breezes in their cheeses, which are carefully aged with controlled exposure to the woodsy air. They make a series of Holmes cheeses, named after one of the ponds surrounding their property, and this is my personal favorite. The texture of the Big Holmes is akin to that of a triple crème, creamy and silky; when young, it is actually spreadable at room temperature. As it ages, it becomes firmer and can be sliced paper-thin if you so desire.

TYPE: Sheep's milk.

PROVENANCE: Grantsburg, northern Wisconsin, USA.

PRODUCER: Mary and David Falk, LoveTree Farmstead.

PRODUCTION: The milk, which is gently pasteurized, comes from the farm's own herd of free-ranging sheep. They graze in flowering pastures all over the farm's 200 acres, 70 of which is a wildlife preserve, allowing the cheeses to capture the unique flavors of the north woods. The curds are hand-ladled and left unpressed. The rinds are formed by dusting the cheeses with rosemary and mint, which allow for development of beneficial molds during the aging period, which last 4 to 6 weeks.

APPEARANCE: The rind is paper-thin, crispy, crunchy, and covered with blue, green, and gray molds. The cheese is topped off with a decoration of cedar and sumac and juniper berries. The paste is off-white to ivory, silky smooth, and subtly layered. Big Holmes comes in stout medium-sized "cakes" approximately 4 inches in diameter, 4 to 6 inches high, weighing about 1 1/2 pounds.

SIMILAR CHEESES: Brin D'Amour, Fleur du Maquis.

SEASONAL NOTE: Available from the end of May through early fall.

RATINGS

QUALITY

79

STRENGTH

3

WINE PAIRINGS: The Big Holmes marries well with a broad spectrum of wine types, but is generally better with floral whites.

WHITE: Albariño; Alsatian Riesling; Sauvignon Blanc (Loire Valley or New Zealand); Chenin Blanc (Savennières).

RED: Chianti Classico (Sangiovese); Merlot (Bordeaux or California).

BLEU D'AUVERGNE

(bluh DOH-vehrn) Legend has it that a local native, Antoine Roussel, developed this cheese in the mid-nineteenth century, discovering the properties and desirability of natural blueing by accident: some Cantalet (a miniature form of Cantal) had come into contact with a moldy loaf of rye bread. By 1854, Roussel had perfected his recipe and was doing brisk business selling his cheeses, known as Bleu de Laqueuille (bluh duh lah-KOY), after his hometown. Soon, the neighbors caught on, its territory expanded, and by the end of the century it had become an established commodity, referred to as Bleu d'Auvergne. It is fairly mild, soft, and buttery for its category. Bleu d'Auvergne is more of a beginner's cheese than, say, Bleu de Gex and Bleu des Causses (see separate entries).

TYPE: Cow's milk blue (pasteurized and raw-milk versions available).

PROVENANCE: The Auvergne region of France's south-central plateau, the Massif Central; originally from the village of Laqueuille, approximately 25 miles west of Clermond-Ferrand in the Puy-de-Dôme (a statue of the original cheesemaker Antoine Roussel now stands in the village square).

PRODUCERS: Local farmhouses and creameries; the genuine raw-milk variety is made by GAEC des Croix de Chazelles.

PRODUCTION: Both raw- and pasteurized-milk versions are available; the raw-milk variety is more highly recommended. Originally made from the milk of the Ferrandaire breed of cows. Made in the style of Roquefort, with the addition of *P. roquefortii* to the curds, and prickings with needles to allow the mold to develop. Stirred, lightly pressed, and poured carefully into molds, which are turned regularly for drainage. Ripened for 4 weeks in humid caves. A.O.C. status granted in 1975.

APPEARANCE: Foil wrapped. The large version is a smallish drum 8 inches in diameter and up to 4 inches high, weighing between $4\frac{1}{2}$ and $6\frac{1}{2}$ pounds. (A smaller version just 4 inches across, weighing up to 2 pounds, is also made.) Some natural bloomy molds on the rind. Interior is well marbled with dark bluish-green mold.

SIMILAR CHEESES: Bleu des Causses, Fourme d'Ambert, Fourme de Montbrison; there is also a Bleu de Laqueuille, which is a local version of Bleu d'Auvergne from the hometown of its originator, Monsieur Roussel.

SEASONAL NOTE: Traditionally best throughout the summer and into winter.

WINE PAIRINGS: Bleu d'Auvergne is tamed with substantial reds and dessert wines.
- **RED:** Madiran (tannic, traditionally rustic wine from southwestern France, made primarily from the tannat grape); Rioja-style Tempranillo blend.
- **DESSERT/FORTIFIED:** Sauternes (late-harvest Sémillon); Tawny Port.

RATINGS

QUALITY

77

STRENGTH

2

BLEU DES CAUSSES

(bluh day KOS) The rugged moorlands of France's large south-central plateau (the Massif Central), encompassing the region of the Causses, represent the ancient heart of the artisanal dairy industry. This is a quintessential cheese of the region. Like its sheep's milk cousin Roquefort, the Bleu des Causses can be fairly piquant without resorting to oversalting. Compared with some of the other rustic French cow's milk blues, it's zestier—almost peppery at times—and less buttery. It offers a full perfume and some real zing, yet, for a blue cheese, it dances lightly on the palate and its flavors are quite refreshing.

TYPE: Cow's milk.

PROVENANCE: The Causses region of south-central France.

PRODUCERS: Authentic raw-milk versions are made by Coopérative Laitière de la Haute Truyere-ULAG and Coopérative Laitière du Malzieu.

PRODUCTION: Made from the milk of the Montbéliarde and Aubrac breeds of cow. Aged 3 to 6 months in the naturally formed underground limestone caves, which are ventilated by cool, humid air currents. A.O.C. protected.

APPEARANCE: Similar to that of Roquefort: smallish drums 8 inches in diameter and 4 inches high, weighing between $5^{1}/_{2}$ and $6^{1}/_{2}$ pounds. Has a moist natural rind, light orangish beige in color, with abundant surface molds. The paste is ivory to light straw colored with cavities of dark blue-gray mold veins somewhat widely spread throughout.

SIMILAR CHEESES: Fourme d'Ambert, Fourme de Montbrison, Bleu d'Auvergne.

SEASONAL NOTE: Due to the character of the milk, the cheeses made in winter are lighter in color and somewhat drier in their interiors than the summer ones.

WINE PAIRINGS: This cheese livens up the rustic reds of southwest France and other Claret-type wines.
RED: Cahors (Malbec-Merlot-Tannat blend from southern France); Madiran (tannic, traditionally rustic wine from southwestern France; made primarily from the Tannat grape); California Cabernet Sauvignon.
DESSERT/FORTIFIED: Banyuls; Quarts de Chaume (late-harvest Chenin Blanc from the Loire Valley).

RATINGS

QUALITY

85

STRENGTH

4

BLEU DE GEX

(bluh duh ZHECKS) One of the older cheeses in France, dating from at least the sixteenth century, it survives in close to its original form. Bleu de Gex has a rich, relatively mild but tantalizing taste for a blue, with a pleasant mineral quality. It is somewhat reminiscent of Stilton but not as firm. Gex is bluer than some other blues due to the presence of *Penicillium glaucum* (as opposed to *P. roquefortii*) and it is also less acidic. The personality of a Gex is unmistakably "mountain cow-style," relying on the qualities and merits of the milk rather than the sting of blueing or excess salting. It is these qualities that set Gex apart from so many other blues—even to this day, when the blueing is aided by piercing. So, to be able to appreciate the Gex at its best, try it younger rather than older, and especially in the latter half of the calendar year; in other words, for summer cheeses, it's fine to consume them at 4 to 5 months of age, but with fall and winter cheeses, they should be eaten at about 2 months (these cheeses have less backbone and thus don't survive the extra aging as well).

TYPE: Raw cow's milk blue.

PROVENANCE: The Juras region of Franche-Comté Province, around the town of Gex, to the north of Geneva, Switzerland. (Both Bleu de Gex and another blue, Bleu de Septmoncel, are protected under the same A.O.C., which is also sometimes referred to as "Bleu du Haut-Jura.")

PRODUCERS: Four local cooperatives (which also produce Comté) make the genuine raw-milk version: Ets Rivoire & Jacquemin; Fromagerie Seignemartin; Juraflore-Société Arnaud Frères; and Coopérative fromagère du Haut-Jura.

PRODUCTION: Made from the milk of the Montbéliarde cows (and also some French Simmentals) that graze high in the mountains of the Jura. The curds are unpressed and uncooked. Air is injected into the paste to promote growth of *P. glaucum* mold during the 1-month aging period in humid caves.

APPEARANCE: Large rounds or millstones about 13½ inches in diameter and 4 inches high, weighing approximately 16 pounds. A thin, beige, natural rind with ivory-colored paste that has bluish green mold distributed throughout its interior.

SIMILAR CHEESES: Fourme d'Ambert, Stilton.

SEASONAL NOTE: September through February.

WINE PAIRINGS: Bleu de Gex is enhanced by Claret-type wines and fruitier, sweeter whites.
- **WHITE:** White Burgundy (Chardonnay); South African Chenin Blanc.
- **RED:** Beaujolais cru (Gamay); red Bordeaux; California Merlot.
- **DESSERT/FORTIFIED:** Banyuls; LBV Port; Sauternes (late-harvest Sémillon).

RATINGS

QUALITY

79

STRENGTH

3

BLEU DE TERMIGNON

(bluh duh tehr-mee-NYON) From high in the Haute-Savoie—not a region you would normally associate with blue cheeses—this is a rustic artisanal blue that is unique, atypical, authentic, and most definitely "farmhouse" in character. Bleu de Termignon was lauded by Charlemagne and, later, King Charles V; records of it were kept by the local priest in the village of Termignon, where it originated. It is semisoft, small-grained, and fine-textured with a relatively dry, crumbly mouthfeel for a blue. When younger, it offers floral lavender- and jasmine-like aromas and flavors that evolve to pronounced musty, moldy ones as the natural blueing progresses. Some fans prefer Bleu de Termignon in its more advanced stages of blueing; others may think of the blue as no more than an afterthought, certainly not the goal. The milk is of such a distinct perfumed quality and the cheese is never overly salty. You won't find another one like this—particularly a blue.

TYPE: Raw cow's milk.

PROVENANCE: The valley of Arc in the Haute-Maurienne area of the mountains of the Savoie, east-central France, south of Lake Geneva; on the French side of the Montcenis or Moncenisio Pass, an area that is also home to Bleu de Bonneval.

PRODUCERS: For years, it was made by farmhouse artisans in the small village of Lanslebourg; it was rediscovered and popularized in the 1980s by Jacques Vernier, a cheesemonger originally from the Savoie who set up shop in Paris. It's now made on several family farms in the area and selected and ripened by Denis Provent.

PRODUCTION: Farmhouse, traditional; made from the milk of brown cows that graze in mountain pastures at over 2,500 meters (over 8,000 feet) elevation.

APPEARANCE: Cylinders or drums of varying dimensions from 7 to 30 pounds. The rind is somewhat rough and rutted, dark beige to light brown with white mold dustings. The paste is off-white to straw colored with a hint of maroon tint, and it turns a darker grayish green toward the rind. There are small striations and pockets of greenish blue and grayish green mold in the paste that start at the rind and gradually move toward the core of the cheese.

SIMILAR CHEESE: Castelmagno.

WINE PAIRING:
RED: Zinfandel (California).

RATINGS

QUALITY

89

STRENGTH

4

BLU DEL MONCENISIO

(bloo del mon-cheh-NEE-see-oh) A fairly rare and refined blue from Piedmont that has a full, intense aroma but a relatively delicate flavor. It comes from the Alps on the Italian side of the Moncenisio Pass; the French delicacy Bleu de Termignon is made on the other side of the pass, in the Haute-Savoie. Blu de Moncenisio also comes in a rare, artisanal alpine version known as Murianengo (moo-ree-ah-NEN-ogh), as in the Vallée de la Maurienne, which is one of the principal place-names associated with Bleu de Termignon; both cheeses also bear some similarity with Castelmagno. All of these cheeses are traditionally subject to natural blueing—that is, without the benefit of piercing—and therefore don't necessarily develop the strong blue veining of a Roquefort, Stilton, or Cabrales. Blu del Moncenisio has a somewhat richer paste and more intense flavors than Castelmagno.

TYPE: Raw cow's milk.

PROVENANCE: Val di Susa, Piedmont, northwestern Italy.

PRODUCERS: Local farmhouses and artisanal dairies; Guffanti is the *affineur* (*stagionatore* in Italian).

PRODUCTION: Made at the upper elevations throughout most of the summer and in the valleys during the winter. Whole milk is coagulated in 30 to 60 minutes, and the curds are cut fairly small. They are left in molds for about 24 hours, then they're removed and salted. The cheeses are ripened for 40 to 80 days.

APPEARANCE: Drums 7 to 12 inches in diameter and 3 to 5 inches tall, weighing $5\frac{1}{2}$ to 7 pounds. The rind is somewhat rough and gray to brown in color. The paste is off-white to slightly yellow with irregularly spaced holes and relatively restrained blueing when at its peak. Murianengo comes in a similar shape but is larger, at about 12 inches in diameter and 4 inches tall, weighing up to 20 pounds. The cheeses made on the French side of the pass are said to have a bluer tint to their molds, while those on the Italian side have a greener one.

SIMILAR CHEESES: Castelmagno, Bleu de Termignon, Fourme d'Ambert, Murianengo.

WINE PAIRINGS: As is the case with many blues, look to pair this cheese with either fruity, full-bodied red wines or, more reliably, with dessert wines.
♥ **WHITE**: California Chardonnay.

♥ **RED**: Beaujolais (Gamay); California Cabernet Sauvignon; California Zinfandel.
♥ **DESSERT/FORTIFIED**: Tawny Port; Sauternes (late-harvest Sémillon).

RATINGS

QUALITY

82

STRENGTH

3

BONDE DE GÂTINE

(bondh duh gah-TEEN) Light, gentle, and slightly sour, this goat's milk cheese develops a blue-gray mold with age. The Bonde de Gâtine is already tasty and pleasant when younger, before the mold begins to show. The cheese reaches its peak when the coating is fully developed and the paste is still moist. At this stage, it develops a flavor and mouthfeel indicative of its provenance, the marshland of the Poitou: slightly salty and claylike but clear and fresh. Considering that it's a rustic artifact, it offers goaty flavors without becoming aggressive or obstreperous; thus, it maintains a very pleasant, approachable character. The Bonde de Gâtine is attractive for its simplicity and desirable for its size: a convenient single portion can be cut out of a whole cheese from top to bottom. If not consumed immediately, the remainder of the cheese keeps well for a day or two if covered in paper and left in a cool, moist place. The word *bonde* means "plug" and is given to these cheeses since their shape is reminiscent of a barrel plug (*bonde de barrique*); Gâtine is a place-name from the town of Mazière-en-Gâtine, where the cheese is made.

TYPE: Raw goat's milk.

PROVENANCE: The Deux-Sevres region of Poitou-Charentes, west-central France.

PRODUCER: Coopérative GAEC de la Fragnée.

PRODUCTION: Artisanal methods, creamery-made. Lactic coagulation; aged 4 to 10 weeks.

APPEARANCE: A small cylinder slightly taller than it is wide, 2 to 2½ inches tall and almost the same width, weighing 5 to 5½ ounces at peak. The rind is off-white in color and wrinkled, with shadings of bluish gray mold. The paste is chalky white and ripening from the outside in to a smooth, creamy consistency and ivory color.

SIMILAR CHEESES: Chabichou du Poitou, Clacbitou.

SEASONAL NOTE: Spring through fall.

WINE PAIRINGS: This cheese works better with crisp, tart white wines.

WHITE: Albariño; Sauvignon Blanc (Pouilly-Fumé, California); Argentinian Torrontés (full-bodied, aromatic white); Vouvray sec or demi-sec (Chenin Blanc).

RED: Bandol (Mourvèdre blend from Provence).

SPARKLING: Brut Champagne.

DESSERT/FORTIFIED: White Port.

RATINGS

QUALITY

89

STRENGTH

1

B R A

(brah) Here is a nourishing cheese you can't easily tire of, one that is equally satisfying but perhaps not as challenging as Fontina. The paste is medium-soft and riddled with very small holes. Its flavor is sour on the attack with a pleasant bitterness gradually building to the finish, altogether a fascinating impression. When young, Bra is fresh, grassy, and mild; it becomes stronger, drier, and more strawlike with age.

TYPE: Cow's milk (sometimes with the addition of small amounts of goat's or sheep's milk).

PROVENANCE: The market town of Bra, in the region of Cuneo, Piedmont, northwestern Italy, near Barolo country.

PRODUCERS: Small cooperative dairies.

PRODUCTION: A pressed, semihard, partially skimmed cheese. There are two versions of Bra sold: a young, soft, fresh one that is ripened for 45 days (Bra Tenero, or "tender Bra," pictured here); and an aged one that is ripened for a minimum of 6 months (Bra Duro, or "hard Bra"). True Bra is made with cow's rennet and of milk from cows that feed only on natural grass. Awarded D.O.C. status in 1982, D.O.P. status in 1996. Note: Guffanti's Bra is made from skimmed cow's, sheep's, and goat's milk. The aged version is hard, crumbly, and difficult to pry open à la Parmesan; there is also a summer mountain version that is the elite among Bras.

APPEARANCE: Wheels from 2¹/₂ to 4³/₄ inches thick and 12 to 17 inches in diameter, weighing between 13 and 22 pounds. The rind is hard and light brown or beige with dustings of white mold. A young Bra has a smooth, semihard paste that is light yellow to golden in color; it hardens to the crumbly, gratable consistency of Parmesan and other similar cheeses, turning a straw color that is darker toward the edges and exhibiting some white flakes of crystallization.

SIMILAR CHEESES: There are two other similar firm, pressed, brine-soaked Piedmontese D.O.C. cheeses from the same area: Castelmagno, which is pierced to encourage blueing, and Raschera. Look for the D.O.C. label on these cheeses as well as the specification "from alpine pastures" or *d'Alpeggio*, the Italian equivalent of the French *alpage*.

SEASONAL NOTE: *Alpeggio* cheeses are made in the summer months only; others year-round.

WINE PAIRINGS: Bra strongly favors red wines, especially those with considerable depth of flavor.
 RED: Barbaresco or Barolo (Nebbiolo); California Cabernet Sauvignon; Dolcetto d'Alba; Beaujolais cru (Gamay).

RATINGS

QUALITY

80

STRENGTH

5

BRESCIANELLA STAGIONATA

(breh-shah-NELL-ah stah-joh-NAH-tah) This cheese features full, pleasant, and melting cow's milk flavors with an irresistible accompanying aroma. Unlike some of the other strong-smelling cheeses, it remains appealing to a wide audience, rather turning off a lot of people with more sensitive noses. Brescianella's peak is smaller than that of similar types—less than a week for optimum enjoyment. This presents a challenge to the *affineur* and cheesemonger or *maître fromager:* to bring the cheese to its peak and then serve it for maximum enjoyment during its narrow window. The Brescianella is a smooth, creamy, highly accessible, and rather mild cheese emanating much of the charm of pure, fresh milk. Very similar to Taleggio and equally alluring; let its aromas and flavors stimulate your nose and mouth just as its evocative name rolls mellifluously off your tongue.

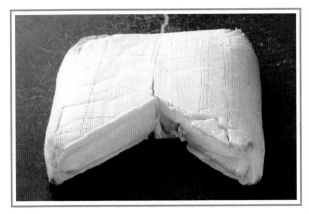

TYPE: Cow's milk.

PROVENANCE: Lombardy, northern Italy, the area between Cremona and Brescia, east-southeast of Milan.

PRODUCER: Luigi Guffanti is the *stagionatore (affineur).*

PRODUCTION: Uncooked, lightly pressed, washed rind, aged 2 to 3 months.

APPEARANCE: A flattened 6-inch square $1\frac{1}{2}$ to $1\frac{1}{4}$ inches high, weighing about 28 ounces, that looks like a somewhat funky smaller version of Taleggio. Its washed rind is a dull orange, ridged and cracked, with splotches of gray-brown and a dusting of white mold. The paste is smooth and off-white.

SIMILAR CHEESES: Quercino, Taleggio.

WINE PAIRINGS: Brescianella finds more synergy with fruity reds than most whites.
WHITE: Pinot Blanc (Alsace).

RED: Amarone della Valpolicella; Barbaresco (Nebbiolo); California Merlot; Beaujolais cru (Gamay).

RATINGS

QUALITY

71

STRENGTH

3

BRIE DE MELUN

(bree duh mel-UNH) When most people think of French cheeses, the first that come to mind are Camembert, Roquefort—and of course Brie. Unfortunately, as is the case with many of the world's most famous cheeses, there are many inferior factory-made and industrial cheeses that manage to reach the market under the name of Brie. Of the genuine, artisanal Brie-type cheeses, the Melun is my favorite. It comes from the southern part of the Brie region and is thought to be the prototype for all the others. For my money, it's also the strongest and fullest version, with a bigger flavor than its better-known younger (and bigger) sister Brie de Meaux. Someone once asked me why people tend to refer casually to just about any bloomy-rind, soft French as Brie; well, they clearly hadn't tasted Brie de Melun—it's in a class by itself. It offers a lovely full dosage of the savory, mouthwatering, creamy sour-milk flavors. It seems to have a fairly wide window of peak ripeness, possibly due to its smaller format, and doesn't seem to fade or go over the hill quite as fast if not consumed immediately.

TYPE: Raw cow's milk.

PROVENANCE: Saint-Simeon, between Paris, Épernay and Melun.

PRODUCERS: Local farmhouses and artisanal dairies. Genuine raw-milk Bries de Meaux are supplied by the following. *Fermiers:* Compagne Fermiere Benjamin et Edmond de Rothschild; Fromagerie Fermier de Juchy. *Laitiers:* Société Fromagère de la Brie; Fromagerie Dongé SA; Sté Fromagère de Meaux St. Faron (Lactalis). *Affineurs:* Société Fromagère de Meaux St. Faron; Fromagère de la Brie, Fromagerie de Pré–Forêt (Rouzaire), Fromagerie Renard-Gillard, Fromagerie Rouzaire and Gratiot Père et Fils.

PRODUCTION: Although many of the cheeses are still hand-ladled and drained on straw mats, the 1970s saw the end of the magnificent tradition of farmhouse and small-scale artisanal Brie-making. Note that despite appearances, Brie de Melun is not merely a smaller version of Brie de Meaux; the Brie de Melun is a product of lactic coagulation (rather than animal rennet coagulation as is Brie de Meaux), and it requires long, slower aging, resulting in a saltier, more assertively flavored cheese. The Brie de Melun A.O.C. was granted in 1969.

RATINGS

QUALITY

87

STRENGTH

2

APPEARANCE: A somewhat irregularly shaped disk or medium-sized wheel 9 to 10 inches in diameter and just over an inch high with a roughish light brown rind that is covered in white mold. It features a light yellow, smooth, creamy paste.

SIMILAR CHEESES: Brie de Meaux (which is a larger, milder cheese), Brie de Nangis, Coulommiers.

SEASONAL NOTE: Traditionally best from May through December, or better June through October. Nowadays, Brie is available year-round and there is less variation.

WINE PAIRINGS: Generally better paired with reds, but we discovered a surprise success with New Zealand Sauvignon Blanc.
WHITE: New Zealand Sauvignon Blanc.

RED: Chilean Merlot; Beaujolais cru (Gamay); southern French Syrah (Languedoc).

BRIN D'AMOUR

(bran dah-MOOR) How could you not fall for a cheese whose name means "a breath of love" in the Corsican dialect? It can also go by the name of Fleur du Maquis ("Flower of the Maquis"), the *maquis* being the local term for the typical thickets of rough underbrush where highway robbers and guerrilla fighters used to hide out. (Technically, the Fleur du Maquis is a subcategory of Brin d'Amour with juniper berries and a few small chili peppers positioned in the center of the cheese's top surface.) Soft, mild, and aromatic. Honestly, I'm usually not a fan of herb-crusted cheese, but this is truly an exceptional one. The flavors of the best Brin d'Amours are subtly enhanced —not overwhelmed—by their herbs.

TYPE: Sheep's milk.

PROVENANCE: The island of Corsica, in the Mediterranean off the south coast of France.

PRODUCERS: Farmhouses and cooperatives; Antoine Ottavi in Ghissonaccia and other comparables.

PRODUCTION: An uncooked, unpressed artisanal cheese, aged a minimum of 1 and up to 3 months, that is sometimes made with goat's milk or mixed milk; but we only see the 100 percent ewe's milk version in the United States.

APPEARANCE: Encrusted with herbs such as rosemary and savory as well as the occasional juniper berry and/or bird's eye chile. A disk weighing up to 28 ounces. The paste color ranges from off-white to ivory.

SIMILAR CHEESE: LoveTree Farmstead's Big Holmes cheese.

SEASONAL NOTE: Shows well year-round but best June to September.

WINE PAIRINGS: A fairly easy partner for many types of wines, but generally works better with whites.

WHITE: Albariño; Chardonnay (Burgundy, California, or Sicilian); Grüner Veltliner; Alsatian Riesling; German Riesling Auslese or Spätlese; Sauvignon Blanc (Sancerre or California).

RED: Barolo (Nebbiolo); red Bordeaux; California Cabernet; California Pinot Noir.

DESSERT/FORTIFIED: Sherry (Oloroso).

RATINGS

QUALITY

80

STRENGTH

CABRALES

(kah-BRAH-less) Among the world's most distinguished blue cheeses (or should that read "...most disturbing...?"), Cabrales forms the famous "international blues quartet" along with Roquefort from France, Gorgonzola from Italy, and Stilton from England. If you're in the mood for a strong aroma and powerful, persistent flavor, this is a good choice. When ripe, Cabrales is fine textured, semisoft, unctuous, slightly granular, dense, crumbly, salty, and almost uniformly blue throughout. It starts out relatively creamy but will eventually turn somewhat dry (most people prefer it in its moist state). Due to its intensity, Cabrales is generally the last cheese in any tasting sequence. It's best enjoyed in its youth before the blueing overtakes the milk. It's also a more interesting cheese when all three types of milk are used. The genuine Cabrales of years past—when it was still wrapped in leaves instead of foil—would have doubtless offered a more subtle impact on the palate.

TYPE: Raw cow's milk blue (traditional Cabrales is made from a mixture of milks—cow, sheep, and goat—mostly in the spring and summer).

PROVENANCE: Twenty villages in the municipalities of Cabrales and Peñamellera Alta, eastern Asturias, in the middle of the Picos de Europa mountain range, northwestern Spain.

PRODUCERS: Originally farmhouse artisans; now there are small family-run dairies throughout the area.

PRODUCTION: Rustic, traditional, handmade. The milk is from livestock that grazes in high mountain pastures. Ripened for a minimum of 2 and often up to 4 months in natural caves under conditions very similar to those of Roquefort: constant cool temperatures, high humidity, and *soplidos* (literally "puffs" or drafts). D.O.P. since 1981. Modern Cabrales is usually made from 100 percent cow's milk; the old-style mixed-milk version is truly exceptional—with a smoother touch from the sheep's milk component and some added bite from the goat's milk. If goat's or sheep's milk is used, it may account for as much as 30 percent of the total.

APPEARANCE: Flattened cylinders between 2 and 4 inches high and 5 to 8½ inches in diameter, weighing between 2½ and 9 pounds. A slightly irregular, bumpy, sticky natural rind covered with brownish mold. Originally wrapped in sycamore leaves (known as *plageru* in Spanish), genuine Cabrales now comes in a light foil. The paste is ivory-colored with bluish green mold striations throughout and some holes and fissures.

SIMILAR CHEESES: Gamonedo, Picon Beyes, Valdeón.

SEASONAL NOTE: For the mixed-milk variety, from late summer to midwinter.

WINE PAIRINGS: Cabrales is a difficult partner for almost all table wines, but it does well with the darker, toastier, raisiny sweet wines. It is also commonly paired with hard apple cider in Asturias.
🍷 **DESSERT/FORTIFIED:** Aged Madeira; Lustau Sherry (Pedro Ximenez).

RATINGS

QUALITY

92

STRENGTH

6

LE CABRI ARIÈGEOIS

(luh kah-BREE ah-ree-eh-ZWAH) When it comes to goat's milk cheeses, this one is pretty much my "Holy Grail." If you can't find it easily, it is definitely worth taking the trouble to seek out—in fact, it's also a great excuse to plan a trip to southern France and the Pyrenees. Consider Le Cabri Ariègeois a goat's milk version of Vacherin Mont d'Or (see page 280). It's this type of cheese that is a sure indication why, of the three principal cheesemaking milks, goat's is best when fresh—that is, before its acids come to the fore, leaving what many find to be an off-putting tang. If this were the first goat's milk cheese people tasted, I believe there would be a much wider circle of chèvre afficionados. The Cabri is soft and, like a Mont d'Or, delivers lovely, fresh milk flavors but is lighter on the palate. The spruce bark waistband lends this cheese an interesting resinous aroma, but that aspect is subtle and restrained when it comes to the overall flavor profile, which is lovely, balanced, goaty without turning obstreperous, tantalizingly bittersweet, and offers an extremely long and satisfying finish.

TYPE: Raw goat's milk.

PROVENANCE: In the Ariège region of the Pyrenees, southwestern France.

PRODUCER: Fromagerie Fermière Cabrioulet.

PRODUCTION: Traditional artisanal farmhouse. Uncooked, lightly pressed, washed rind. Aged 3 to 6 weeks.

APPEARANCE: Similar to a small Vacherin Mont d'Or; it is presented in a wood-chip box encircled with spruce bark and comes in a miniature wheel less than 2 inches tall and no more than 5 inches across. The rind is moist and dark orange with a screen pattern; the paste is shiny, smooth, and off-white.

SIMILAR CHEESES: Vacherin Mont d'Or, Chevrotin des Aravis (young).

WINE PAIRINGS: A lovely cheese on its own, but it does find a couple of pleasant pairings.
 RED: California Pinot Noir.

SPARKLING: California Champagne-style cuvee (Chardonnay).

RATINGS

QUALITY

92

STRENGTH

2

CAERPHILLY

(kaer-FILLY) I like cheeses that make a bold, emphatic statement. But I also like the subtler, less ostentatious ones. Caerphilly is an eloquent cheese, and Gorwydd's variety (see below) can speak volumes about the grandest style of cheesemaking. It is simple, direct, and incredibly delicious—a cheesy cheese in the best sense of the word and certainly no wallflower. It's the kind of delicacy that elicits a reaction along the lines of, "Now *that's* real cheese!" I often think it comes close to being my "desert-island cheese." Caerphilly is firm, smooth, and creamy, approaching the consistency and weight of a farmhouse butter, albeit with more palpable texture. It tastes clean, mild, and buttery with hints of lemon.

TYPE: Cow's milk.

PROVENANCE: Wales and southwestern England.

PRODUCERS: Chris Duckett used to make it on his family's farm, near Wedmore, Somerset, but recently moved his cheesemaking operation to nearby Westcombe Farm (which also produces a fine farmhouse Cheddar). Martin Trethowan (aka Todd) of Gorwydd ("Gore-with") Farm, Ceredigion, Wales, also makes a genuine Caerphilly. Todd apprenticed with Charlie Westhead, Dougal Cambell (maker of T'yn Grug), and Chris Duckett, whose recipes for starter and cheese he uses. Todd, in turn, taught Simon Jones, who makes Lincolnshire Poacher.

PRODUCTION: Duckett's is made from pasteurized milk, Trethowan's from raw milk. Caerphilly was traditionally consumed young and fresh, after just a few weeks of maturing. At this stage, it is drier, more crumbly, and acidic; as it ripens from the outside in, the paste becomes softer and smoother in texture while the flavors get stronger and more integrated. At age 3 months, which is when we receive it from Neal's Yard Dairy, there is a definite contrast between the ripened paste toward the crust and the fresher portion toward the core. Allowed to ripen all the way through (i.e., up to 4 months), it can become quite funky.

APPEARANCE: 8-pound millstones with light brown, mold-dusted rinds. The paste is light golden yellow, ripening to a darker hue from the outside in.

SIMILAR CHEESES: Llangloffan, Single Gloucester.

WINE PAIRINGS: Gorwydd's Caerphilly is a versatile partner for wines, so keep your cellar well stocked.
WHITE: White Burgundy (Chardonnay); Condrieu (Viognier); Alsatian Gewurztraminer; Grüner Veltliner; Alsatian Riesling; Vouvray demi-sec (Chenin Blanc).
RED: Northern Rhône Syrah; California Pinot Noir.
SPARKLING: Moscato d'Asti.

RATINGS

QUALITY

93

STRENGTH

3

CAMEMBERT

(KAHM-uhm-behr) In many people's minds the word *Camembert* is somehow synonymous with "French cheese." Unfortunately, like many other big names in the world of cheese, this one suffers from the consequences of excessive demand, including especially countless poor imitations. The real deal is labeled Camembert de Normandie A.O.C. and is made by traditional methods from the unpasteurized milk of the Normande breed of cows. An authentic Camembert should have a generous flavor and its texture should be soft but not runny. Because it contains a high degree of moisture, its best days are in its youth before it overferments and loses its resolve entirely. Camembert is one of those types we forget to enjoy when it's at its peak stage of ripeness—although some don't reach this stage—and/or its best season of the year; it can be such a disappointment outside this window. Marie Harel is credited with inventing Camembert in 1791 and she has been elevated to the status of French national heroine. Legend has it the recipe was passed down to her by a refugee priest she helped. A statue in honor of "The Mother of Camembert," stands in the village of Camembert (there is also a Camembert Museum there in the shape of a Camembert box). The poplar-wood box was invented in the late nineteenth century by an engineer named Monsieur Ridel, and this allowed the fragile cheeses to be shipped all over the world.

RATINGS

QUALITY

86

STRENGTH

3

TYPE: Cow's milk (raw and pasteurized).

PROVENANCE: Normandy, northwestern France; specifically the areas around Livarot and Calvados.

PRODUCERS: Recommended brands of genuine Camembert de Normandie are as follows. *Fermier:* Ferme de la Héronnière. *Laitiers:* Château de la Tremblaye; Compagnie des Fromages Domaine de Saint Loup; Fromagerie de la Perelle; Fromagerie du Val de Sienne; Gillot SA laiterie; Lactalis; Laiterie de Bernières; Laiterie du Val d'Ay—Ets Th. Réaux; Sté Fromagère de Saint-Maclou; Vallée SA; and the cooperative Isigny-Sainte-Mère.

PRODUCTION: Formerly, milk from the Normande breed of cow was used exclusively to make this cheese. The curds are hand-ladled into molds and drained naturally. It takes over 2 quarts of milk to make each 9-ounce Camembert. The cheeses are salted, then ripened for 3 weeks in a *hâloir* (drying room) with turnings every 48 hours. Genuine Camembert de Normandie is protected by an A.O.C. granted in 1983. Cheeses made with pasteurized milk may not claim A.O.C. status; however, they are permitted to state *fabriqué en Normandie* (made in

Normandy) on the label to signify authenticity of origin. (Unfortunately, the A.O.C. designation seems to be insufficient in its protection of the genuine article.)

APPEARANCE: A small white wheel about 4½ inches wide and 1¼ inches high, weighing 250 grams (almost 9 ounces). The rind is orangish beige to light brown, with rumples and undulations; it has regular tightly spaced ridges on top and bottom from the draining slats and has an almost complete dusting of bloomy white mold. The paste is light yellow to golden straw colored, smooth, creamy, and somewhat open textured.

SIMILAR CHEESES: Brie, Chaource, Coulommiers.

SEASONAL NOTE: Best November to April.

WINE PAIRINGS: Camembert generally melds well with a variety of reds, but it also finds happiness with various expressions of Chardonnay and Sémillon.

WHITE: Chardonnay (white Burgundy or California). Note: One white wine to avoid is Sauvignon Blanc, or at least all the ones I've tasted with Camembert.

RED: Beaujolais cru (Gamay); Cabernet Sauvignon (Bordeaux or California); red Burgundy (Pinot Noir); Chianti Classico (Sangiovese); Rioja (Tempranillo blend); California Zinfandel.

SPARKLING: Brut Champagne (Blanc de Noirs).

DESSERT/FORTIFIED: Sauternes (late-harvest Sémillon).

CANESTRATO PUGLIESE

(kah-neh-STRAH-toh poo-LYEH-zeh) A rather brash and sultry sheep's milk cheese; it is not afraid and in fact it's rather sly. Tasted on its own terms, Canestrato Pugliese is a reminder that a little bit of cheese—especially hard sheep's cheese—can go a long way. It's a traditional cheese named after the woven baskets used to form and drain the curds (*canestrato* meaning "basketed"). In Homer's *Odyssey*, the cyclops Polyphemus was portrayed as a shepherd who made cheese from the milk of his ewes in this manner. A nearly identical cheese is also made in the mountains of the nearby Abbruzzi; in fact, the shepherds from Puglia traditionally spent summers making cheeses in those high pastures. There are a number of other Italian "basket" cheeses—including those from Crotona and Sicily—but Pugliese is the one I recommend for a genuine taste of rustic southern artistry. The Canestrato Pugliese is considered among the best Pecorino cheeses made; as compared with less subtle versions, it has a grainier consistency and is less sharp and salty, due in large part to the richer grasslands of its production zone. By comparison, a Pecorino Romano is probably too sharp and biting to be enjoyed on its own and is really only suitable for cooking, whereas the Puglieses stand alone very nicely.

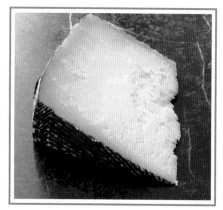

TYPE: Sheep's milk (both raw and pasteurized versions available; a small amount of goat's milk may be added).

PROVENANCE: The area around Foggia in the province of Puglia, the heel of the Italian boot.

PRODUCERS: Two small cheese factories produce fine D.O.P.-status cheeses: Cooperativa Latteria di Santeramo, a co-op, and Cordisco, a private firm.

PRODUCTION: Pressed, drained in baskets and aged from 2 months to 1 year. It received D.O.C. status in 1985 and D.O.P. in 1996.

APPEARANCE: The cheeses come in flattened drums of varying dimensions (anywhere from about 4 to 6 inches tall and 5½ to 14 inches in diameter), weighing 5 to 30 pounds. The rind is shiny and light brown to darker reddish brown with a basket pattern imprinted on it; and the paste is straw-colored, fairly dense, and somewhat flaky.

SIMILAR CHEESES: Canestrato Abbruzzese, Pecorino Romano.

WINE PAIRINGS: Canestrato Pugliese comes off as a bossy cheese partner for most wines but succumbs to Sauvignon Blanc and the less assertive Pinot Noirs.

🍷 **WHITE**: White Bordeaux (Sauvignon Blanc blend).

 RED: California Pinot Noir.

RATINGS

QUALITY

91

STRENGTH

4

CANTAL

(kahn-TAHL) This venerable cheese has ancient roots in its production zone and was mentioned by food writers and historians through the ages, beginning with Pliny the Elder in the first century A.D. For many, Cantal is the master of ceremonies, and no party would be complete without it. In the arena of French cheeses, along with Beaufort and Comté, it can take the stage anytime of the year. Cantal has a semihard paste, and its overall impression is formidable yet sublime. I like to think of it as "The Big Easy." It is a straightforward cheese from a very traditional, recognizable, and extremely approachable category—all of which belies the painstaking labor that goes into it. Like many similar mountain cheeses, Cantal develops deliciously melded, complex, and nutty flavors when well-aged. It has smooth and buttery flavors with a gentle presence that lingers gracefully.

TYPE: Cow's milk (raw or pasteurized).

PROVENANCE: The town of Cantal and forty-one surrounding communes in the Aubrac Plateau of the Auvergne region, south-central France.

PRODUCERS: In addition to over 100 farmhouse producers, there are approximately thirty co-op and dairy producers of Cantal, which are supplied by as many as 4,000 milk producers. Recommended makers of the genuine raw-milk version are Jean-Paul Bonal; Coopérative laitière de Valuejols; Coopérative laitière de Thérondels; Fromagerie Morin-Mopalait; and Laiterie Condutier.

PRODUCTION: Mountain farms, located at elevations of between 700 and 1,000 meters, make Cantal in the summer, and commercial plants make it year-round. The curds are pressed three times, broken up, milled, salted, and molded, then wrapped in cloth. The cheeses are aged in cool, damp cellars with regular turnings and brushings. Cantal Jeune (young) is aged up to 3 months; regular Cantal undergoes 3 to 6 months' ripening; Cantal Vieux undergoes further aging. Cantal received A.O.C. protection in 1956; its "delimited production zone" extends to a large area of the Auvergne.

APPEARANCE: Standard-sized Cantal comes in large drums—also known locally as *fourmes*—14 to 18 inches in diameter and 14 to 16 inches tall weighing from 77 to 99 pounds: tall enough to last but short enough to lend the cheese maturity at a relatively young age. A medium-sized Petit Cantal weighs 44 pounds or 20 kilos; the smaller version, Cantalet, weighs 22 pounds or 10 kilos. Each authentic Cantal has an aluminum plate attached to its rind as a "guarantee of quality." The rind is thick and gray; it can become bumpy and take on a yellow hue with age. The paste is smooth and ivory colored; with age, it becomes darker and more golden in color.

(continued)

RATINGS

QUALITY

89

STRENGTH

3

SIMILAR CHEESES: Laguiole, Lancashire, Salers.

WINE PAIRINGS: Cantal works well with a range of table wines.
WHITE: White Bordeuax (Sauvignon Blanc).

RED: Beaujolais cru (Gamay); California Cabernet Sauvignon; California Merlot; California Pinot Noir.
SPARKLING: Champagne-style Blanc de Noirs.

DESSERT/FORTIFIED: LBV Port.

CAPRINO NOCE

(kah-PREE-noh NOH-cheh) The term *caprino* encompasses a fairly broad category of charming little goat's milk cheeses from the mountains of northwestern and southern Italy. While not nearly as well known or widespread as the French chèvres, they are certainly worthy of investigation. *Caprino* cheeses are sold either fresh, briefly aged (1 or 2 weeks), or aged 1 to 3 months. Some of them are sprinkled with herbs, spices, or vegetal ash; but this is one of my favorites, and it requires no such manipulation. Young Caprino Noce is wrapped in walnut leaves and allowed to ripen sufficiently to acquire pleasing and distinct flavors; a well-aged example is straightforward, soft, moist, and edible right through to the rind just inside the leaves. That these little gems of the Italian cheesemaking world can travel so well is a testament not only to the skilled team of *affineurs* at Cora but also to the vastly improved distribution systems in place today.

TYPE: Mixed milk: cow's, sheep's, and goat's.

PROVENANCE: The Langhe, comprising the hill country near the towns of Asti, Allesandria, and Cuneo, Piedmont, northwestern Italy.

PRODUCERS: The *stagionatura* (*affineur*) of these rustic farmhouse-style cheeses is Cora.

PRODUCTION: The recipe of walnut leaf-wrapping followed by careful aging seems to be particularly effective for cheeses of this dimension. The milk is all produced on the farms where the cheeses are made; they are selected and ripened for 20 to 30 days by the experts at Cora who travel thousands of kilometers throughout the alpine foothills and valleys of Piedmont each year to seek out and collect the best local artisanal cheeses.

APPEARANCE: Small drums 2 to 2½ inches in diameter and about 2½ inches high, weighing 5 to 6 ounces and wrapped in leaves. The paste is compact and chalky white; it ripens, from the outside in, to a smooth, melting consistency and off-white color.

SIMILAR CHEESE: Banon.

WINE PAIRINGS: Blends well with the softer, grapier reds.
RED: Beaujolais cru (Gamay); red Burgundy (Pinot Noir); Argentinian Malbec; Rioja (Tempranillo blend); Australian Shiraz; Chianti Classico (Sangiovese).

RATINGS

QUALITY

87

STRENGTH

1

CAPRINO NOCCETTO

(kah-PREE-noh noh-CHET-oh) This is essentially a smaller version of the Caprino Noce, except that it is made exclusively with goat's milk—a delightful, superbly balanced little delicacy selected and ripened by the exacting team of *affineurs* at Cora. As Pecorino is the diminutive name for sheep cheese, so Caprino is the same with respect to goat (*capra*). In addition, this particular cheese refers to itself on its label as a Tomino—that is, the Italian version of a small *tomme*. The Cora firm is based in Monesiglio in the province of Cuneo; their cheese selectors scour all the hills and valleys of Piedmont for the best artisan cheeses to ripen and sell throughout Italy and the rest of the cheese-loving world. Because of its small size, the influence of the black walnut leaves on this cheese is more pronounced than the Caprino Noce. The Noccetto can pack a big nutty flavor.

TYPE: Raw goat's milk.

PROVENANCE: Piedmont, northwestern Italy.

PRODUCER: The firm of Cora selects and ripens these cheeses from among the best of the local artisanal producers.

PRODUCTION: Maximum 90 days aging.

APPEARANCE: A beautiful little package 1½ to 2 inches in diameter and the same height, weighing 50 grams (1¾ ounces), wrapped in walnut leaves with strips of raffia holding them in place.

SIMILAR CHEESES: Banon, Caprino Noce.

WINE PAIRINGS: The Caprino Noccetto favors light-bodied, dry, crisp white wines.
WHITE: White Bordeaux (Sauvignon Blanc); California Chardonnay; New Zealand Sauvignon Blanc; Savennières (Chenin Blanc from the Loire Valley).
RED: California Cabernet Sauvignon.

DESSERT/FORTIFIED: Moscadello di Montalcino (late-harvest Muscat from Tuscany).

RATINGS

QUALITY

86

STRENGTH

2

CARDINAL SIN

A monastery-style cheese with a good balance of pleasantly sour and bitter, lactic and piquant, flavors. My approach is to hold on to the Cardinal as long as I dare, allowing it to become as "sinful" as possible. Short of that, it can be quite tame. This is also a cheese you might want to give a bath if it looks too dry: simply place it in a small bowl or saucer with a tablespoon or so of water with a little white wine added, and get its surface wet.

TYPE: Cow's milk.

PROVENANCE: Quantock Hills, Somerset, southwest England.

PRODUCER: Monastery Cheeses Ltd.

PRODUCTION: The recipe was developed by Monastery's cheesemaker Amode Katiyar under the guidance of the late, great cheese guru James Aldridge. Friesian cow's milk is obtained from a local farm and/or cooperative in Somerset. The milk is pasteurized and vegetarian rennet is added; the curds are cut, stirred, and placed by hand into draining molds. The cheeses are brine salted, then matured for 6 to 8 weeks in caves where they receive regular turnings as well as washings in a brine solution that includes *B. linens*.

APPEARANCE: A somewhat irregularly shaped medium-sized wheel, 8 inches in diameter and 3 inches tall, weighing about 4 pounds. The rind is moist and beige to brownish orange in color with orange tinges and a cross-hatch draining-rack pattern top and bottom. The paste is smooth, semifirm, pliant, and orange tinted. It ripens from a slightly chalky consistency to a smoother one from the outside in.

SIMILAR CHEESES: Munster, Reblochon.

WINE PAIRINGS: Melds smoothly with many wine types, especially the sweeter whites.
- **RED**: Beaujolais (Gamay); Carignan (medium-bodied, fruity, spicy red from the Languedoc-Roussillon, southern France); Oregon Pinot Noir.
- **SPARKLING**: Champagne (Blanc de Blancs).
- **DESSERT/FORTIFIED**: Jurançon (late-harvest, made from the Petit Mensang grape in southwestern France); Madeira.

RATINGS

QUALITY

72

STRENGTH

2

CASHEL BLUE

(KAH-shel) In the late eighteenth century, the Grubb family was part of a sect called the Anabaptists who were persecuted in England. They fled to County Tipperary, Ireland, where they became millers and butter makers. In the mid-1980s, Jane and Louis Grubb created this wonderful farmstead blue cheese, the first of its kind in Ireland to my knowledge. It rarely disappoints and it keeps well; consequently, I think of it as "Reliable Cashel"—and the name fits since a cashel was an enclosure for herds of cows in the Middle Ages. The cheese is moist, creamy, and semisoft with a voluptuous texture. It can melt in your mouth and its taste is relatively mellow for a blue, featuring a distinct sweetness along with the expected salted butter and tangy notes. Cashel Blue compares favorably to the great Gorgonzola and may be even more reliable. It's an excellent "dessert cheese"—the perfect choice for a festive after-dinner cheese course.

TYPE: Pasteurized cow's milk blue.

PROVENANCE: Beechmount, Fethard (near Cashel), County Tipperary, south-central Ireland.

PRODUCERS: The Grubb family.

PRODUCTION AND AGING: Farmhouse-made; aged from 6 months to a year.

APPEARANCE: 3- to 4-pound cylinders about 6 inches across and 5 inches high with naturally wet rinds that come enclosed in gold foil. The paste is bone-colored with well-spaced striations of blue-gray mold.

SIMILAR CHEESES: Gorgonzola, Bleu d'Auvergne.

WINE PAIRINGS: An amenable cheese partner for dessert wines and various expressions of Chardonnay.
WHITE: White Burgundy (Chardonnay); California Chardonnay.

RED: California Pinot Noir.

DESSERT/FORTIFIED: Late-harvest California Chardonnay; Madeira; Tawny Port; Hungarian Tokaji; Sherry (Oloroso and Lustau).

RATINGS
QUALITY
84

STRENGTH
2

CATAHOULA

(kah-tah-HOO-lah) Be forewarned! Here is a cheese that is most definitely for the daring and adventurous palates. I call it dangerous—in the best sense of the word. My colleague Daphne Zepos, *affineur* at the Artisanal Cheese Center, says: "It's the bungee jumping of cheeses!" Put it in the category of eye-opening "stinky" cheeses; it can easily stand up to a really ripe Afuega'l Pitu (page 71), an Innerschweizer Weicher (page 249), or a Stanser Fladä (page 248). Its maker is Roberto Molina, a dedicated, independent, and hard-working artisan who has carved out a niche for himself at his farmstead in Louisiana. (He also makes about seven other cheeses, each proudly named after a different parish.) Catahoula has a powerful, pungent aroma and fairly strong flavors; its paste evolves to a creamy, soft consistency with aging. Given its washed-rind aging and its Louisiana *terroir*, who would be surprised that Catahoula emerges as funky and individualistic as any American original?

TYPE: Raw cow's milk.

PROVENANCE: Metairie, Washington Parish, Louisiana, USA, a few miles north of New Orleans.

PRODUCER: Roberto Molina, Chicory Farm.

PRODUCTION: Made from the high-quality raw whole milk of a herd of cows on a nearby farm. Uncooked, unpressed; aged at least 60 days and sometimes as much as 12 weeks. The rinds are washed with brine to promote the development of *B. linens*, which lends the cheese its powerful aromas and complex flavor profile.

APPEARANCE: Catahoula comes in two sizes of rounds: small, about 3 inches in diameter and 1 1/2 high and weighing about 1/4 pound; and large, 6 inches in diameter and weighing about 1 pound. The rind is beige and moist with splotches of brownish, gray, and white mold. The paste is cream colored or off-white and ripens to a smooth consistency from the outside in.

SIMILAR CHEESES: Époisses, Livarot, Pont l'Éveque.

WINE PAIRING: A cheese of strong, assertive character that can be tamed by spicier, crisp whites.
 WHITE: Alsatian Pinot Blanc.

RATINGS

QUALITY

71

STRENGTH

6

CENTOVALLI TICINO

(chen-toh-VAH-lee tee-CHEE-noh) How would I describe this cheese in a phrase or two? Grace with dignity; unending finesse. . . . It's an expertly crafted mountain cheese that's been enjoyed by emperors and common folk alike over the past millennium. Its paste is firm with a smooth, sweet, buttery flavor. The first big taste impression is a gentle smokiness; the finish leaves a lingering impression of sweet heavy cream. The Centovalli is unlike other alpine cheeses in that its flavors manage to linger without relying on excessive rind washings or oversalting—the methods that give so many other cooked, pressed, aged mountain cheeses their stout, sharper, mouthwatering qualities. Instead, the finish of a well-aged Centovalli is especially smooth and milky, a testament to the restraint of the cheesemakers and ripeners as well as the high quality of the milk.

TYPE: Raw cow's milk.

PROVENANCE: Valle Leventina in the Ticino canton, southeastern Switzerland.

PRODUCERS: Alpine farmhouse production; local artisanal cheesemakers come and go (not too many people spend every summer high in the Alps herding cows and making cheese).

PRODUCTION: A mountain-style cheese, Ticino is made strictly in summer with no salt added, a rarity. The milk comes from a rare breed of white cows found only in these alps, which are steep and feature a fairly extreme climate. The curds are cooked over a wood fire then pressed. The cheeses are aged first in stone cellars up in the mountains till the end of summer, then in the aging rooms of local dairies that buy the wheels from the cheesemakers. High humidity promotes the growth of furry, grayish white cat's hair mold that is pressed down to help form the rind. The total maturation period is from 9 to 12 months.

APPEARANCE: Comes in 14-pound wheels, 11½ to 12 inches in diameter and about 3 inches high, fairly cylindrical but with slightly rounded edges. The rind is light brown, slightly rough, riddled with very tiny holes, and dusted with white mold. The paste is light yellow to straw colored, smooth and dense, with round holes widely spaced throughout.

RATINGS

QUALITY

91

STRENGTH

3

SIMILAR CHEESES: Abondance, Prättigauer; also the Italian mountain cheeses produced in the Valtellina region across the border.

SEASONAL NOTE: Cheeses bought from the end of winter through spring and summer will probably have sufficient aging to yield the best volume of flavors.

WINE PAIRINGS: Centovalli's smooth flavor profile makes it a highly versatile partner, offering a much broader range of pairings than other cheeses of its type. As spectacular as those other mountain cheeses may be, few are as affable with wines as this one.

WHITE: Alsatian Gewurztraminer; Grüner Veltliner; Savennières (Chenin Blanc from the Loire Valley).

RED: Barbaresco (Nebbiolo); southern Rhône Syrah-Grenache blends; Australian Shiraz.

DESSERT/FORTIFIED: Sauternes (late-harvest Sémillon); Sherry (Oloroso).

CHABICHOU DE POITOU

(shah-bee-SHOO duh pwah-TOO) This is a delightful, refreshing little rustic goat's milk cheese that is believed to have been initiated by the Saracens, who ruled parts of France in the eighth century A.D. The word *chabi* and its diminutive *chabichou* come from the Arabic *chebli* ("goat"). It is the progenitor of so many other goat's milk cheeses of northern and western France. Over the centuries—and especially throughout the last one—there's been a temptation to alter it, coat it with something or break it up and incorporate it into a recipe. Why not just leave it alone and enjoy it at its fairly wide window of peak ripeness? Chabichou's appeal lies in its simplicity. The flavor of good, clean goat's milk comes through every time I taste it. Its dimensions allow it to ripen early so it can retain its freshness while developing enough texture to offer a satisfying mouthfeel.

TYPE: Goat's milk.

PROVENANCE: The limestone plateau of Haut Poitou in central western France.

PRODUCERS: More than a handful of farmhouses and at least eight creameries (*laiteries*) make authentic A.O.C. Chabichou de Poitu. *Laitiers:* Chèvrechard; Coop. Sèvre et Belle; Eurial Poituraine; Fromagerie des Gors; Fromagerie de Fontenille; La Bonde de Gâtine; and SARL le villageois. *Affineurs:* Le Père Bafien; and EURL Paul Georgelet—SCEA Le Petit Boisselage.

PRODUCTION: Made with whole goat's milk. Hand-ladled into cylindrical molds called *bondes* (which means "plug," as in a barrel plug—roughly the shape of these little cheeses; see also Bonde de Gâtine, page 95). Aged 10 days in a *hâloir* (drying room). A.O.C. protected.

APPEARANCE: A picturesque small cylinder up to 2½ inches high and 2¼ inches across, weighing up to 5¼ ounces. The rind is rough, squiggly, and off-white to light beige in color; it eventually develops a thin coating of grayish blue mold as it matures. The paste is chalky white.

SIMILAR CHEESES: Crottin de Chavignol, Sancerre.

WINE PAIRINGS: Gentle Chabichou clashes with few wines, but especially favors light, crisp whites.
WHITE: Northern Italian Chardonnay blend; Alsatian Pinot Blanc; Tokay Pinot Gris (Alsace); Sauvignon Blanc (California, Sancerre, or New Zealand).
RED: Chianti Classico (Sangiovese).

SPARKLING: Moscato d'Asti.

DESSERT/FORTIFIED: Tawny Port.

RATINGS

QUALITY

88

STRENGTH

CHAOURCE

(shah-OORSE) Chaource is named after the small town where it originated; no one really knows whether it was created in a monastery or on a farm, but it has been handcrafted on at least one local farm for the past 600 years. Chaource is meant to be enjoyed relatively young—no more than 2 months old. Compared with other bloomy-rind types it has a certain plump fluffiness, an appealing "lightness of being." With 50 percent fat in dry matter, it qualifies as a double crème yet it can deliver all the satisfaction of a triple crème (75percent or more f.d.m.). I'd recommend it as somewhat lighter but potentially just as pleasingly rich as its triple-crème cousins. Although it can be inconsistent—either a little salty or a little flat on the palate—when Chaource is at its best, it is delightfully smooth and creamy.

TYPE: Cow's milk.

PROVENANCE: The Champagne region, in the *départment* of Aube, around the towns of Coulommiers and St. Simeon, just to the southeast of Paris. Also in the northwestern part of Burgundy.

PRODUCERS: Various local creameries including Fromagerie de la Brie; Fromagerie de Champagne; Fromagerie de L'Auxon; Fromagerie du Pré-Fôret (Rouzaire); GAEC des Tourelles; and Lincet. There is also a farmhouse version that is ripened and exported by the *affineur-fromager* François Millet.

PRODUCTION: A.O.C. protected. From the milk of the Brunes des Alpes, Tachetées de l'Est and Frisonnes breeds. The curds are unpressed, uncooked, and hand-ladled; the cheeses are aged from 2 weeks up to 2 months.

APPEARANCE: Somewhat loose, white bloomy rind that may exhibit streaks of gold or red. Made in two formats: 200 grams (or about 7 ounces) and 450 grams (1 pound). Comes in small drums 3 to 4½ inches in diameter and 2½ inches tall with a light yellow rind covered in velvety white mold that may begin to exhibit some reddish tints with age. Once the rind and paste of a Chaource begin to go gray and the cheese becomes very soft, it is past its prime.

SIMILAR CHEESES: Coulommiers, Explorateur, Roucoulons.

RATINGS

QUALITY

74

STRENGTH

2

SEASONAL NOTE: Best summer through fall.

WINE PAIRINGS: Chaource is a versatile partner for many wine types.

 WHITE: Chardonnay (California, white Burgundy, or northern Italian); Alsatian Pinot Blanc.

 RED: Barbaresco (Nebbiolo); Beaujolais cru (Gamay); California Merlot; Rioja (Tempranillo blend).

 SPARKLING: Champagne (Blanc de Noirs).

 DESSERT/FORTIFIED: LBV Port.

CHAPUT VACHERIN MONT D'OR

(shah-POO vash-RAN mon-DORE) The distinguished Québec creamery Chaput makes a fairly large variety of cheeses, many of which have caught my eye over the years and even captured my fancy. At one point, I had a list of ten or more of them as possible candidates for inclusion in this book. To summarize, Chaput cheeses can be very good, albeit somewhat inconsistent. I've decided to include a listing only for this, my current favorite (as of this writing), but I do recommend you try some of the other Chaput offerings, because you're likely to encounter some pleasant surprises. Chaput's version of Mont d'Or hints at the velvety soft texture of the French original and, although its flavor is different, it is nevertheless delightful—and maybe even a little fresher. At peak, it's not as unctuous as the French original, but still very tasty.

TYPE: Raw cow's milk.

PROVENANCE: Chateauguay, suburban Montréal, Québec, Canada.

PRODUCER: Fromagerie Chaput (Patrick Chaput).

PRODUCTION: Artisanal and in the traditional style of Vacherin Mont d'Or. The milk comes from a select herd of cows, raised on a farm where no pesticides are used, in the Vallée du Saint-Laurent (St. Lawrence River Valley). The cheeses are aged in a humid cave at 54 degrees Fahrenheit for five weeks with regular rubbings in brine for the first 3 weeks to promote development of the *candidum* ripening mold; they are then placed in their wooden boxes and stored for an additional 2 weeks in a cool place.

APPEARANCE: Small wheels about 4 inches in diameter and 1³/4 inches tall, weighing about 1 pound, encircled in a band of spruce sapwood (the layer between the bark and the tree's interior). The rind is damp and yellowish to light brown in color with some white and brownish red molds as well as ridged draining-rack imprints; the interior is off-white in color and very smooth in texture. (There is also a large version of the cheese, 7¹/2 to 8 inches in diameter and 1³/4 inches tall, weighing about 3 pounds.)

SIMILAR CHEESES: Krümmenswiler Försterkäse, Vacherin Mont d'Or.

RATINGS

QUALITY

76

STRENGTH

2

WINE PAIRINGS: Chaput's Mont d'Or favors medium-bodied raisiny red wines.
- **WHITE:** Alsatian Gewurztraminer; Tokay Pinot Gris (Alsace); Vouvray demi-sec (Chenin Blanc).
- **RED:** Amarone della Valpolicella; Barbera d'Asti; Beaujolais cru (Gamay); Chianti Classico (Sangiovese); California Merlot; southern French Syrah blend (Languedoc).
- **SPARKLING:** Blanc de Blancs Champagne (and other Chardonnay-based wines).

CHEDDAR

Because of an accident of British history—or maybe it could be better described as an unfortunate evolutionary quirk—much of the cheese sold today under the name of Cheddar doesn't deserve to bear the name. Unlike other venerable national treasures, "Cheddar" was never legally protected or defined. The rare, remaining genuine British Cheddars are superb examples of the potential of a raw-milk farmhouse cheese. But they can be counted on the fingers of one hand: Keen's, Montgomery's, Lincolnshire Poacher, Reade's (from the Isle of Mull, Scotland), and another recent addition to the list, Westcombe's. Across the Atlantic, there are several respectable farmhouse Cheddars, including Grafton's special aged reserve and Fiscalini Farms Bandage Cheddar. Real Cheddar features a hard paste and dry, subtle consistency with a remarkable range of fruity, sharp, and nutty flavors. It's another one of those delectable artifacts that, upon first tasting, is practically guaranteed to elicit an exclamation such as "Now *that* is cheese!"

TYPE: Raw cow's milk.

PRODUCTION: Classic farmhouse Cheddars are cloth wrapped and aged at higher temperatures and humidities than standard Cheddars; they receive 10 to 18 months-plus aging.

APPEARANCE: Large drums of between 54 and 60 pounds. Keen's makes a 28- to 30-pounder for export. Westcombe is 8½ inches high and 13 inches in diameter (54 pounds, clothbound). Montgomery's is 13 inches in diameter. Lincolnshire Poacher is a bit smaller, at around 40 pounds.

SIMILAR CHEESES: Nothing compares with a real British farmhouse Cheddar; in America, we have a few cheeses that come admirably close, so we've chosen to include them in this category.

WINE PAIRINGS: Farmhouse Cheddars are versatile partners with many wine types; they're especially reliable with Pinot Noirs, domestic and French.
WHITE: White Burgundy (Chardonnay); German Gewürztraminer Spätlese; Alsatian Pinot Blanc.
RED: Barbaresco or Barolo (Nebbiolo); red Bordeaux (Cabernet Sauvignon blend); red Burgundy (Pinot Noir); Rhône reds (Syrah); California Pinot Noir.
SPARKLING: Brut Champagne.

DESSERT/FORTIFIED: LBV Port; Tawny Port; Sherry (Oloroso).

FISCALINI BANDAGE CHEDDAR

The third generation of the Fiscalini family continues the livestock-raising and cheesemaking traditions of its Swiss ancestors. They make a number of cheeses, including a traditional farmhouse bandage-wrapped Cheddar-style cheese that comes in 60-pound drums, 18 inches in diameter and 12 inches tall, like its British counterparts. The cheeses are bandaged in cheesecloth in preparation for their aging period of at least 16 and up to 36 months; the bandage develops a natural protective mold covering. The paste is straw colored with firm, crumbly texture and a nutty, slightly smoky taste—more complex than most American aged Cheddars. Fiscalini's Bandage Cheddar won a first place in its category in 2003 from the American Cheese Society.

PROVENANCE: Modesto, in the Central Valley of California, directly east of San Francisco Bay.

PRODUCER: Fiscalini Farms

RATINGS

QUALITY

88

STRENGTH

4

GRAFTON

This is the standard-bearer of Vermont Cheddars, made from the raw milk of select herds of local Jersey cows. Grafton sells its cheeses at different levels of maturity beginning with a standard 1-year-old. They come in 1-pound bricks and 2-pound blocks sealed in wax. I recommend the Four-Star (4 years) or the Gold (30 to 36 months).

PROVENANCE: Grafton, Vermont, USA.

PRODUCER: Grafton Village Cheese Company.

RATINGS

QUALITY

89

STRENGTH

5

KEEN'S

Keen's is a classic full-flavored, sharp, tangy firm-bodied Cheddar with a smoother texture and that familiar "bite." It is one of the two greatest English farmhouse Cheddars. Its sharpness or bite is a result of the pinpoint, precise focus of its distinct flavors. Keen's is highly self-assured and relies less on fruitiness (a characteristic more easily recognized in Montgomery's).

PROVENANCE: Somerset, southwestern England.

PRODUCER: Keen family.

RATINGS
QUALITY

97

STRENGTH

5

LINCOLNSHIRE POACHER

Despite its wonderfully evocative name, which might lead you to believe it's something other than a stolid, respectable British farmhouse Cheddar, this cheese is effectively just that. The Joneses tend and milk their own herd of 170 Holsteins. The cheeses are made from October to May and aged 2 years plus additional time at Neal's Yard Dairy. Unlike other Cheddars and Cheddar-type cheeses, Lincolnshire Poacher is not clothbound. It has a tough, sandy-colored plasticote rind, mottled with mold. Plasticote is a synthetic, artificial rind that is painted on young cheeses. It does not crack but at the same time allows the cheeses to breathe. In the case of Lincolnshire Poacher, it eventually wears off, leaving a natural rind.

PROVENANCE: Alford, Lincolnshire, east-central England.

PRODUCER: Simon and Tim Jones, Ulceby Grange.

RATINGS
QUALITY

93

STRENGTH

5

MONTGOMERY'S

Montgomery's offers a complex spectrum of flavors and aromas with a touch of sweetness and the suggestion of a Sunday roast. It is truly the modern benchmark of all great Cheddars. Taste Monty's and compare all the rest!

PROVENANCE: Somerset, southwestern England.

PRODUCER: Montgomery family.

RATINGS
QUALITY

98

STRENGTH

5

READE'S

This Scottish Cheddar-style cheese is made in the same way as the great farmhouse Cheddars of Somerset, England. Compared with the English types, Reade's Isle of Mull Cheddar (aka Tobermory) is less fruity and has a defining hint of bitterness, which I find a highly pleasant and desirable reflection of *terroir*. The cheese has been through changes in its development to achieve a signature flavor; in that sense, you might say it has been inconsistent, but I would say it's found its measure.

PROVENANCE: Isle of Mull, off the western coast of Scotland.

PRODUCER: Chris Reade.

RATINGS
QUALITY

92

STRENGTH

5

WESTCOMBE

Richard Calver revived a 100-year-old farmhouse Cheddar-making tradition in the late 1990s with the intention of creating a cheese as good as Montgomery's or Keen's. The farm now produces about 19 cheeses a day, 4 days a week. They are clothbound and aged 12 to 14 months. Westcombe is not as dry or as nutty-flavored as Montgomery's and not as sticky as Keen's. It is smooth textured and firm. Its flavors are fruity and gentle with considerable subtlety and depth. It has a bit more acidity than Monty's but not as much as Keen's. A "new classic."

PROVENANCE: Somerset, southwestern England.

PRODUCER: Richard Calver, Westcombe Farm.

RATINGS

QUALITY

91

STRENGTH

5

CHESHIRE

(CHESH-uhr) Timeless and exemplary, Cheshire has been called a cheese of "gritty simplicity" in the best sense of the phrase. Cheshire is England's oldest and one of its most revered cheeses. While most of Cheshire consists of factory-made imitations, there is one surviving genuine cheese: Appleby's. It is semihard but nevertheless moist, with a wonderful light, flaky, crumbly texture; a savory, slightly salty full-bodied tang; and a long, lingering finish. With 6 months or more of aging, the flavors of the larger cheeses become richer, deeper, and more powerful with perhaps a hint of smokiness. The county of Shropshire encompasses an area south of Cheshire along the border with Wales and abutting the counties of Worcestershire, Herefordshire, and Staffordshire. (There was also a traditional and virtually identical cheese called Shropshire.) Its northern plains offer rich grazing and have been a fertile dairy-producing area for centuries. The salt flats of the Cheshire basin are considered to be the source of the cheese's distinct character. Both Cheshire and Shropshire are prone to a phenomenon referred to as "green fade": they go slightly blue or green with mold. Although this is a hit-and-miss business not entirely under control of the cheesemaker or ripener, it is quite popular with many cheese aficionados.

TYPE: Raw cow's milk.

PROVENANCE: Shropshire, west-central England.

PRODUCER: The Appleby family, at Hawkestone Abbey Farm.

PRODUCTION: Genuine farmhouse; the Applebys and staff tend and milk their own herd of nearly 300 Friesians. The curds are cooked (but less than Cheddar) and pressed. The cheeses are aged for 6 weeks (smaller versions) or 2 to 10 months (larger ones).

APPEARANCE: Clothbound tall cylinders weighing 18 pounds. There is a light-colored version and a yellower version, made with the addition of annatto.

SIMILAR CHEESES: Double Gloucester, Llangloffan.

WINE PAIRINGS: Apart from an interesting combination of reds and whites, including at least two expressions of the Muscat grape, Cheshire pairs well with a good glass of traditional ale.
  WHITE: California Chardonnay; German Muskateller Kabinett; Pouilly-Fumé (Sauvignon Blanc).
  RED: Beaujolais cru (Gamay); Dolcetto d'Alba; Chianti Classico (Sangiovese).
  DESSERT/FORTIFIED: Lustau Sherry (Moscatel).

RATINGS
QUALITY
84

STRENGTH
3

LE CHÈVRE NOIR

(luh shev NWAHR) Delightful and sweet, this is a cheese that reflects the dedication of its makers to deliver a consistent, refreshing, clean, and lean product. It has a firm ivory-white paste with an underlying crystalline texture, which provides one of the more remarkable taste sensations of any cheese. Imagine a medium to full-flavored Cheddar-style cheese with a touch of sweetness on the attack, buttery and caramelly notes, a pleasantly goaty finish, and a dense texture that has a hint of crunch when you bite into it—and there you have Le Chèvre Noir. It has won first place in Canadian local and national competitions as well as a first at the American Cheese Society convention.

TYPE: Goat's milk.

PROVENANCE: Chesterville, Québec, Canada.

PRODUCER: Fromagerie Tournevent.

PRODUCTION: A Cheddar-type recipe but made with fresh goat's milk, pasteurized at low temperature to preserve its flavors. The aging process, which lasts a minimum of 12 months, yields "flavor crystals" (converted lactose sugars) that give this cheese its special mouthfeel.

APPEARANCE: 2.4-pound bricks encased in black wax.

WINE PAIRINGS: Blends nicely with soft, raisiny reds and bright whites.
WHITE: Malvasia Bianca; Tokay Pinot Gris (Alsace); California Sauvignon Blanc.
RED: Barbera d'Alba; California Syrah; Zinfandel (California).

RATINGS

QUALITY

74

STRENGTH

2

CHEVROTIN DES ARAVIS

(shev-roh-TAN days ah-rah-VEE) This is a goat cheese with a difference—most definitely *not* your typical chalky white Loire Valley chèvre. It offers a soft, mild flavor with a pleasant, somewhat musty, goaty finish. It's a small goat's milk version of Reblochon, a mountain cheese benefiting from the animals' high-pasture summer grazing season. Compared with the cow's milk Reblochons, the Chevrotin des Aravis, at peak, is softer and may be a little younger. A Chevrotin has its moments—or rather its several days—of absolute peak ripeness within its season, which is summer through fall.

TYPE: Raw goat's milk.

PROVENANCE: From the Haute-Savoie region of France, along the Swiss border, south of Lake Geneva; named after the Aravis mountain range near Megève.

PRODUCERS: Produced on only a few local farms and ripened by the *affineur* Fromagerie Missillier.

PRODUCTION: Made by a recipe similar to that of Reblochon—that is, uncooked, lightly pressed, and with a washed rind. Aged 3 to 6 months.

APPEARANCE: The washed rind has a pinkish to orangish yellow color with some whitish powdery mold. Comes in rounds up to 4 inches in diameter and 1½ inches thick, weighing about 9 ounces, with a smooth, supple off-white paste.

SIMILAR CHEESE: Consider this a goat's milk version of Reblochon.

SEASONAL NOTE: Summer through fall.

WINE PAIRINGS: Chevrotin des Aravis favors both the crisp, light-bodied whites and the sweeter ones.
- **WHITE:** Grüner Veltliner; German Riesling Kabinett; Sauvignon Blanc (white Bordeaux or Sancerre); Tokay Pinot Gris (Alsace); Vouvray demi-sec (Chenin Blanc).
- **RED:** California Cabernet; northern Rhône Syrah.

- **DESSERT/FORTIFIED:** Sauternes (late-harvest Sémillon).

RATINGS

QUALITY

82

STRENGTH

2

CLASSIC BLUE

Here is something a little different, an artisanal product of western Massachusetts, to liven up your cheese plate, pique your curiosity, and stimulate your taste buds. Classic Blue is designated a "surface-ripened blue goat's milk cheese," which places it in an unusual if not unique category. It is semisoft and fluffy and features a gentle, mellow goat milk flavor with a nice little bit of zip from the mold.

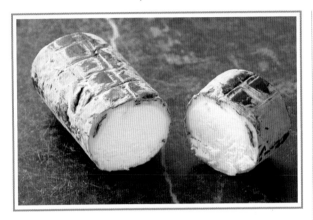

TYPE: Pasteurized goat's milk.

PROVENANCE: Westfield Farm, Hubbardston, north-central Massachusetts, USA.

PRODUCER: Proprietor-cheesemakers Bob and Letitia Kilmoyer retired in 1996 and handed the reins to Bob and Debby Stetson.

PRODUCTION: Classic Blue starts off with fresh white chèvre-type curds that are inoculated with the Roquefort mold (*P. roquefortii*). The cheeses dry over a period of about 2 weeks, evaporating from 10 ounces to about 7 and developing an exterior covering of blue mold. Then they are wrapped in permeable cellophane and shipped after about 1 week; they are best sold and consumed after an additional 2 to 4 weeks' curing in a refrigerator.

APPEARANCE: Logs about 5¹/₂ inches long and 2 inches in diameter, with a blue moldy exterior and chalky white paste.

SIMILAR CHEESE: Monte Enebro.

WINE PAIRINGS: Pairs well with fruity reds.
RED: Chianti Classico (Sangiovese); Syrah from the Languedoc.
SPARKLING: Brut Champagne.

RATINGS

QUALITY

73

STRENGTH

1

CONSTANT BLISS

A buttery soft cow's milk cheese whose window of peak ripeness is actually longer than its outward appearance might indicate. From its youngest stage, when very white and perfectly cylindrical, to its darker, almost brown and misshapen look, Constant Bliss remains a very tasty cheese. Its producer, a relative newcomer, Jasper Hill Farm, is located on 225 acres in a fairly remote corner of Vermont, fondly referred to by its residents and visitors as the Northeast Kingdom. Constant Bliss is named after a settler who was killed by local natives while guarding the Hazen Military Road in 1781. Its sister cheese, Bayley Hazen (page 81), also made by the Kehler brothers, is named after the two Revolutionary War–era generals, Bayley and Hazen, who built the road in anticipation of battling the English on a Canadian Front, which never actually developed.

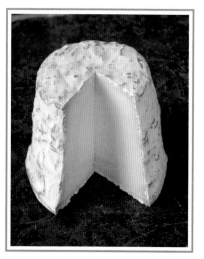

TYPE: Raw cow's milk.

PROVENANCE: Greensboro, northeastern Vermont.

PRODUCERS: Andy and Mateo Kehler, Jasper Hill Farm.

PRODUCTION: Farmhouse-style, using the milk of the farm's small herd of Ayrshire cows (23 head as of this writing). Only fresh, uncooled evening milk is used (the morning milk is used to make the Bayley Hazen). The curds are predominately lactic, although a small amount of traditional rennet is used. The curds are hand-ladled. The cheeses are individually salted and turned by hand every day for their first 30 days and matured at the farm for a total of 60 days.

APPEARANCE: Short, irregularly shaped, slightly conical cylinders approximately 3 inches in diameter at the base, 2 inches at the top and 2 to 2½ inches tall, weighing about 6 ounces. The rind is rough, bumpy, and undulating; it is orangish beige in color with a nearly complete thin covering of white mold. The paste is bone white and ripens to an ivory or off-white cream color from outside in.

SIMILAR CHEESE: Chaource.

SEASONAL NOTE: Made year-round; summer cheeses will develop a wide variety of molds, yeasts, and bacteria on their fluffy white rinds, yielding many different shades of red, pink, yellow, black, blue, and green.

WINE PAIRINGS: Constant Bliss balances well with many full-flavored red wines, but it also works well with less acidic whites.
WHITE: White Burgundy (Chardonnay); Vouvray demi-sec (Chenin Blanc).
RED: Barbera d'Asti; Bordeaux (Cabernet Sauvignon blend); red Burgundy (Pinot Noir); Super Tuscan blend (Sangiovese-Merlot).
SPARKLING: Champagne-style Blanc de Blancs (Chardonnay-dominant) or Blanc de Noirs (Pinot Noir-dominant).

RATINGS

QUALITY

74

STRENGTH

2

COOLEA

(koo-LAY) A superb Gouda-style farmhouse cheese made by a family of Dutch restaurateurs who immigrated to Ireland. Coolea measures up to any of the best Boeren Kaases (Dutch aged farmhouse Gouda), which are hard-pressed (pun intended) to equal its creaminess and sweetness. In confirmation of this, Coolea has won competitions back on Gouda's home turf in Holland. Coolea has a semihard to hard paste with a mild and creamy flavor when young; when aged, it is well-rounded, nutty, piquant, and quite hard with deliciously lingering aftertastes that feature hints of butterscotch.

TYPE: Cow's milk.

PROVENANCE: Coolea, northwest County Cork, southwestern Ireland.

PRODUCER: Willems family (Dick and Helene and their son, Dickie).

PRODUCTION: Cooked, pressed, and aged 4 to 8 weeks (young); or 9 to 12 months, sometimes up to 2 years (aged).

APPEARANCE: Three sizes of round-edged millstones: 17 pounds, 9 pounds, and 2 pounds. Plasticote rind (synthetic, waxy, but allows for breathing). The paste is light yellow to straw-colored, and semihard, with a layered texture and some eyelet holes.

SIMILAR CHEESES: Aged Gouda (Boeren Kaas); Mimolette.

WINE PAIRINGS: Coolea finds good pairings with softer, fruitier reds and whites.
🍷 **WHITE**: Albariño; Vouvray demi-sec (Chenin Blanc).

🍷 **RED**: Rhône red (Syrah-Grenache-Mourvèdre blend); Beaujolais cru (Gamay); California Pinot Noir; Australian Shiraz; Zinfandel (California).
SPARKLING: Moscato d'Asti.

RATINGS

QUALITY

88

STRENGTH

3

COULOMMIERS

(koo-lum-ee-YAY) Coulommiers is one of those "just-barely-cheese" cheeses—lovely and ready when young, no need to wait for it to ripen to a more profound maturity. Encased in a thin rind of bloomy white mold, the cheese-milk on the inside should be clean and uncompromised by heat treatment. Its flavor is milky and mild with a slight nuttiness. The *fermier*, or farmhouse, versions are far superior—always the case—so try one if you can get hold of it.

TYPE: Cow's milk (raw and pasteurized versions).

PROVENANCE: Île-de-France, the region around Paris; the town of Coulommiers is to the east-southeast of the capital.

PRODUCERS: *Fermier:* Compagnie Fermière Benjamin et Edmond de Rothschild. *Laitiers:* Fromagerie Dongé S; Lactalis. *Affineurs:* Fromagerie Renard-Gillard; Fromagerie Rouzaire.

PRODUCTION: Like all the artisanal cheeses of the Brie family, the best Coulommiers are made from pure, high-quality milk of local herds. The curds are unpressed, uncooked, and hand-ladled; the cheeses are aged 1 to 4 weeks.

APPEARANCE: Very similar to Brie, although smaller: it comes in medium-sized flattened drums 5 to 6 inches in diameter and up to 1 1/2 inches high, weighing approximately 1 pound. The bloomy rind is somewhat rough and undulating; it has cross-hatch markings top and bottom from the draining molds. The cheese should be a pure, downy white due to its velvety smooth (*velouté* as the French say) mold covering with occasional reddish splotches. The paste is off-white to bright yellow, satiny smooth and shiny with occasional holes and small air cavities.

SIMILAR CHEESE: Brie.

WINE PAIRINGS: Favors softer reds as well as dry whites.
WHITE: White Burgundy (Chardonnay); Sauvignon Blanc (California or Languedoc).
RED: Red Burgundy (Pinot Noir); Chilean Carmenère-Merlot blend (spicy, ripe red).
DESSERT/FORTIFIED: LBV Port.

RATINGS
QUALITY
76
STRENGTH

1

CROTTIN DE CHAVIGNOL

(kroh-TAN duh shah-veen-NYOL) A quintessential chèvre, among a mere handful of France's most famous and revered Loire Valley goat cheeses. Although there are legions of imitators worldwide, there is nothing quite like a well-made, perfectly ripened, genuine chèvre. Depending on its degree of aging, Crottin de Chavignol is semisoft to semihard, creamy and mild to sharp and salty. The younger cheeses are called *mou* or "wet"; their flavor is less pronounced. Although some fans of this type of cheese prefer it more aged, hence drier and chalkier, for the Crottins and many similar chèvres, the flavor and texture peak is a little younger—past the wet phase yet with some mold on the exterior.

TYPE: Goat's milk.

PROVENANCE: The Berry region, around the town of Sancerre, Loire Valley, France.

PRODUCERS: There are more than 30 artisanal farmhouse producers and at least 15 dairies and *affineurs*, including the following recommended producers. *Fermiers:* Chèvrerie de la Tour; EARL Meunier; EURL de la Motte; Ferme de Port Aubry; Ferme des Places; Fromagerie des Pellets; Magalie Legras; Philippe Jay. *Laitiers:* Coop. Agricole producteurs de fromage chèvre vallée du Cher; Domaine des Garennes; Ets Denizot; Laiterie de la Cloche d'Or; Laiteries H. Triballat. *Affineurs:* Fromagerie Claude Crochet SA; Fromagerie Pasdeloup; Sté Dubois-Boulay.

PRODUCTION: Unfortunately, the A.O.C. for this cheese allows for the use of frozen curds and as little as 10 days' ripening. It also doesn't sufficiently pinpoint the cheese's provenance.

APPEARANCE: Comes in small flattened spheres up to about 2 inches in diameter and up to 1½ inches high, weighing 1½ to 5 ounces. As a *crottin* ages, it gradually shrinks. Its rind starts out cream colored, then develops a thin coating of grayish blue mold and also some fuzzy white areas, eventually hardening and offering sharper aromas and flavors after about 5 weeks. The paste is off-white, dryish, and whiter toward the middle with a creamier, yellower striation toward the rind.

SIMILAR CHEESES: Chabichou de Poitou, Pouligny-Saint-Pierre, Sancerrois, Selles-sur-Cher, Valençay.

SEASONAL NOTE: May through November.

WINE PAIRINGS: Strongly favors light crisp whites.
- **WHITE**: Albariño; Chenin Blanc (Vouvray sec or South African); Sauvingon Blanc (white Bordeaux or Sancerre); California Viognier; Zierfandler (fruity, medium-bodied, from Austria).
- **RED**: Cahors (made from the Malbec grape in southwestern France); Chianti Classico (Sangiovese).

RATINGS

QUALITY

78

STRENGTH

2

DODDINGTON

I place this relatively new artifact firmly in the category of British Boss Cheeses; it offers so much pleasure and has texture, aromas, and flavors galore. Imagine a cross between a fine Cheddar and a top farmhouse Gouda and you have a pretty good idea of what Doddington is all about. The flavor notes combine elements of both types: nutty, sharp, sweet, and fruity with a long but balanced finish. The Doddington is a little more crunchy and less crumbly than many other British farmhouse-type cheeses. Its flavor is saltier with a savory tang. Doddington is also a versatile cheese for pairings; it satisfies on its own but also shows restraint so as not to annihilate wine partners (as long as it's not too old).

TYPE: Raw cow's milk.

PROVENANCE: Wooler, Northumberland, northern England.

PRODUCER: Maggie Maxwell, Doddington Dairy.

PRODUCTION: The dairy is engaged in small-scale cheese production (much of the milk is used to make ice cream). The curds are heat treated, not scalded. The cheeses are aged approximately 1 year. They have rinds made of plasticote, a synthetic material that is waxy but nevertheless allows for breathing.

APPEARANCE: Comes in a brick-red "flying saucer" shape (a flattened cylinder with a ridge around the upper/outer edge), about 14 inches in diameter and 5 inches high, that weighs about 24 pounds. It looks something like it is: a cross between a Cheddar and a fine aged Gouda—unique and vastly appealing. Its paste is golden colored with a crumbly texture and consistency reminiscent of not only Cheddar but also Parmesan-style cheeses.

SIMILAR CHEESES: Farmhouse Cheddars or farmhouse-style aged Goudas.

WINE PAIRINGS: Doddington works best with softer reds and fuller-flavored whites.
WHITE: Chardonnay (California or northern Italian); Alsatian Riesling.
RED: California Cabernet; California Merlot; Pinot Noir (California or red Burgundy).
SPARKLING: California Blanc de Blancs (Champagne-style, Chardonnay-dominant); Moscato d'Asti.
DESSERT/FORTIFIED: LBV Port.

RATINGS
QUALITY
92
STRENGTH
5

DURRUS

When I think of this lovely, delicious treasure, I can't help but think of a catchphrase, "Pretty in pink." Durrus is complex yet subtle—and a true farmhouse artifact. It features a rich, smooth, creamy semisoft paste with small airholes in it; the typical texture is oozy rather than runny. Its flavor is milky, sweet, fruity, and very approachable. As the cheese matures, it goes from semihard to nearly liquefied at room temperature, always a good sign. Its flavors go from mild, mellow, and fruity to something a bit stronger and more challenging but never offensive, and it can be enjoyed at ages up to 5 or even 6 months. Durrus is a survivor—one of the last in Ireland to be made from uncompromised milk supplied by a genuine, reliable source close to the farmhouse where it's made.

TYPE: Raw cow's milk washed rind.

PROVENANCE: Coomkeen, Bantry, in the western part of County Cork, southwestern Ireland.

PRODUCER: Jeffa Gill.

PRODUCTION: Jeffa began making cheeses in her kitchen in the late 1970s. She started out using the milk of her eight cows, but she now buys it from a "very particular" farmer six miles down the road. The cheese is made following certain traditional Swiss practices, including the use of a copper rather than stainless steel vat and a harp with a vertical blade to cut the curds. The cheeses are sprayed to encourage the development of *B. linens* and matured for 3 to 5 weeks on the farm.

APPEARANCE: 2-pound cylinders, 8 inches across and 2 inches high with a slightly pink-shaded rind.

SIMILAR CHEESES: Reblochon or Saint Nectaire; also reminiscent of Tomme de Savoie, although somewhat more vegetal.

SEASONAL NOTE: Jeffa tells me she prefers the winter cheeses, but I've enjoyed them most in the late summer and early fall.

WINE PAIRINGS: A versatile partner for many wine types, but most successful with whites that have some residual sugar.
WHITE: German Gewürztraminer Spätlese; German Riesling Auslese; Vouvray demi-sec (Chenin Blanc).
RED: Barolo (Nebbiolo); Beaujolais cru (Gamay); red Bordeaux (Cabernet Sauvignon-Merlot blend.
SPARKLING: Brut Champagne.

DESSERT/FORTIFIED: Sauternes (late-harvest Sémillon).

RATINGS

QUALITY

91

STRENGTH

3

ÉPOISSES DE BOURGOGNE

(OR SIMPLY "ÉPOISSES") (ay-PWAHSS duh boor-GUHN-nyuh)

Époisses is one of the more frequently requested cheeses at fine dining establishments and epicurean locales. Like many of its sister washed-rind cheeses, it was probably developed in an abbey during the late Middle Ages (in this case, Cistercian monks in the environs of Dijon). Époisses became famous during the reign of Louis XIV and is said to have been one of Napoleon's favorite cheeses. (But it isn't the only French cheese that claims to have been blessed by the emperor.) The great food scribe Brillat-Savarin called Époisses "The King of Cheeses." It nearly went extinct in the 1930s and was dormant throughout the World War II years but was revived in the 1950s. It features a smooth and pliant pâte that becomes gooey and spoonable at room temperature when ripe. Although "pungent" might be a euphemism or gross understatement of the aroma of a ripe Époisses, it offers a remarkably diverse spectrum of soft, rich, and mouthwatering flavors. It's amazing how it can smell so funky and taste so balanced and well rounded. This is one of Époisses's most cogent features: it can be quite salty yet simultaneously rich, creamy, luxurious, and balanced. If you are looking for the quintessential French washed-rind delicacy, this would be the place to start. Then you might want to branch out and try Langres and L'Ami du Chambertin for comparison. Take it out of the fridge, put it on a plate, wait for it to turn meltingly soft and alluring, then cut in and enjoy the beautiful essence of controlled milk spoilage.

RATINGS

QUALITY

90

STRENGTH

3

TYPE: Cow's milk.

PROVENANCE: Burgundy, particularly the area west-northwest of the city of Dijon around the village of the same name (A.O.C. protected).

PRODUCERS: Berthaut is recommended; Germain is also excellent. Producers of the raw-milk version are GAEC de la Roche Fontaine and Laiterie de La Cote.

PRODUCTION: An uncooked, unpressed cheese, made by slow curdling of the milk at low temperatures with small amounts of rennet, a process the French call *caillé lactique* ("lactic coagulation" in English). Its rind is built up from repeated baths in brine, then in wine or, more often, *marc* (brandy distilled from the leftover grape skins and seeds after wine-pressing). Époisses is ripened for a total of 5 to 6 weeks and should be eaten *à point*.

APPEARANCE: A shiny, reddish orange washed rind and a smooth off-white or yellowish paste. Comes in several sizes of flattened cylinder or disk—small 2-inch minidrums (about the size of Crottin de Chavignol); regular or medium (about 4 inches in diameter, weighing 9 ounces); and large (about 6$^{1}/_{2}$ inches in diameter and 1$^{1}/_{2}$ high, weighing nearly 2 pounds). The larger is known as an Époisses Coupe and is less salty.

SIMILAR CHEESES: L'Ami du Chambertin (essentially a brand of Époisses that comes in a 9-ounce size); Livarot; Munster. Berthaut also makes a notable variation on Époisses called Affidélice (ah-fee-day-LEESE), which is essentially a smaller version of the original washed in brine and Chablis wine rather than Marc de Bourgogne, ultimately yielding a slightly fruitier flavor and potentially more subtle flavor. Affidélice comes in relatively small (4 inches in diameter, 1$^{1}/_{2}$ inches high) dull reddish-orange-colored drums with slightly rounded edges weighing about 7 ounces; its top surface is rough, squiggly, and wet or slimy. Like Époisses, Livarot, and other similar washed-rind cheeses, it comes in its own little wooden box.

SEASONAL NOTE: Best season is July through February.

WINE PAIRINGS: Époisses is a good partner for many wines.
WHITE: Alsatian Riesling; Alsatian Pinot Blanc; Condrieu (Viognier).
RED: California Cabernet; Pinot Noir (California or Oregon); Ribera del Duero (Tempranillo blend).
DESSERT/FORTIFIED: Coteaux de Layon (late-harvest Chenin Blanc from the Loire Valley); Sauternes (late-harvest Sémillon).

EVORA

(OR QUEIJO EVORA) (EH-vaw-rah) An elemental, unabashed sheep cheese; the preservation of an older, sheepier type of milk flavor, one that I hope can survive. It features a semihard paste whose flavor is creamy and somewhat salty, with peachy, plummy overtones and a slightly acidic finish. It has a meatiness that gets progressively sheepier with age. The Evora is a type of cheese that may not grab you at first bite but is one that you'll remember and go back to without hesitation, especially if your first one is not too old. Then you may find yourself working your way up the age scale.

TYPE: Raw sheep's milk.

PROVENANCE: From the town of the same name in the Alentejo region east of Lisbon, Portugal.

PRODUCERS: Local farmhouses.

PRODUCTION: Thistle coagulated. Matured from 6 to 12 months. D.O.P. protected.

APPEARANCE: Evora comes in two sizes: the larger one is 4 inches in diameter and 1 inch high and weighs 6 ounces; the smaller is 2½ inches in diameter, just over half an inch tall and weighs about 3½ ounces. Its rind is bright beige to light yellow, with the cross-hatched markings of the drainage mats; its paste is pale ivory with small eyelets or holes.

SIMILAR CHEESES: Berkswell, Trade Lake Cedar.

SEASONAL NOTE: Made beginning in November, with peak production in March and April.

WINE PAIRINGS: Evora matches well with dry, crisp whites and fruit-driven reds.
WHITE: White Bordeaux (Sauvignon Blanc–Sémillon blend); New Zealand Sauvignon Blanc.
RED: Malbec (Argentina); Rioja-type wines (Tempranillo–Garnacha blend); Sangiovese (Brunello di Montalcino, Chianti Classico, or Vino Nobile di Montepulciano); Australian Shiraz.
DESSERT/FORTIFIED: White Port.

RATINGS
QUALITY
84
STRENGTH
3

FIUMORBU BRÉBIS

(fyoom-OR-boh bray-BEE) This is a cheese about which can be said, "A little bit goes a long way"—in the best sense of the expression. Your quest for a tiny but exceedingly tasty morsel of carefully fermented milk will reach a happy conclusion when you find this prize. The uncertain caseophile may circle around the Fiumorbu twice before landing. The taste is sheepy and persistent but not overly funky or barnyardy. Although it looks a bit like a small Munster or perhaps an Affidélice, it is most definitely a sheep's milk cheese. The attack is somewhat salty if not definitively sharp and strong, while the mouthfeel is slightly dry, mouthwatering, and satisfying. The finish is long and savory. The cheese's name comes from that of a small river in northern Corsica.

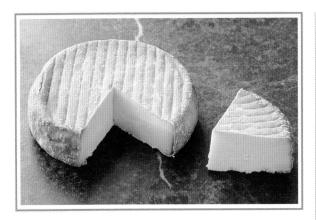

TYPE: Raw sheep's milk. (There is also a goat's milk version.)

PROVENANCE: The island of Corsica, in the Mediterranean off the south coast of France.

PRODUCERS: Local artisanal farmhouses and dairies including the Fromagerie Ottavi.

PRODUCTION: A handmade artisanal washed-rind sheep's milk cheese aged for 2 months with turnings every 2 days.

APPEARANCE: A medium-sized disk 4 inches in diameter and 1 to 1$\frac{1}{2}$ inches high, weighing about 8 ounces, with a light orange moist rind that has the ridged drying-rack pattern on its top. The paste is semihard, off-white to ivory in color, smooth and regular.

SIMILAR CHEESE: Stanser Schafkäse.

WINE PAIRINGS: This is a friendly cheese vis-à-vis many wine types, but especially the less complex ones—both red and white.
- **WHITE:** Grüner Veltliner; Alsatian Pinot Gris; Sancerre (Sauvignon Blanc).
- **RED:** Aglianico del Vulture (smoky, spicy, rich red from southern Italy); Barbera d'Asti; Rioja (Tempranillo blend).
- **DESSERT/FORTIFIED:** Sauternes (late-harvest Sémillon).

RATINGS

QUALITY

84

STRENGTH

3

FLIXER

(FLICK-ser) A rare type of alpine sheep's milk cheese from Canton Graubünden in Switzerland. The cheese is firm and moist, and the flavor is complex yet subtle at the same time. There are also interesting variations in flavor from one batch to the next depending on the sheep's diet. This cheese can easily be overlooked as it is quite unassuming. But it is expertly crafted and unique. The Flixer also has a remarkably stable shelf life once cut. It is best enjoyed on its own; in the company of other braggart cheeses, it may be overshadowed. Its overall impression is dense, solid, and upstanding—both in flavor and texture.

TYPE: Raw sheep's milk.

PROVENANCE: Alp Flixer, a tiny place above Davos in Graubünden, easternmost Switzerland.

PRODUCER: Mario Cotti.

PRODUCTION: The milk comes exclusively from the herd of about 12 Lacaune sheep on the alp. The curds are cooked in a copper cauldron over a wood fire in the center of the one-room farmhouse. The cheeses are lightly pressed, hand salted, and dry brushed during a 4-month aging period.

APPEARANCE: Smallish drums 5 inches in diameter and $2^{1}/_{4}$ inches high. Features a brownish beige rind with some white mold dustings and a distinctive raised-dot draining mold pattern. The paste is light yellow and hard with occasional irregularly shaped holes of uneven distribution.

SIMILAR CHEESES: Spenwood, Stanser Schafkäse (though the Flixer is more restrained); some of the Ossau-Iraty-type sheep cheeses of the western Pyrenees.

SEASONAL NOTE: Produced only from May until October.

WINE PAIRINGS: Flixer prefers most whites—from dry and crisp to sweeter and spicier—to most reds.
WHITE: Sicilian Chardonnay; Alsatian Gewurztraminer; Alsatian Pinot Blanc; Alsatian Riesling; Sauvignon Blanc (Pouilly-Fumé and Sancerre).
SPARKLING: Champagne-style sparkling wines (Pinot Noir-Chardonnay-Pinot Meunier blend).
DESSERT/FORTIFIED: LBV Port; Lustau Sherry.

RATINGS

QUALITY

91

STRENGTH

2

FOIN D'ODEUR

(fwan doe-DURR) If you're looking for a relatively unknown thriller from Canada (and you want to impress your friends with your French pronunciation skills), try this one. It's a washed-rind sheep's milk cheese that exhibits a great deal of character and individuality. While it may not be so subtle, it is balanced when in good form. Its first impression—after you take in its moist, rustic appearance—is usually a very attractive yeasty aroma. The semisoft interior, which will ripen to a partially liquid state, yields a stimulating dryish mouthfeel, pleasing sour and bittersweet flavors, and more delicious yeastiness. The Foin d'Odeur can be variable but improved packaging and shipping methods and/or the hoped-for switch to raw-milk production will yield a stunning artifact. Its mellifluous name comes from the local term for sweet grass, an herb that the natives believed attracts positive energy and whose pleasant odors suffuse the hay barn and grazing pastures at La Moutonnière.

TYPE: Pasteurized sheep's milk.

PROVENANCE: Ste. Helene-de-Chester, Québec, Canada.

PRODUCER: Fromagerie La Moutonnière.

PRODUCTION: The milk comes mostly from the farm's own flock of East Friesian sheep. The curds are cut large, then hand-ladled to drain for 24 hours before an aging period of 10 to 14 days in the cave under cool, humid conditions. The mixed cultured rind (*croûte fleurie*) is formed by applying special formulas of lactic cultures—first directly into the curds and then to the exterior by hand-spraying.

APPEARANCE: Except for the six carefully arranged blades of sweet grass (Foin d'Odeur) that adorn its top, it looks like nothing so much as a recently rolled-out slab of biscuit dough. An irregularly shaped disk or small wheel 7 to 7$\frac{1}{2}$ inches in diameter and 1$\frac{1}{4}$ to 1$\frac{1}{2}$ inches tall. The rind, when mature, is wet and slightly sticky, somewhat loose and undulating, and has six blades of sweet grass arranged decoratively on top; it is light beige in color with a cross-hatch draining mold pattern on top and bottom. The paste is off-white to ivory colored and somewhat chalky in appearance.

SIMILAR CHEESES: Fiumorbu Brébis, Innerschweizer Schafkäse (although the Foin is milder than either of these).

RATINGS

QUALITY

72

STRENGTH

2

WINE PAIRINGS:
WHITE: Southern French Chardonnay (Languedoc); Tokay Pinot Gris (Alsace).
RED: Salice Salentino (powerful, spicy Negroamaro-Malvasia Negra blend from Apulia, southern Italy); Brunello di Montalcino (Sangiovese).

FONTINA D'AOSTA

(fon-TEEN-ah dah-OST-ah) If imitation is the sincerest form of flattery, then Fontina has been very well flattered. Genuine Fontina should not to be confused with the many imitation versions—mostly sandwich cheeses or cheeses-as-nutrition—that hail from countries other than Italy. This is an ancient cheese and one of Italy's greatest. Historical references to the name date back more than 700 years, but it's likely much older. Fontina is at once luscious and subtle, capturing the essence of milk from cows that feast on the succulent flowers and grasses of the Italian Alps. It does not beg or shout for your attention; rather, it commands your respect and ultimate admiration. Its paste is semihard, smooth, and fairly elastic. Fontina is buttery, nutty, round, and full-flavored with characteristic underlying sweetness including hints of honey. It's an excellent cooking cheese but when you can enjoy the real deal, why not have it on its own? As with all the real cheeses, a little bit does go a long way.

TYPE: Raw cow's milk.

PROVENANCE: Val d'Aosta, northwestern Italy, not far from Geneva, Switzerland.

PRODUCERS: The Fontina Consortium consists of approximately 400 producers, including factories, cooperatives, and small independent dairies. The best Fontina I've tasted is made by Pietro Vallet (sometimes listed as Vallet Pietro).

PRODUCTION: A pressed, cooked cheese made from whole milk and aged for 7 months in cool, humid caves excavated from rock. The cheeses are salted and brushed on alternate days for the first 3 months of their aging to promote development of the rind. Ten liters of fresh milk from the Valdaostan breed of cows go into each kilo of cheese (that's nearly 5 quarts for every pound of this rather dense cheese). Signore Vallet buys milk only from his brother's farm. He makes cheeses for the five or six spring and summer months every year and ages them another seven. Vallet's curds are heated more gently than those in the cooperatives and factories. Fontina received D.O.P. status in 1996.

RATINGS

QUALITY

86

STRENGTH

3

APPEARANCE: Wheels weighing 19 to 40 pounds that are 12 to 18 inches across and 3 to 4 inches high with a thin, slightly concave natural rind, light reddish brown in color. The distinctive green stamped label has a silhouette of the high alps, which frame the Aosta Valley, as its backdrop.

SIMILAR CHEESES: Beaufort, Gruyère, Vacherin Fribourgeois.

SEASONAL NOTE: October through June peak.

WINE PAIRINGS: Fontina is a good partner with various expressions of Chardonnay and also some softer reds.

WHITE: Chardonnay (California, Burgundy, Sicily, and northern Italy); California Pinot Blanc.

RED: Barbera d'Alba; Chianti Classico (Sangiovese); Dolcetto d'Alba; Minervois (Syrah–Grenache blend from the Languedoc-Roussillon region of southernmost France); California Pinot Noir.

FOUGERUS

(foo-zhay-ROO) Here is a soft, bloomy-rind cheese that bears certain similarities and resemblances to Brie and Coulommiers. It can be outstanding and easily the best-showing bloomy rind at the counter. Robert Rouzaire is the originator of this delicacy and its name comes from the French word for fern, *fougère*. The pretty fern should not be discounted as merely a cosmetic device (although it does add points in terms of visual assessment); it also seems to tone down the soapiness that can creep into the flavor profile of many bloomy-rind cheeses. Fougerus has a mild, creamy, smooth, soft paste that rarely—if ever—suffers from oversalting.

TYPE: Cow's milk.

PROVENANCE: From the Île-de-France region, not far south of Paris.

PRODUCER: Robert Rouzaire's artisanal dairy, Fromagerie Rouzaire, Tournans-en-Brie.

PRODUCTION: Originally handmade in the farmhouse and meant for rapid consumption, it is now made by similar methods in the Rouzaire factory. Aged for 4 weeks.

APPEARANCE: Disks $5^1/_2$ to 6 inches in diameter and $1^1/_2$ to 2 inches high, weighing about 23 ounces. An orangish beige, ridged rind with white mold dustings and small bunch of fern leaves resting on top. The paste is satiny smooth and cream-colored.

SIMILAR CHEESES: Brillat-Savarin, Coulommiers, Pierre-Robert.

WINE PAIRINGS: Fougerus is most successfully paired with light-bodied, softer wines, both whites and reds.
  WHITE: White Bordeaux (Sauvignon Blanc–Sémillon blend); Alsatian Pinot Blanc; Vouvray sec (Chenin Blanc).
  RED: Beaujolais cru (Gamay); Chianti Classico (Sangiovese); California Merlot.
  DESSERT/FORTIFIED: Tawny Port.

RATINGS

QUALITY

76

STRENGTH

2

FOURME D'AMBERT

(foorme dom-BEHR) I like to think of this cheese as France's answer to Stilton. Another ancient cheese from the Auvergne, heartland of France's rustic dairy industry, Fourme d'Ambert's origins can be traced back to the ninth century A.D., but it probably existed in close to its present form during Roman times. Its paste is semisoft, smooth, rich, and creamy—not dry or crumbly. The flavor is more buttery and less salty or bitter than many—an important standard of superiority among fine blue cheeses. "Fourme," by the way, is a very old name for a cheese that comes from the bucketlike cylindrical or drum-shaped molds that the curds were hand-ladled into to drain and shape the cheeses.

TYPE: Raw cow's milk blue (pasteurized also available).

PROVENANCE: Auvergne region, Massif Central, south-central France.

PRODUCERS: Ten local cooperative dairies and several farmhouse producers. *Fermiers:* Ferme de Brugeailles; GAEC de Croix de Chazelles; Fromagerie des Hautes Chaumes, for Fourme de Montbrison (foorme duh mon-bree-SON).

PRODUCTION: The milk is from cows that graze at altitudes of about 2,000 to 5,000 feet. Similar to Stilton but pressed, so it's less crumbly. Aged a minimum of 28 days. Beginning in 1972, this cheese shared A.O.C. status and protection with Fourme de Montbrison; in 2002, the two A.O.C.s were separated.

APPEARANCE: An upright cylinder or drum, similar to Stilton, albeit a bit smaller at about 4 inches across and 8 inches tall, weighing about 5 pounds (the characteristic shape of the *fourme* or mold into which the curds are poured). It has a mottled natural rind with fuzzy gray mold on its surface. The interior has cavities of gray-green mold distributed throughout.

SIMILAR CHEESES: Fourme de Montbrison (essentially the same cheese as Fourme d'Ambert, but originating around the town of Montbrison, near the upper Loire River in the Auvergne), Bleu d'Auvergne, Bleu des Causses, Blu de Moncenisio.

WINE PAIRINGS: As is the case with many of the blues, this is a particularly amiable cheese partner for sweet wines.
WHITE: Alsatian Pinot Blanc.

RED: Chianti Classico (Sangiovese).

DESSERT/FORTIFIED: Banyuls; Sauternes (late-harvest Sémillon); Sherry (Oloroso); Tawny Port.

RATINGS

QUALITY

84

STRENGTH

3

GAMONEDO

(hah-moh-NAY-doh) A rustic, traditional, naturally blueing cheese—one of the last of its kind—with a pleasant hint of apple-smoke flavor. As compared with its more famous Asturian cousin Cabrales, Gamonedo is drier, not as sticky, less acidic, and less funky-smelling. It is nevertheless a fairly piquant blue with a semihard paste, somewhat grainy texture, and delightfully complex flavors. It's an excellent cheese for anyone who wants a real taste of the blues but isn't quite ready to tolerate the intense—almost noxious—flavors and aromas of a mature Cabrales.

TYPE: Raw cow's milk blue.

PROVENANCE: The municipalities of Onis and Cangas de Onis in southern Asturias, near the Picos de Europa range, northern Spain.

PRODUCERS: Artisanal, family farms.

PRODUCTION: Gamonedo was traditionally a *transhumance* (migratory grazing) cheese made with cow's, goat's, and sheep's milk; it is now made year-round principally with cow's milk. The curds are gently pressed and, once formed, lightly applewood-smoked and matured in natural caves for a minimum of 2 months and usually 4 to 5. (As with other rustic or peasant-style Spanish cheeses, the smoking was originally accidental as the cheeses were set on shelves in mountain cabins kept warm by small fires.)

APPEARANCE: Cylinders that weigh 2 to 8 kilos (up to nearly 18 pounds); generally a larger cheese than its fellow Asturian blues, Cabrales, Valdeón, and Picon Beyes, although there is significant variation depending on which family makes it. The rind is somewhat bumpy and grayish beige with black, orange, and bluish green patches. The paste is yellowish white in younger cheeses, and turning more yellow with maturity, and eventually develops veins of bluish green mold throughout. Its paste is more compact with fewer holes and less veining than similar blues due to the somewhat less humid conditions in its natural ripening caves.

SIMILAR CHEESES: Cabrales, Picon Beyes, Valdeón.

WINE PAIRINGS: Gamonedo's natural blueing and well-balanced character make it a good partner for an intriguing range of wines.

WHITE: White Burgundy (Chardonnay).

RED: Beaujolais cru (Gamay); Periquita (soft, low-tannin, light-bodied Portuguese red); Ribera del Duero (Tempranillo blend).

DESSERT/FORTIFIED: Dulce de Monastrell (fortified dessert wine from Jumilla, southeastern Spain); late-harvest Pinot Gris dessert wine; Sherry (Moscatel and Pedro Ximenez).

RATINGS

QUALITY

86

STRENGTH

5

GARROTXA, QUESO DE LA

(gah-ROTCH-ah, KAY-soh day lah) A traditional "rustic" cheese, indigenous to Catalonia, Garrotxa had all but died out by the early 1980s but was revived, becoming a star among the so-called New Artisanal Cheeses ("Los Nuevos Quesos Artesanos"). Its paste is firm, almost flaky, yet moist and smooth. When properly ripened, it melts on the tongue, revealing mild herbal flavors to go along with its wonderfully tangy mouthfeel and a hint of hazelnuts in the aftertaste. Garrotxa, which is also known as *"pell florida,"* or "bloomy rind" in the Catalan dialect, reaches its peak at approximately 4 weeks. It also enjoys a fairly long window for maximum enjoyment and can keep well, without drying or fading, when left out for serving purposes.

TYPE: Pasteurized goat's milk.

PROVENANCE: Throughout Catalonia, in northeastern Spain, but principally in Garrotxa in the north-central part of the province, close to the Pyrenees.

PRODUCERS: Made by an influx of youthful city dwellers who moved back to the land and chose cheesemaking as their new vocation. Blancfort is the best brand.

PRODUCTION: Aged for a minimum of 20 days in natural caves at high humidity.

APPEARANCE: A cylinder with rounded edges weighing 2–3 pounds that has a bluish gray moldy, rind from the growth of *P. glaucum.* The paste is pure bone white and occasionally fissured.

SIMILAR CHEESES: Ticklemore, Pau.

WINE PAIRINGS: Garrotxa is most appropriately paired with dry but fruit-driven white wines and soft, rounded reds.
- **WHITE:** Albariño; Chardonnay (white Burgundy, California, or Sicilian); Alsatian Riesling; German Riesling Kabinett or Spätlese; California Sauvignon Blanc.
- **RED:** Ribera del Duero (Tempranillo blend); Super Tuscan (Sangiovese-Merlot blend).
- **SPARKLING:** Champagne (Blanc de Blancs).
- **DESSERT/FORTIFIED:** Sherry (Pedro Ximenez).

RATINGS

QUALITY

85

STRENGTH

1

GORGONZOLA

(gore-gon-ZOH-lah) From ancient times, the town of Gorgonzola was a stop for herds on their summer and fall treks from the valleys of Lombardy to the alpine pastures and back. Local farmers had always made cheese there, aging it on wooden slats. At one point, a cheesemaker discovered the properties of *Penicillium* mold and thereafter the cheeses were encouraged to go blue. (Legend has it that a young cheesemaking Romeo, rushing out to meet his Juliet, left a vat of curds open all night, returned later, and, in order to cover up his mistake, added more fresh curds. In a few weeks, he found that a bluish mold had invaded his cheeses and rendered them far more delicious and interesting than before.) Gorgonzola features a firm, moist, buttery consistency and a flavor that is both sharp and sweet, giving it an admirable balance. Regular aged Gorgonzola is now generally known as *Gorgonzola Piccante;* it was formerly known as *Gorgonzola Naturale* or *Stagionato* ("aged"). There is another younger, milder version called *Gorgonzola Dolce* ("sweet"), which is creamier, more buttery, less moldy, and more spreadable; it contains a lot of moisture and is better suited for salad dressing or cooking rather than as a table cheese. The ones I respect most are the "mountain" or *piccante* versions. I've noticed some inconsistency and even the occasional serious flaw, particularly in the *dolce* category, which is unfortunate and should be remedied—especially in the case of such a highly esteemed blue.

TYPE: Cow's milk.

PROVENANCE: Originally from around the town of Gorgonzola, Lombardy, in the center of northern Italy, the cheese is now aged, according to D.O.C. regulations, in the environs of Novara, an industrial suburb of Milan.

PRODUCER: Two of the best Gorgonzola manufacturers are Jean-Battista Arrigoni and Luigi Guffanti. Arrigoni begins maturing the cheeses at his factory in Novara on the plains of Lombardy and then sends them back up to the Taleggio Valley for final aging. Guffanti is a family business launched in 1876 and named after its founder; the current cheesemaker, Giovanni Fiori, is fifth generation. (Guffanti is also a selector and *affineur* of an impressive range of other Italian cheeses, including virtually all the D.O.P. ones.) Guffanti sells some "super-aged" Gorgonzola—200 days old and sometimes more—that can get pretty radical.

RATINGS

QUALITY

85

STRENGTH

5

PRODUCTION: Made with essentially the same type of milk as Taleggio. Aged a minimum of 3 months. The cheeses arrive in the United States aged about 5 months. Inspectors rate Gorgonzolas according to the amount of mold in their interiors; the ones with the most green-blue striations are placed in the premium category. Gorgonzola received D.O.C. status in 1955 and D.O.P. in 1996.

APPEARANCE: Gorgonzolas are made in medium-large drums from 8½ inches to about 12 inches in diameter and 6 to 10 inches in height; they weigh in the range of 9½ kilos or about 21 pounds. Gorgonzolas for export start out as full drums that are cut in half either horizontally or vertically, then foil wrapped. Guffanti's Gorgonzola Piccante Extra Affinato, a fine aged example of this cheese, has a light brown cracked, bumpy natural rind with plenty of puncture holes. The interior is full of greenish blue striations of mold and also exhibits the elongated puncture marks of needles that aerate the cheeses, encouraging mold development. Younger Gorgonzolas start out with relatively little interior mold development and off-white to straw-colored pastes; as they age, they take on more interior mold and darker colors.

SIMILAR CHEESES: Cashel Blue, Fourme d'Ambert.

SEASONAL NOTE: Made year-round.

WINE PAIRINGS: The younger, milder Dolces tolerate less sweet red wines so long as they offer plenty of fruit; the more aged Piccantes require more sweetness in their wine partners.

🍷 RED: California Cabernet.

🍷 DESSERT/FORTIFIED: Banyuls; Dulce de Monastrell (fortified dessert wine from Jumilla, southeastern Spain); Madeira; Muscat de Rivesaltes (sweet fortified dessert wine from the Languedoc); Sherry (Moscatel); Vin Santo.

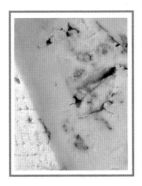

G O U D A

(HOW-dah) Most of us grew up pronouncing its name "*Goo*-dah" and consuming large quantities of supermarket-bought mild, semihard cheese that came encased in the familiar red wax. Well, the correct pronunciation is quite different, and the genuine raw-milk farmhouse variety is a legitimate gourmet delicacy, a far cry from that commercial manifestation you may remember. One version of this cheese I like is a raw-milk farmhouse product called Goudse Boerenkaas (HOWD-seh BOOR-en-kahs) (the latter term meaning "farmer cheese"). Properly aged, it is hard, grainy, salty, tangy, and sharp with a hint of butterscotch on the finish. If you like a firm, dense, crystalline, almost crumbly cheese with deep, mouthwatering flavors and a lingering aftertaste, this is the one for you. The genuine article will age up to 6 years, but past that they start to lose flavor.

TYPE: Cow's milk.

PROVENANCE: Schooenrewoerd, southern Holland.

PRODUCERS: Local artisanal dairies and farmhouse makers who bring their cheeses to the central aging facility in the village of Schooenrewoerd, where they begin the long maturing process.

PRODUCTION: Goudse Boerenkaas has a pressed, semihard paste, a natural brushed rind, and is saleable after 4 months of aging but only becomes interesting when matured for 3 years or more.

APPEARANCE: Wheels about 15 inches in diameter, up to 5 inches high, weighing 18 to 29 pounds, with bulging, convex sides. The paste can be hard and crumbly and will take on a dark golden or straw-colored hue when well aged.

SIMILAR CHEESES: Coolea, Mimolette, Roomano (Edam is another widely exported and extremely popular cooked cow's milk cheese from Holland that in well-aged versions can be delicious).

SEASONAL NOTE: Year-round.

WINE PAIRINGS: An aged Gouda pairs best with reds that have a toasty, raisiny quality; it also goes well with the more syrupy dessert wines.
WHITE: California Chardonnay; Tokay Pinot Gris (Alsace).
RED: Amarone della Valpolicella; California Cabernet Sauvignon; Rhône reds (Syrah-Grenache-Mourvèdre blends); Merlot (California or Long Island).
DESSERT/FORTIFIED: Muscat de Rivesaltes or Jurançon Petit Manseng (late-harvest sweet dessert wine from southern France).

RATINGS

QUALITY

96

STRENGTH

6

GREAT HILL BLUE

The Great Hill Dairy farm has been in the Stone family since the early twentieth century; David Frisone, an accomplished former chef, is now the head cheesemaker. The cheese is firm and robust with a balanced finish; the blue is refreshing but at the same time piercing. It features a more dense, yellower curd and a richer, creamier-tasting cheese than is possible in a more industrial milieu.

TYPE: Raw cow's milk blue.

PROVENANCE: Marion, Massachusetts, on the shores of Buzzard's Bay, about fifty miles south of Boston.

PRODUCER: The Stone family (Tim and Nancy), Great Hill Dairy.

PRODUCTION: Made from the milk of local Jersey and Holstein cows by traditional manufacturing methods. Aged at least 6 months.

APPEARANCE: 6-pound wheels. The paste is creamy, smooth, moist, and crumbly at the same time. Its color is off-white with deep striations and cavities of bluish and grayish green mold.

SIMILAR CHEESES: Bleu d'Auvergne, Bleu des Causses, Fourme d'Ambert.

WINE PAIRINGS: This is a cheese that marries best with fruitier white wines.
WHITE: German Gewürztraminer Spätlese; Alsatian Riesling; Vouvray demi-sec (Chenin Blanc).
RED: Cornas (northern Rhône Syrah); California Merlot; late-harvest Muscatel or Chenin Blanc.

RATINGS

QUALITY

79

STRENGTH

4

GRUYÈRE

(groo-YEHR) Gruyère is one of Switzerland's better-known, most prevalent, and finest cheeses, a big beautiful repository of alpine flora and *terroir*. Its hard to semihard paste melts in your mouth and reveals a nutty, slightly sweet taste with complex musty, mushroomy flavor notes. It offers a long, full aftertaste with distinct hints of spoiled milk. One of the best things about Gruyère is that it's a little salty on the attack but not on the finish. I much prefer the well-aged variety—at least 1½ years old, with its crunchy bite from the sugar crystals. A fine genuine Gruyère is a great place to start if you want to experience the best of Swiss mountain cheese production. There is, however, a fairly wide range of quality among Gruyères, so it is certainly worth paying a little more for one of the expertly crafted, selected, and aged versions. The extra aging yields a far superior cheese that is delicious start to finish.

TYPE: Raw cow's milk.

PROVENANCE: The unofficial capital of Gruyère production is the Bulle region of the Canton of Fribourg in western French-speaking Switzerland, but it is made over a wide area of this part of the country. Some of the most interesting Gruyères come from the Brevine Plateau close to the French border in the Juras mountain range, an area known as "the Siberia of Switzerland" due to its extreme climate.

PRODUCERS: Local co-ops and dairies; one of my favorite authentic Gruyères is made by the showcase dairy in the village of Le Pont de Martel by two young, educated cheesemakers whose facility is state of the art but whose methods remain traditional and artisanal—just the way they should be.

PRODUCTION: Genuine farmhouse Gruyère is meticulously handcrafted from the highest-quality milk of the Fribourgeois breed and aged about 16 months, allowing it to reach its full potential. The large cheeses are regularly hand washed with brine. After about 12 months, they begin to emit gasses and begin to develop a few evenly placed tiny interior holes. Don't fall for the overused and even abused term "cave aged"; most cheeses receive this treatment. It's far more important that, during their *affinage*, the cheeses are allowed enough time to ripen properly. Sixteen months—rather than the usual 6 to 10—make a huge difference.

RATINGS

QUALITY

97

STRENGTH

6

APPEARANCE: Very large wheels about 2 feet across and 4 inches high with slightly convex sides, weighing up to 40 kilos (88 pounds). In the old days, all Gruyères had pea- or small cherry-sized holes spread throughout their interiors; modern factory-made versions have very few if any holes. In any case, they should exhibit no cracks, blemishes, or bruises.

SIMILAR CHEESES: Appenzeller, Beaufort, Fontina d'Aosta, Hoch Ybrig.

SEASONAL NOTE: Year-round, but the wheels made in spring and summer offer more intense flavors.

WINE PAIRINGS: A well-aged Gruyère flatters full-bodied berry-flavored reds; it also works well with sparkling wines.

WHITE: California Sauvignon Blanc.

RED: Southern Rhône Syrah–Grenache blend; Tuscan Sangiovese; Australian Shiraz; California Zinfandel.

SPARKLING: Champagne (Blanc de Blancs or Blanc de Noirs).

GUBBEEN

Gubbeen represents an eloquent expression of its wild Irish *terroir*, outgoing and forward but with appropriate restraint. It's a lovely, plump cheese, approachable and buttery—one you'll want to come back to (to paraphrase some of the marketing for the Emerald Isle). This farmhouse beauty has a semisoft paste with a silky smooth, pliable texture and an intriguing mushroomy aroma with the pleasant, slightly musty, earthy ambiance of an old cellar. It offers a fresh, milky taste with a mild buttery, nutty flavor and smoky accents.

TYPE: Pasteurized cow's milk washed-rind.

PROVENANCE: Western County Cork, Ireland.

PRODUCERS: Tom and Giana Ferguson.

PRODUCTION: Farmhouse; the rind is washed with salt water.

APPEARANCE: The rind is is orangish beige and often has a light coating of white *P. candidum*. The paste is golden and light-yellow hued, semihard with small holes, reminiscent of the *tomme*-style cheeses of the European continent.

SIMILAR CHEESES: Ardrahan, Chimay, Durrus, Pont l'Évêque.

WINE PAIRINGS: Gubbeen pairs best with floral or spicier white wines.
WHITE: German Gewürztraminer Spätlese; Alsatian Riesling; Vouvray demi-sec (Chenin Blanc).
RED: Cornas (northern Rhône red).

RATINGS

QUALITY

83

STRENGTH

2

HARBOURNE BLUE

(HAR-born) Here is one of the great small-production British artisanal cheeses, created by master cheesemaker Robin Congdon. I consider it an unconventional "hybrid"—a blue-veined goat cheese—of which there are few if any other successful examples. Harbourne is among the most "desserty" of the blue cheeses, an enthralling artifact that can be sublime when at its peak. It is normally aged from 4 to 8 months; despite its pleasing balance of sweetness, it can become quite fierce when it gets older than that, so I recommend enjoying it only when young and fresh-cut. Harbourne is firm, creamy, almost fudgy in texture with a pleasingly dry mouthfeel. Its flavor is sharp, pronounced, and lingering yet it maintains a certain mellow sweetness and complexity, an attractive and rare trait among blues. It is also not oversalted, a common fault of many blues and another big plus in favor of Harbourne.

TYPE: Pasteurized goat's milk blue.

PROVENANCE: Sharpham Barton, South Devon, southwestern England.

PRODUCER: Robin Congdon.

PRODUCTION: Aged from 4 to 8 months. Now that it's made with pasteurized milk, it tends to fade more rapidly and, once cut, doesn't have the shelf life it had when it was made with raw milk.

APPEARANCE: 8-pound cylinders with natural wet rinds. Its paste is bright white with an evenly spread web of blue-green veins.

SIMILAR CHEESES: Beenleigh Blue, Monte Enebro, Persillé de Tignes.

SEASONAL NOTE: Made from spring to fall and is generally available in fall and winter.

WINE PAIRINGS: Harbourne Blue favors dessert wines from northern climes, but it also does well alongside heartier table reds.
  WHITE: German Gewürztraminer Spätlese; Grüner Veltliner; Vouvray demi-sec (Chenin Blanc).
  RED: Amarone della Valpolicella; Cabernet Sauvignon blends (Bordeaux or California).
  SPARKLING: Moscato d'Asti.
  DESSERT/FORTIFIED: Late-harvest Muscat and late-harvest Chenin Blanc dessert wines (e.g., Bonnezeaux and Coteaux du Layon, from the Loire Valley); Hungarian Tokaji.

RATINGS

QUALITY

90

STRENGTH

3

HARVEST MOON

Harvest Moon is the product of the relatively young and highly successful Bingham Hill Cheese Co. It is a washed-rind cheese with barnyardy aromas that shares some traits with its European counterparts such as Livarot (page 167) and Pont l'Évêque (page 207); Tom Johnson designed it to be a gentler, larger version of those French classics. When they sell it at the local farmer's market, he calls it a "Brie with a serious attitude." It's also been favorably compared with Reblochon (page 210); I'd call it a Reblochon with *some* attitude. It's pliant, sturdy, not all that strong, holds up well on a cheese board, and is actually very pleasant. Harvest Moon presents a strong, arresting aroma; its flavors include milkiness, yeastiness, sweetness, and grassiness. The paste is semisoft at 2 months and meltingly soft at 3½ months.

TYPE: Pasteurized cow's milk.

PROVENANCE: Fort Collins, Colorado.

PRODUCER: Tom and Kristi Johnson, Bingham Hill Cheese Company.

PRODUCTION: The milk is gently pasteurized (145°F for 30 minutes) and coagulated with microbial rennet. The curds are cut and drained in hand-tied cheesecloth, broken by hand and salted, then molded to drain. The molded curds are turned, stacked, and restacked to press under their own weight. For the first 2 weeks of aging, the cheeses are washed daily to develop their characteristic rinds. Then they are aged for another 2 months.

APPEARANCE: A somewhat lumpy medium to small-sized wheel with rounded edges, approximately 8 inches in diameter and 1½ inches high, weighing approximately 3 pounds. The rind is light beige in color with pink and orange tints. It is doughy in appearance, with occasional cracks, as if the dough had been kneaded, giving the cheese a resemblance to its namesake. The paste is light ivory in color, semisoft, pliable, and somewhat chalky in texture, ripening to a uniform smoothness near the rind. It has some irregularly shaped holes and fissures.

SIMILAR CHEESES: Brescianella Stagionata, Taleggio, Reblochon.

RATINGS

QUALITY

72

STRENGTH

2

WINE PAIRINGS: Harvest Moon pairs best with less-dry whites as well as the less-aggressive, younger reds.
- **WHITE**: California Chardonnay; Vouvray demi-sec (Chenin Blanc).
- **RED**: Aglianico del Vulture (smoky, spicy, rich red from southern Italy); Negroamaro-Malvasia blend from Sicily.
- **SPARKLING**: California Champagne-style (Pinot Noir-Chardonnay blend).

HILLTOWN WHEEL

This fine American original is made in the style of the hard-aged goat cheeses of the French Alps with some techniques cleverly adapted from other European artisanal treasures (including even Roomano). It delivers complex flavors with hints of a burnt-sugar sweetness and nuttiness. As the cheeses age, they develop a piquant, lingering finish, but what I like best about them is they retain their fresh, mild, creamy flavors—a delicate balance not easily attained in an aged goat cheese and a tribute to the skill of its makers and ripeners.

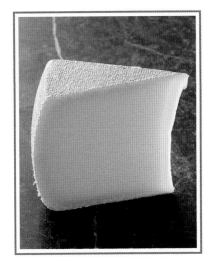

TYPE: Raw goat's milk.

PROVENANCE: Northeast foothills of the Berkshire Mountains, western Massachusetts, USA.

PRODUCER: Carolyn and Joe Hillman, Hillman Farm.

PRODUCTION: Made strictly by traditional farmstead methods (including the use of a wood fire) from the milk of the farm's own herd of goats, which graze in its lovely organic hillside pasture of native grasses, herbs, and wild berries and also feast on the farm's own clover-flower hay. The curds are cut, stirred, and molded by hand, then pressed and brine salted. The cheeses are aged 5 to 8 months in a partially buried concrete cellar with frequent brushings and brine washings.

APPEARANCE: A medium-sized small drum or wheel 8 inches in diameter and 4 inches tall, weighing approximately 8 pounds. The rind is dark cream to reddish brown in color with a slight roughness and the imprint of the draining molds. The paste is firm, compact, yet quite smooth and yielding with some small spaces and holes; its color is ivory ripening to a creamy tan.

SIMILAR CHEESES: Tomme de Chèvre, Chevrotin, Tumalo Tomme. The Hillmans also make Harvest Cheese, which is similar to the Hilltown Wheel but aged 3 to 7 months and made year-round.

SEASONAL NOTE: The Hilltown Wheel is made seasonally from the rich spring and fall milk.

WINE PAIRINGS: The Hilltown Wheel pairs favorably with light-bodied fruity wines.
WHITE: South African Chenin Blanc.

RED: Beaujolais (Gamay).

SPARKLING: Champagne (Blanc de Blancs).

RATINGS

QUALITY

84

STRENGTH

2

HOCH YBRIG

(hohk ee-BRIG) Overall, I rate this lesser-known cheese as a superlative rendition of what most people consider the classic Swiss taste—in a word, it's one of Switzerland's great hidden treasures. It's been one of my top cheeses since I first encountered it; for those who say they don't like Swiss cheeses, I defy them to bad-mouth this one. A mature Hoch Ybrig is positively mouthwatering. It has a wonderfully smooth and sumptuous yet dense texture. At about 9 months, it has the consistency of butter; like a good Gruyère, it then starts to become more crystalline and concentrated. Its flavors are complex, harmonious, and lingering; they include salty, nutty, sweet, and tangy with a hint of butterscotch.

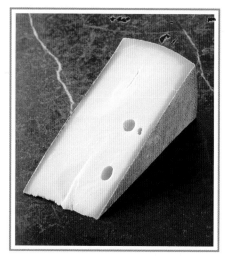

TYPE: Raw cow's milk.

PROVENANCE: Canton Schwyz, north-central Switzerland, about 50 miles east of Zurich, specifically the villages of Oberiberg, Ybergeregg, and surrounding areas, in the heart of Swiss ski country.

PRODUCERS: The Hoch Ybrig I buy is ripened by Rolf Beeler; it is made in a dairy in the town of Küssnacht—hence its generic name, Küssnachter (KUSS-nack-ter)—then aged by Beeler, after which it is permitted to bear the name Hoch Ybrig.

PRODUCTION: Made by farmhouse/artisanal methods from the milk of local Simmental cows. The curds are pressed and salted. The best Hoch Ybrigs are aged from 9 up to 14 months. During maturation, the cheeses are washed at least three times a week with a white wine brine, which lends a sweet undercurrent to their flavor.

APPEARANCE: Wheels weighing about 16 pounds. As the cheeses age, their rinds develop a reddish coating with white dustings of mold. Their interiors change from white to gold as the flavors intensify.

SIMILAR CHEESES: Appenzeller, Bundner Alpkäse, Genuine Swiss Gruyère, Urner Bergkäse.

SEASONAL NOTE: Available year-round but best from late spring through summer when it's more likely to have acquired sufficient age.

WINE PAIRINGS: Hoch Ybrig pairs especially well with various vinifications of the Riesling grape but also with some of the grapier big reds.

WHITE: German Riesling Auslese or Spätlese; Vouvray demi-sec (Chenin Blanc).

RED: Beaujolais cru (Gamay); California Merlot; Australian Shiraz.

SPARKLING: Champagne (Blanc de Noirs); rosé Champagne.

DESSERT/FORTIFIED: Late-harvest Alsatian Riesling.

RATINGS

QUALITY

97

STRENGTH

5

HOJA SANTA

(OH-ha SAHN-tah)   What gives this cheese its special character—beyond the fresh, clean, and mild pasteurized goat's milk flavor—is the wrapping in leaves of Hoja Santa, a plant indigenous to Texas and Mexico. The leaf itself is a bit prickly, zesty, and weedlike but it does impart a warm, savory character to the paste that renders the cheese unique and desirable. Some tasters have detected hints of sassafrass and/or anise in its flavor profile. Apparently, the southern states of the United States are better suited to goat's milk production (I've tasted several successful goat cheesees from this part of the country); cattle farming in the area supplies the meat industry, but unfortunately there's been little effort or success diverting cow's milk to cheesemaking. Paula Lambert devised this cheese after tasting Hoja Santa leaves in Veracruz and Oaxaca, Mexico, where they are used for wrapping fish and chicken before steaming in banana leaves. It was a clever and delicious way for her to regionalize her Banon-style artisanal goat's milk cheese.

TYPE: Goat's milk.

PROVENANCE: Dallas, Texas, USA.

PRODUCER: Paula Lambert, The Mozzarella Company.

PRODUCTION: The milk comes from small family farms and is delivered fresh to The Mozzarella Company in 5-gallon pails. The milk is slowly pasteurized, then inoculated with cultures and rennet to develop soft, lactic curds. The curds are hand-ladled into molds and drained overnight, then unmolded, salted, and left in an aging room for 2 days with turnings and further saltings. After a week of curing, they are wrapped in the Hoja Santa leaves and allowed to mature for several days up to several weeks.

APPEARANCE: Small flattened drum shape 2$\frac{1}{2}$ inches in diameter and 1$\frac{1}{2}$ inches high, weighing 5 to 6 ounces, wrapped in dark green leaves tied with small strands of raffia. The paste is white, soft, and moist. It becomes more dense with age and may develop beneficial surface molds with additional *affinage*.

SIMILAR CHEESES: Banon, Sally Jackson's goat's milk cheeses.

SEASONAL NOTE: Made year-round, but winter production is limited due to scarcity of local Hoja Santa leaves.

WINE PAIRINGS: Hoja Santa complements rustic reds from the warmer climes.
  WHITE: California Sauvignon Blanc.

  RED: Beaujolais (Gamay); Madiran (tannic, traditionally rustic wine from southwestern France, made primarily from the Tannat grape); California Zinfandel.
  SPARKLING: Champagne (Blanc de Blancs).

RATINGS

QUALITY

74

STRENGTH

1

HUDSON VALLEY CAMEMBERT

This award-winning cheese gives the continental double and triple crèmes a run for their money, adding an extra dimension with the inclusion of sheep's milk. It is semisoft with a mild buttery flavor and possesses a good balance of the two milk types. Its maker, the Old Chatham Sheepherding Company, was founded by Tom and Nancy Clark in 1993. Their marketing pitch proclaims "we make sheep's milk cheeses using traditional European methods to create new 'American Originals'," and I believe they're doing a great job fulfilling that mission.

TYPE: Sheep's and cow's milk.

PROVENANCE: Old Chatham, New York, in Shaker Country, southeast of Albany, USA.

PRODUCER: Old Chatham Sheepherding Company.

PRODUCTION: A Camembert-style cheese, cured 18 to 20 days. Old Chatham has the largest flock of dairy sheep in the country; they began with 150 in 1994 and now have more than 1,200 grazing on 600 acres of lush, organically managed rolling pastureland. The cow's milk component comes from the neighboring Hollrock Farm in Kinderhook. The cheeses are handmade under the supervision of cheesemakers Benoît Maillol and Brian Booth.

APPEARANCE: 5-ounce squares with a white, bloomy, edible rind. It is also sold in two variations, named after the farm's founders: Nancy's Hudson Valley Camembert, a 2-pound wheel, and Tom's Hudson Valley Camembert, which is a 1-pound wheel (and isn't it nice that Nancy is the big wheel?).

SIMILAR CHEESE: Roucoulons.

WINE PAIRINGS: Hudson Valley Camembert is an agreeable partner for fruitier whites—from dry to sweet.

WHITE: White Burgundy (Chardonnay); white Bordeaux (Graves/Sauvignon Blanc-Sémillon); German Riesling Kabinett.

SPARKLING: Brut Champagne.

DESSERT/FORTIFIED: Late-harvest ice wines.

RATINGS

QUALITY

76

STRENGTH

1

HUMBOLDT FOG

This is a very nice and deservedly popular American chèvre-style cheese that reflects its *terroir* and evokes the prevailing foggy conditions of its Northern California locale. Humboldt Fog has a light, creamy, yet earthy flavor when young. With age, it turns stronger and develops more complexity. Goats survive in a variety of climactic and geographical conditions and are able to yield delicious milk of a sufficient heft to justify the effort of artisanal cheesemaking. Well-crafted goat cheeses, even when made from pasteurized milk like this prizewinning one, can be quite pleasant and yield much pleasure to their legions of fans.

TYPE: Goat's milk.

PROVENANCE: McKinleyville, Humboldt County, Northern California, USA.

PRODUCER: Cypress Grove Chevre, Inc.; Mary Keehn is the cheesemaker.

PRODUCTION: Humboldt Fog is a mold-ripened *tomme* made according to traditional methods. The milk is sourced from small family-owned farms in the area, which is second only to certain parts of England in terms of its amount of rain per annum. Its shelf life is generally anywhere from 3 to 15 weeks, but it can be enjoyed at ages up to 6 months if properly cared for. Several years ago, Mary instituted a bonus program under which she pays the dairy farmers who supply her milk premiums based on exceptional quality. Among the criteria are butterfat, protein content, and cleanliness.

APPEARANCE: Rounds about 2 inches tall and 3½ inches across that weigh 11 to 14 ounces. (There are also larger rounds, 7 inches in diameter and weighing around 4½ pounds.) The cheeses have a center layer of vegetable ash; their rinds are dusted with ash and develop a covering of white mold that reminded the cheesemakers of the morning fog, hence the name. The rind is gray to bluish gray and covered almost uniformly with white mold. The paste is chalky but moist and bone white, gradually ripening to a creamy smoothness from the outside in.

SIMILAR CHEESES: Wabash Cannonball, Valençay.

SEASONAL NOTE: Available year-round.

WINE PAIRING: Humboldt Fog is a fitting partner for dry whites and softer reds.
WHITE: Pouilly-Fumé (Sauvignon Blanc); white Burgundy (Chardonnay).
RED: Beaujolais cru (Gamay).

SPARKLING: Moscato d'Asti.

RATINGS
QUALITY
75
STRENGTH

IBORES

(OR QUESO IBORES) (ee-BOR-ess) Here is a delightfully accessible, zesty aged goat cheese that has been made in the primordial sheep country of the Extremadura since Roman times. Without sacrificing its distinct and distinguished character, Ibores is more gregarious and cooperative than almost any other cheese of its genre. Ibores features a semisoft to semihard paste and a light airy consistency; it is compact yet open-textured with small eyeholes. Its flavors are a little salty and moderately acidic with earthy notes; there's an agreeable tinge of bitterness balanced by an underlying sweetness amid pleasant reminders of sour milk as well as hints of wildflowers. There is a pleasing aftertaste of dried fruits and a hint of spiciness in the pigmented cheeses, which are the ones I prefer. It's unmistakably a goat cheese but always seems to stop short of intense goaty or barnyardy aromas or flavors. Ibores is also a very wine-friendly cheese.

TYPE: Raw goat's milk.

PROVENANCE: In the environs of four small towns—Trujillo, La Jara, Villuercas, Ibores—in the province of Caceres (between Trujillo and Plasencia), Extremadura, western Spain.

PRODUCERS: Local artisanal dairies and farmhouses.

PRODUCTION: Made from the milk of the Retinta and Verata breeds of goats. Molded, pressed (originally by hand), uncooked. The D.O. regulations (pending final approval) define two types: normal, with a minimum of 60 days maturation; and artisanal (*artesano*), made with milk from the producer's own herd and with a minimum of 100 days aging. Genuine Ibores cheeses also have several types of rinds: some are natural and whitish to yellowish in color; some are rubbed with olive oil; and others have an additional rub of sweet paprika (*pimenton*), which lends their exterior a reddish orange tint.

APPEARANCE: Irregular upright cylindrical shapes weighing 1 to 3 pounds. A reddish, somewhat mottled rind and an off-white smooth paste with air pockets.

SIMILAR CHEESE: Garrotxa.

SEASONAL NOTE: Late fall to summer.

WINE PAIRINGS: Ibores is a very wide-ranging crowd-pleaser when it comes to wine pairings; it is especially recommended with spicy wines, red or white.
  WHITE: Albariño; Chardonnay (California or white Burgundy); Pouilly-Fumé (Sauvignon Blanc); Alsatian Riesling; German Riesling Spätlese.
  RED: Barbaresco (Nebbiolo); red Burgundy (Pinot Noir); California Merlot; Rhône reds (Syrah and Syrah blends).

RATINGS

QUALITY

89

STRENGTH

3

JERSEY BLUE

Karen Galayda has been farming and making cheese since the early 1990s and is considered a pioneer of fine American farmstead mold-ripened cheeses. In this time, she's produced formidable versions of Camembert and Brie as well as this delectable blue. Jersey Blue features a firm, dense, creamy curd that marries perfectly with the flavors of the *Penicillium* mold to produce well-balanced flavors.

TYPE: Raw cow's milk.

PROVENANCE: Corinth, northeastern Vermont, USA.

PRODUCER: Karen Galayda, Blythedale Farm.

PRODUCTION: Karen manages her own herd of about thirty Jersey cows and makes her cheeses by hand according to a Stilton-type recipe. To promote proper flavor development, Karen very conscientiously tries to limit the amount of salt used. (I wish more cheesemakers were cognizant of this pitfall.) *P. roquefortii*, however (the famous blue mold), requires salt to develop. Because of this difficult balancing act, the cheese doesn't always have a lot of blue veining in it when Karen sells it.

APPEARANCE: 5-pound drums or wheels 8 inches in diameter and 4 inches high with a brown, bumpy rind that has grayish white mold growth. The interior is off-white to yellowish ivory with a variable amount of greenish blue mold striations. The paste is dense, firm, and slightly moist.

SIMILAR CHEESE: Stilton.

WINE PAIRINGS:
🍷 **DESSERT/FORTIFIED**: Madeira; Tawny Port; vintage Port.

RATINGS

QUALITY

74

STRENGTH

5

KRÜMMENSWILER FÖRSTERKÄSE

(krummens-VEE-ler FERST-er-keh-she) This wonderful Swiss artifact is similar in appearance to a Vacherin Mont d'Or or a Vacherin du Haut-Doubs (page 280) and it also shares some of the most attractive characteristics of its venerable French cousins: it is smooth-textured, delightfully creamy yet full-flavored, and meltingly unctuous at peak ripeness. When ripe, it is served *torta* style—that is, by cutting a disk out of the top and spooning out dollops of the melting paste. The Krümmenswiler's flavor is spicier and more resinous than any of those cheeses; it also features some mustard or horseradish notes, making it a very interesting and memorable cheese. The quality of the milk and the use of fir bark encircling the wheel no doubt contribute to its exquisite and wide-ranging flavor profile.

TYPE: Raw cow's milk.

PROVENANCE: Canton Thurgau, Switzerland.

PRODUCER: Diriwaechter & Schmid, a dairy well known for producing new cheeses in traditional ways (they also make Wildmannli).

PRODUCTION: Using traditional methods, the curds are poured into the molds, which are encircled in fir bark. The cheeses are washed several times to stimulate the development of beneficial *B. linens* bacteria.

APPEARANCE: An irregular flattish oval shape, 6 to 7 inches in diameter and $1^3/_4$ inches high with an undulating orangish beige washed rind that has some yellowish moldy splotches. It weighs about $22^1/_2$ ounces and comes wrapped in a thick belt of dark fir bark to keep its shape when meltingly ripe. The paste is light straw to ivory colored, smooth and shiny.

SIMILAR CHEESE: Vacherin Mont d'Or.

SEASONAL NOTE: Although available year-round, it is best from early summer though winter.

WINE PAIRINGS: This is a wine-friendly cheese that should be reserved for the more flavorful red wine types.
WHITE: Tokay Pinot Gris (Alsace).

RED: Amarone della Valpolicella; red Bordeaux (Cabernet Sauvignon blend); red Burgundy (Pinot Noir); Beaujolais cru (Gamay); Tempranillo (Rioja-style blend).
SPARKLING: Blanc de Blancs Champagne (and other Chardonnay-based wines).

RATINGS

QUALITY

92

STRENGTH

4

LAGUIOLE

(lie-OLE) References to similar cheeses occur as far back as the Roman times, but the cheese under the current name Laguiole was "invented" at a monastery in the twelfth century. The paste is firm, substantial, and melts in your mouth to reveal a satisfying array of clean flavors—flowery, sweet, and mildly sour. Laguiole reminds me of several of the British traditional farmhouse cheeses; I'd place it somewhere between a Lancashire and a Cheddar, with equally pleasing heft but less of a bite.

TYPE: Raw cow's milk.

PROVENANCE: The town of Laguiole and thirty surrounding communities in the Aubrac Plateau of the Auvergne region in south-central France.

PRODUCERS: Daniel Cestrieres (*fermier*) and Coopérative Jeune Montagne (*laitier*) make the genuine raw-milk version.

PRODUCTION: Made from 95 percent milk of the French Simmental breed of cows—milk that's rich and ideally suited for making this sturdy, upstanding type of cheese. The curds are uncooked, broken, and pressed, then broken again prior to placing them in a cloth-lined mold for further pressing. The cheeses are aged from 4 months to 9 months. A.O.C. protected.

APPEARANCE: Large regularly shaped cylinders just under 16 inches in diameter and 16 inches across, weighing up to 105 pounds. The rinds are orangish brown to light amber colored; the paste is light yellow, quite dense, and somewhat crumbly (or Cheddar-like) in texture. The signals of authenticity are a stamp of a bull and the cheese's name on the rind.

SIMILAR CHEESES: Cantal, Salers.

SEASONAL NOTE: The best cheeses are made during the *transhumance*, or summer migration of the herds to the high-mountain pastures from May to October.

WINE PAIRINGS: Laguiole most decidedly sides with reds.
RED: Beaujolais cru (Gamay); Pinot Noir (Burgundy and California); Rhône reds (Syrah and Syrah blends); California Zinfandel.

RATINGS

QUALITY

91

STRENGTH

4

LANCASHIRE

(LANG-ka-shur) Lancashire is what I like to call one of the "British Boss Cheeses." It manages to stay simultaneously subtle and delicate, hardy and robust. A good Lancashire features a texture described locally as "buttery crumble," a sumptuous almost breadlike consistency, both creamy and flaky at the same time—if you can imagine that. Its flavor should be mildly acidic with a lemony tang, buttery and full but not strong or overpowering. It maintains a sublimely light, airy, moist consistency, at times almost as if it were a hardened version of cottage cheese. Not much authentic farmhouse Lancashire is being made anymore, but the Kirkham family is maintaining this great tradition. Mrs. Kirkham's method has been passed down through three generations—from her grandmother to her mother and then to her. Let's hope and pray it continues.

TYPE: Raw cow's milk.

PROVENANCE: Goosnargh, Lancashire, northwest England.

PRODUCER: John, Ruth, and Graham Kirkham, Beesley Farm.

PRODUCTION: One key to the Kirkham's method is the blending of 2- and 3-day-old curds, which have higher acidity and drier texture. They are cut, crumbled by hand three times, and set aside, then blended, milled, and pressed into cheeses. The cheeses are aged for 4 to 8 months in the Neal's Yard Dairy caves.

APPEARANCE: Comes in cylinders of 50 pounds, 25 pounds, 6½ pounds, or 3 pounds. (Note: the smaller cheeses tend to dry out faster.) Some are waxed, but the ones I buy from Neal's Yard Dairy have the natural buttered, cloth-covered rinds, one important sign of a genuine British farmhouse artifact.

SIMILAR CHEESES: Caerphilly, Cheshire, Double Gloucester, Llangloffan.

WINE PAIRINGS: Lancashire has proven to be more in sync with the softer reds, but it can also pair well with a fruity white.
WHITE: German Gewürztraminer Spätlese; Grüner Veltliner; German Riesling Kabinett and Spätlese.
RED: Barbaresco (Nebbiolo); Barbera d'Alba; Pinot Noir (California and Burgundy); California Cabernet Sauvignon; Rhône reds (Syrah and Syrah blends).

RATINGS

QUALITY

92

STRENGTH

4

LANGRES

(LON-gruh) Here is a cheese for anybody who doesn't like a strong or sharp taste but appreciates worldly, sophisticated flavors that linger lovingly on the palate. It features a curdy, somewhat springy texture with smooth, subtle flavors, distinct notes of sour milk, and a long finish. It also offers good pairings with a wide range of wines.

TYPE: Cow's milk.

PROVENANCE: From Champagne country, northeast of Dijon, France, hence its full formal name of Langres de Champenois.

PRODUCERS: La ferme du Modia (farmhouse) and Schertenleib (creamery) make authentic raw-milk A.O.C. versions.

PRODUCTION: Receives washings of Marc de Champagne during its ripening period of 15 to 21 days. The rind is colored with annatto (rouco).

APPEARANCE: This is among the most intriguing-looking cheeses you'll encounter (not to mention its eye-opening flavors!). It is a small drum with a concave top. Its apricot-colored light orangish rind has an irregular, undulating bumpy surface and white mold dustings. It comes in two sizes: the larger one is $6\frac{1}{2}$ to $7\frac{1}{2}$ inches in diameter, 2 to $2\frac{3}{4}$ inches tall and weighs $1\frac{3}{4}$ pounds; the smaller is 3 to $3\frac{1}{2}$ inches in diameter and $1\frac{1}{2}$ to $2\frac{1}{2}$ inches high, weighing about 6 ounces. (I prefer the smaller ones due to the beneficial ripening effect of a higher surface-to-paste ratio.) The paste is dry, off-white to light yellow in color, and it ripens (softens) from the outside in.

SIMILAR CHEESES: L'Ami du Chambertin, Époisses, Krümmenswiler Försterkäse.

SEASONAL NOTE: Best summer through fall.

WINE PAIRINGS: Langres is a versatile wine partner that works better with whites and sparkling wines, but also melds nicely into velvety reds.
  WHITE: Albariño; Sauvignon Blanc (California and Sancerre); German Riesling.
  RED: Pinot Noir (California and Burgundy); California Zinfandel.
  SPARKLING: Blanc de Blancs Champagne (and other Chardonnay-based sparkling wines).
  DESSERT/FORTIFIED: Sauternes (late-harvest Sémillon); Sherry (Pedro Ximenez).

RATINGS

QUALITY

88

STRENGTH

3

LAVORT

(lah-VOR) Although this cheese has an ancient and rustic appearance, it was actually created in the 1990s by cheesemaker Patrick Beaumont at the suggestion of the great chef Pierre Troisgros. The mold for its rare shape—it has a "crater" in its top and looks like a bagel or doughnut with an incomplete hole—came from Spain. The texture is firm and smooth. With proper aging, it attains a hard, crystalline, Parmesan-like consistency while retaining signature sheep's milk flavors à la Zamorano, Roncal, and Berkswell with grassy notes. Overall, it's a relatively milky "snacking"-type sheep cheese.

TYPE: Raw sheep's milk.

PROVENANCE: Dore Valley, Auvergne region, south-central France.

PRODUCER: Fromagerie de Terre-Dieu.

PRODUCTION: Lavort is made from the same raw material—the milk of the Lacaune breed of sheep—as several other distinguished cheeses, including Roquefort, and it comes from a renowned cheesemaking region. It is ripened for 3½ months.

APPEARANCE: A unique shape: a drum with a donut-shaped top side and a concave bottom rim that is about 6½ inches in diameter and 4½ inches tall and weighs around 4¾ pounds. It features a mottled natural rind with splotchy shades of white, beige, brown, and rust. The paste is straw colored, crumbly, and flaky.

SIMILAR CHEESES: The Ossau-Iraty Brébis family.

WINE PAIRINGS: Like many fine sheep's milk cheeses, the Lavort is an agreeable partner for many wines types.
WHITE: Sancerre (Sauvignon Blanc).

RED: Bordeaux (Cabernet Sauvignon blend); California Merlot.

SPARKLING: Brut Champagne (and other Champagne-style sparkling wines).
DESSERT/FORTIFIED: LBV Port; Sauternes (late-harvest Sémillon).

RATINGS
QUALITY
71
STRENGTH
2

LIVAROT

(lee-vah-ROH) Like several of its close relatives in the washed-rind family, Livarot is an ancient and noble cheese with a well-deserved lofty reputation. It originated more than 700 years ago, with cheesemaking monks in the abbeys of the Middle Ages, and is another key component of Norman gastronomic pride. By the middle of the nineteenth century, when it was dubbed *la viande du pauvre* ("the poor man's meat"), there were 4.5 million Livarots produced annually, making it the most consumed Norman cheese. Livarot is also a classic stinky cheese: its nearly noxious aroma is much stronger than its pleasant nutty flavor. Its paste is semisoft, creamy, and smooth in texture, with small holes, and it can become quite runny when ripe at room temperature.

TYPE: Cow's milk.

PROVENANCE: The market towns of Livarot and Vimoutiers, in the Calvados zone of the Pays d'Auge, southern Normandy, France.

PRODUCERS: Look for the A.O.C. label to guarantee quality and authenticity (A.O.C. status was granted in 1975). Recommended producers are as follows. *Fermier:* UNOG. *Laitiers:* Domaine du Plessis; Fromagerie Eugene Graindorge; Fromagerie de la Perelle; and the cooperative Isigny-Sainte-Mère.

PRODUCTION: The curds are cut and stirred, and then, still uncooked and unpressed, poured into molds. The cheeses are drained and salted, then aged from 3 weeks to nearly 3 months with regular washings in brine.

APPEARANCE: Livarot is also known as "The Little Colonel" because of its "insignia"— five strips of sedge or raffia that traditionally encircle the cheese to hold its shape. It comes in small to medium-sized rounds about 2 inches high that are wrapped in paper and packed in a box. Its rind should be smooth and moist, not sticky or slimy, and pinkish brown with reddish yellow or orange shading. Graindorge's Livarots come in two sizes: regular, which is about 5 inches across and 2 inches high, weighing $17\frac{1}{2}$ ounces; and Petit Livarot, just over $3\frac{1}{2}$ inches in diameter and weighing $9\frac{1}{2}$ ounces. As with similar cheeses, there is also a (third) large-size Livarot Coupe, which is 8 inches in diameter and $1\frac{3}{4}$ inches high, and weighing about 3 pounds. In general, the larger versions don't have the flavor of the smaller sizes. The paste is creamy light yellow, smooth, and fairly dense with abundant air pockets. It should have a little give and will ooze or melt at room temperature when ripe. The rind should not be cracked; the paste shouldn't be too hard (neither should the rind) or too thick.

RATINGS

QUALITY

75

STRENGTH

2

(continued)

SIMILAR CHEESES: Époisses, Munster, Pont L'Évêque.

SEASONAL NOTE: Livarots made with spring and early-summer milk attain ripeness from late summer through early winter, which is consequently the best time to eat this cheese.

WINE PAIRINGS: Livarot much prefers fruitier and/or spicier white wines.

WHITE: Alsatian Gewurztraminer; Grüner Veltliner; Alsatian Riesling; German Riesling (Kabinett, Spätlese, or Auslese); Tokay Pinot Gris (Alsace).

RED: Beaujolais cru (Gamay).

DESSERT/FORTIFIED: Hungarian Tokaji.

ADDITIONAL BEVERAGE PAIRING: In keeping with the principle of local pairings, try hard cider—a traditional specialty of the region.

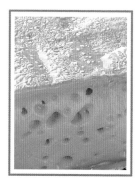

LLANGLOFFAN

(lang-LOFF-an) Since his retirement as principal viola for the Halle orchestra, Leon Downey, along with his wife, Joan, has been making beautiful music with this cheese. Llangloffan is firm with a light, pleasantly flaky texture reminiscent of Cheshire, yet it remains full-bodied, buttery, and luxurious, with concentrated flavors attributable to its careful aging. It's definitely in my category of British (or should I say Welsh?) Boss Cheeses, and I would recommend it to anyone who's looking for a strong, dry cow's milk cheese.

TYPE: Raw cow's milk.

PROVENANCE: Ty Uchaf, Castle Morris, Llangloffan, Pembrokeshire, on the western coast of Wales.

PRODUCER: Leon and Joan Downey.

PRODUCTION: Made according to a recipe almost identical to that of farmhouse Cheshire. The Downeys use both Brown Swiss and Jersey cow's milk, giving Llangloffan an additional richness due to the creamier milk. It is aged 2 to 6 months.

APPEARANCE: Comes in medium-sized wheels 9 inches in diameter and 3½ inches high that weigh 9 to 9½ pounds. The rind is thin and brownish beige with splotches of gray and white molds and a slightly rough surface. The paste is dark yellowish, straw colored, compact and firm, somewhat flaky and Cheddarlike but a bit smoother, more like Caerphilly.

SIMILAR CHEESE: Cheshire.

WINE PAIRINGS: Llangloffan works best with softer reds; for white pairings, look for the fruitier wines.
WHITE: German Gewürztraminer Spätlese; Alsatian Riesling; Vouvray demi-sec (Chenin Blanc).
RED: Barbera d'Alba; Cabernet Sauvignon (Bordeaux or California); Rhône Syrah; Malbec (Argentina).
DESSERT/FORTIFIED: Vintage Port.

RATINGS
QUALITY
82
STRENGTH
4

MAHÓN

(mah-HOHN) Menorca is known as a resort island but it can also boast a long and successful history of dairy production. Cheese has been made there since ancient times, from the epoch of Muslim rule and even before, but the full beneficial aging process was not perfected until the nineteenth century. Mahón is exemplary of the island's ancient dairy tradition—a straightforward cheese with textures and flavors fully capable of charming its consumers, if not downright enchanting them. It delivers tangy, sharp, sourish, and salty taste sensations that constitute an enticing reflection of its *terroir*—quite literally, a taste of the Mediterranean. As the cheese ages, the rind darkens, the paste turns yellower and harder, and the flavor intensifies to the point where it might rival even a mature Cabrales. I'm tempted to call Mahón Spain's answer to genuine English farmhouse Cheddar—at peak, it is equally solid, reliable, and delicious—but that might not account for its subtler, more seductive aspects.

TYPE: Cow's milk.

PROVENANCE: Menorca, the northernmost of the Balearic Islands, in the Mediterranean off the eastern coast of Spain (named after the principal port of the island).

PRODUCERS: Approximately 600 farms that either make their own cheese or sell their milk to smaller farmhouse-style cheesemakers or larger cooperative dairies.

PRODUCTION: Pressed, uncooked, drained in cheesecloth bags, and aged in natural caves. Farmhouse or *artesano* versions are made with unpasteurized milk; industrial ones from pasteurized. The artisanal versions show the imprint of the cloth mold, which is tied tightly around the curds to drain and squeeze out the whey. Mahón is sold in four categories by age: *tierno* (young), 15–30 days old; *semicurado*, up to 2 months of aging; *curado*, 3 to 6 months; and *añejo*, 9 to 12 months. The artisanal raw-milk *viejo* or *añejo* variety, aged for 10 months, is superior; the industrial pasteurized version is simply not the same cheese. Mahón acquired D.O.P. status in 1985.

APPEARANCE: Approximately 8-inch squares that are about 2 inches thick with rounded edges and weigh 5 to 6 pounds. The paste is ivory white to light yellow; it is dryish, somewhat crumbly, and Parmesan-like in texture, but it should not be rock hard. The rind is light yellowish or orangish brown, depending on whether it's rubbed with olive oil, butter, or sweet paprika, and dusted with white mold.

RATINGS

QUALITY

87

STRENGTH

4

SIMILAR CHEESES: Queso de los Beyos; a sharp Cheddar.

SEASONAL NOTE: Produced from September to June.

WINE PAIRINGS: Mahón requires generous fruit from its wine partners if not a lot of sweetness.

WHITE: California Chardonnay; Grüner Veltliner.

RED: Barbera d'Alba (Nebbiolo); red Bordeaux (Cabernet Sauvignon blend); Ribera del Duero (Tempranillo blend; also Almendralejo, from the Extremadura).

DESSERT/FORTIFIED: Madeira; Sherry (Oloroso); Tawny Port.

MAJORERO

(OR QUESO MAJORERO) (mah-ho-REH-roh) The island where this distinguished cheese is produced is just 60 miles off the coast of Africa and 700 miles from the Spanish mainland. Nevertheless, it is one of Spain's finest goat cheeses. It features a distinct, mildly goaty, sweet, mouthwatering taste, with a creamy, semihard texture, and a delicate aftertaste reminiscent of dried fruits, nuts, and grasses. It has a stimulating dryish, chalky attack on the palate and then it melts into a fascinating complexity of flavors. Raw-milk Majorero has an open texture, with small eyeholes throughout, and is slightly more acidic in flavor; it is toasty, not too salty, and has a pleasing bite to it. This is a cheese of great character that trumpets its *terroir* beautifully; it has hints of bitter, sour, salty, and dusty volcanic terrain. In its native archipelago, Majorero is typically served with potatoes boiled in their skins or as a dessert with quince paste or guavas.

TYPE: Goat's milk (raw and pasteurized).

PROVENANCE: Fuerteventura, Canary Islands (the name comes from the medieval name for the island: *Maxorata*).

PRODUCERS: Look for the D.O. label. The genuine farmhouse raw-milk version is far superior; the more commercial pasteurized version is not the same cheese. Julian Diáz is the best producer of this cheese I've found to date.

PRODUCTION: Artisanal cheeses are made from the raw milk of the local breed of goats; the industrial ones from pasteurized milk. (D.O. regulations allow for up to 15% local sheep's milk as well.) The goats manage to survive in desertlike conditions, munching on all kinds of scrubby vegetation—including lichen attached to volcanic rocks—and produce a relatively dense milk. Majorero is pressed, uncooked, and rubbed in lard or olive oil during its maturation period. It comes in three categories by age: young (8 to 20 days); *semicurado* (20 to 60 days); *curado* (more than 60 days). Look for the D.O.P. label and the genuine farmhouse raw-milk version—if available.

APPEARANCE: Flattened cylinders or wheels weighing from about 6½ pounds (3 kilos) to as much as 15 pounds (7 kilos). The diamond pattern on the rind comes from the forming molds, which are made from plaited palm fronds (or from plastic imitating them). The rind is off-white in young cheeses and turns to brownish beige in the more aged ones. It comes in three variations: rubbed with oil, rubbed with brownish orange *pimentón* (paprika), or rubbed with *gofio* (roasted cornmeal).

RATINGS

QUALITY

90

STRENGTH

2

SIMILAR CHEESES: Ibores, Ticklemore.

SEASONAL NOTE: Made in winter and spring.

WINE PAIRINGS: Majorero blends best with light, crisp whites and soft reds.

WHITE: Albariño; Tokay Pinot Gris (Alsace); Alsatian Riesling; Vinho Verde (lively, acidic wine from northern Portugal).

RED: Barbaresco (Nebbiolo); California Pinot Noir.

SPARKLING: Moscato d'Asti.

DESSERT/FORTIFIED: Sauternes (late-harvest Sémillon).

MANCHEGO

(mahn-CHEH-goh) You've heard of Don Quixote, Man of La Mancha? Well, this is the cheese of La Mancha, Spain's best-known and most popular worldwide—and also one of its most ancient. Food scribes in Roman times—including Columela—noted the animal husbandry and cheesemaking of Spain's arid central plain. (The region's name, La Mancha, given during the Moorish conquest of Spain in the Middle Ages, comes from an Arab word for "waterless.") Manchego is the quintessential representation of a Spanish sheep's milk cheese. Artisanal, unpasteurized versions can be truly excellent. Since so much of it is produced, however, there are large variations in quality and many mediocre cheeses bear the name; look for the genuine D.O. versions. A young Manchego is mild and even somewhat bland—a worthy sandwich cheese. The best aged ones develop depth of flavor with that pleasant bite and underlying sweetness characteristic of the finest sheep's milk cheeses. The paste is hard and it features the rich, buttery, oily heft and mouthfeel typical of sheep's milk cheeses.

TYPE: Sheep's milk.

PROVENANCE: The region of La Mancha, including the provinces of Albacete, Ciudad Real, Cuenca, and Toledo in the high plain of central Spain. An area of roughly 35,000 square kilometers of high plain (650 to 800 meters altitude) with a relatively harsh and extreme climate.

PRODUCERS: Industrial (large scale) and artisanal (small and medium-sized farms). Pasamontes is my preferred brand.

PRODUCTION: Made from the milk of the local ("oveja manchega") breed of sheep. Artisanal (raw milk) and industrial (pasteurized); aged a minium of 60 days. Pressed, uncooked, salted. D.O.P. regulated since 1984. Occasionally, Manchegos are rubbed in olive oil toward the end of ripening.

APPEARANCE: Drums with slightly convex sides of 7 and 8½ inches in diameter and 3 and 5 inches in height, weighing from 5½ to 7½ pounds. The rind is straw to dark brown colored with zigzag striations on the sides. These are imprints of the esparto grass, which is woven together to make the draining molds in traditional production. The top and bottom faces of the cheese also exhibit a characteristic and traditional flower pattern from the ridges in the wooden shelves on which the cheeses were cured and aged. The paste is ivory colored with irregularly spaced small eyelets.

RATINGS

QUALITY

82

STRENGTH

2

SIMILAR CHEESES: Castellano, Roncal, Zamorano.

SEASONAL NOTE: Available year-round but best consumed summer through winter.

WINE PAIRINGS: Manchego is more appropriate for fruity red wines.
RED: Barbera del Monferrato; Beaujolais cru (Gamay); California Pinot Noir.

MAROILLES

(mar-WAH) One of the original washed-rind monastery cow's milk cheeses of northern France. Typical of its regional traditions, Maroilles has a very pungent aroma and a strong, salty taste. It's definitely a strong cheese, not for the squeamish. It's been called "The King of the North." For most people, a little bit goes a long way. The paste is soft to semisoft. Important note: if it starts to turn brown and crumble up around the edges like a pie crust, it may be past peak and start to turn bitter.

TYPE: Cow's milk.

PROVENANCE: Eastern Flanders, France, in the Ardennes Forest near the border with Belgium; it was created by monks at the Benedictine Abbey of Saint-Humbert over 1,000 years ago.

PRODUCERS: Now made by about a dozen local artisanal farmhouses and dairies. Traditional raw-milk farmhouse versions of this A.O.C. cheese are made by La Ferme Blanche; Ferme du Pont de Sains; and GAEC de la Fontaine Orion.

PRODUCTION: My favorite version is called Gris de Lille (gree duh LEEL), a cheese whose nickname translates literally as "The Stinker from Lille." A washed-rind cheese, the raw-milk version is aged less than 2 months; others are aged up to 4 months.

APPEARANCE: Within the Maroilles A.O.C., there are numerous cheeses made in different shapes according to the same recipe. They range from little 5- to 7-ounce heart shapes to larger bricks that weigh from 1½ to almost 2 pounds. They have slightly beveled, moist rinds, and most of them come in square wooden boxes. The standard-sized Maroilles is a 5-inch square 1¾ inches high, weighing approximately 1½ pounds with an appearance similar to a Pont l'Évêque. It has a yellowish washed rind that matures to pinkish orange with bulging, collapsing sides and some cracking. The paste is off-white to light yellow, and it has small irregularly shaped holes throughout.

SIMILAR CHEESES: Livarot, Munster, Pavé d'Auge.

SEASONAL NOTE: Best in summer and autumn.

WINE PAIRINGS: Maroilles strikes a good balance with fruity reds and sweeter whites.
WHITE: Alsatian Gewurztraminer.

RED: Côtes-du-Rhône (Grenache-Syrah-Carignan blend); Rioja (Tempranillo blend); California Zinfandel.
DESSERT/FORTIFIED: Late-harvest Muscat (Moscadello di Montalcino/Tuscany).

RATINGS

QUALITY

77

STRENGTH

3

MATOS ST. GEORGE

(MAH-tohs saint-GEORGE) Mary and Joe Matos and their daughter, Sylvia Tucker, represent the fourth and fifth generations of cheesemakers in the family. Mary and Joe immigrated in 1979 from the Azores to Sonoma County, California, and started their family farm, amid familiar *terroir* and, not surprisingly, a large Portuguese community. Matos St. George is like a cross between a Cheddar and a Monterey Jack. It has a full, buttery, cream flavor with a firm texture. With age it becomes more tangy and crumbly.

TYPE: Raw cow's milk.

PROVENANCE: Santa Rosa, Sonoma County, California, USA.

PRODUCERS: Matos family.

PRODUCTION: Made in the traditional style of Queijo de São Jorge, the cheese from the island of the same name in the central Azores, ancestral home of the producers' family. The milk comes from the Matos' own herd of fifty Jersey and Holstein, lovingly cared for by the family. Coagulated with vegetarian rennet and aged for up to 7 months in the dairy's custom-built aging room.

APPEARANCE: There are three sizes of thick wheels: small (8 to 10 pounds, 9 inches in diameter and 4–5 inches tall); medium (12 to 15 pounds, 11–12 inches in diameter and 6 inches talk); and large (18 to 22 pounds, about 15 inches in diameter and 7 inches tall). The natural rind is hard and waxy yellow to light beige in color with white mold dustings. The paste is light yellow to ivory, firm and somewhat open textured with small airholes.

SIMILAR CHEESES: Lancashire, Fiscalini Bandage Cheddar, Cantal.

WINE PAIRINGS: Leans toward light to medium-bodied fruity red wines.
WHITE: California Viognier; Zierfandler (fruity, medium-bodied, from Austria).
RED: Cahors (made from the Malbec grape in southwestern France); Pinot Noir (Burgundy and California); Chianti Classico (Sangiovese).

RATINGS

QUALITY

75

STRENGTH

2

MIMOLETTE

(mee-moh-LET) Young Mimolette is an undistinguished, pedestrian cheese with a semihard interior; unless one hits you in the head, it won't make much of an impression. (Its name comes from the word *demi-molle*—"semisoft.") But once the cheeses are subject to careful aging, the magic emerges: they harden, turn a deeper orange on the interior, and take on an exceptionally mouthwatering array of fruity, nutty flavors, with notes of butterscotch and caramel. A well-aged Mimolette is pretty to look at—inside and out—and wonderful to taste. It's packed with lip-smacking, jaw-clacking flavor; like a comparable aged farmhouse Gouda, it will leave a nice impression on your palate.

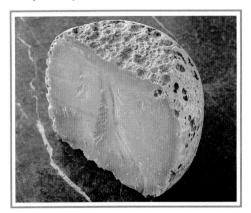

TYPE: Pasteurized cow's milk.

PROVENANCE: Around the town of Lille, in French Flanders, primarily the northernmost *department* of Pas de Calais, south and west of Belgium. Mimolette is also traditionally known as Boule de Lille (bool duh LEEL), after its rounded shape and the fact that its original ripening caves were in Lille.

PRODUCER: Factory made by the Coopérative Isigny-Sainte-Mere.

PRODUCTION: A pressed, cooked cheese. Its degrees of aging are young (*jeune*, 3 months), half old (*demi-vieille* or *demi-etuvée*, 6 months), old (*vieille* or *etuvée*, 12 months), and very old (*extra-vieille*, 24 months). Two fascinating quirks of Mimolette: producers use a wooden mallet to "sound" the cheeses and determine their stage of ripeness; and the rind is inhabited by mites that bore holes in it, which allows the ripening cheese inside to breathe.

APPEARANCE: Comes in the shape of a cannonball, about 8 inches in diameter with a flattened top, weighing up to 7 pounds with a hard natural brushed rind, brownish beige in color, that becomes rough and cratered with age. The paste is a deep orange color.

SIMILAR CHEESES: Aged Edam or Gouda (Goudse Boerenkaas).

WINE PAIRINGS: Mimolette pairs well with lighter reds and gentle dessert wines.
RED: Cahors (a rustic red made with the Malbec grape in southwestern France); Carignan (rustic red from southwestern France); Malbec (Argentina).
DESSERT/FORTIFIED: Malvasia Delle Lipari (Sicilian dessert wine); Quarts de Chaume (late-harvest Chenin Blanc from the Loire Valley).

RATINGS

QUALITY

77

STRENGTH

2

MONT ST. FRANCIS

This is a semihard aged monastery-style goat cheese from American master cheesemaker Judy Schad, whose cheeses are rated by some experts higher than the great French chèvres. Mont St. Francis is named for a local retreat that was once a Franciscan monastery and represents fond childhood memories for Judy. It's her favorite among her own cheeses—about a dozen total. The Mont St. Francis features a washed rind and the pungent aromas that go with it. Its semihard paste ripens to semisoft with aging. The company line goes something like this: "For years we produced these cheeses from pasteurized milk. The difference with raw milk is so distinctive, we've become true believers." Those are heartening words indeed, and I believe you'll taste the difference in the cheese's intense, beefy, earthy, hearty flavors.

TYPE: Raw goat's milk.

PROVENANCE: Greenville, Indiana, USA.

PRODUCER: Judy Schad, Capriole, Inc.

PRODUCTION: Made from the raw milk of the farm's own herd of Alpine, Saanens, and Nubian goats, which graze on rich natural woodlands and grasslands and have been subject to years of selective breeding for flavor. The milk is heated, ripened, and renneted. The curds are cut, cooked, unpressed, and hand-ladled. The cheeses are brine soaked and washed with a solution containing *B. linens*. They are aged from 3½ to about 8 months with regular brine washings for the first 7 to 8 days. (Select cheeses during the spring "flush" milking period are preaged for a time before being washed to create their rinds.)

APPEARANCE: A 3 ½- to 5-pound wheel with a reddish orange, somewhat moist and wrinkled rind that may exhibit patches or coatings of white and/or occasional bluish molds. The paste is open textured, semifirm, slightly shiny and white. The paste softens and becomes shinier with age, while the rind will become darker and somewhat crusty.

SIMILAR CHEESES: Munster-Geromé (but firmer), Chevrotin des Aravis.

SEASONAL NOTE: Available year-round but supply may be short January to April.

WINE PAIRINGS: Mont St. Francis finds its best match in a crisp Sauvignon Blanc.
🍷 **WHITE:** Pouilly-Fumé (Sauvignon Blanc); California Sauvignon Blanc; California Sémillon.

RATINGS

QUALITY

84

STRENGTH

2

MONTASIO

(mon-TAH-zee-oh) Present-day Montasio is probably not all that different from the cheese produced in an abbey called Moggio beginning in the thirteenth century. Like many other distinguished cheeses of northern Italy, it began as strictly an alpine cheese, but in the nineteenth century its production expanded to the valleys and surrounding areas. When young, Montasio is pliable, aromatic, and mild with grassy, fruity flavors. With age, it gradually takes on deeper, nutty flavors and eventually becomes hard and gratable.

TYPE: Cow's milk.

PROVENANCE: From the Alpe Giulie (Giulian Alps) in the province of Friuli, near the city of Udine, the extreme northeast corner of Italy close to the border with Slovenia.

PRODUCERS: Produced in factories and dairies throughout Friuli and the eastern part of the Veneto. D.O.C. protected since 1986 and D.O.P. since 1996.

PRODUCTION: There are three categories of this pressed, cooked cheese: young (aged 2 months); partially aged (4 to 10 months); and aged (1 year plus). Like Asiago, it can be aged up to 4 years.

APPEARANCE: Medium-sized wheels that have a yellowish gray natural brushed rind with cloth indentations and possibly some reddish brown shading. The paste is a light straw color, which turns yellower with age, and it has tiny holes throughout.

SIMILAR CHEESES: Asiago, Piave.

WINE PAIRINGS: Montasio favors smooth red wines.
WHITE: Getariako Txakolina (light-bodied floral white from Basque country); California Pinot Blanc.
RED: Barbaresco (Nebbiolo); Bordeaux (Cabernet Sauvignon blend); Carignan (rustic red from southwestern France); California Merlot.

RATINGS

QUALITY

88

STRENGTH

3

MONTE ENEBRO

(MON-te eh-NEB-roh) Monte Enebro's creator, Señor Baez, is considered a Spanish cheese hero, and his creation is recognized as one of the nation's premier alimentary artifacts. A delightfully unusual cheese, it features a semisoft, smooth, pure chalky-white, creamy paste that yields tangy, lingering, insistent, and complex goaty flavors. Monte Enebro (alternate spelling: Montenebro) is for fans of the classic flavor and mouthfeel of a goat cheese. It can be a dense mouthful; a classic French chèvre from the Loire Valley may seem light and fluffy in comparison.

TYPE: Pasteurized goat's milk.

PROVENANCE: Avila, west of Madrid.

PRODUCER: Rafael Baez and his daughter, Paloma.

PRODUCTION: Farmhouse; aged 21 days.

APPEARANCE: Loaves with rounded edges about the size and shape of a brick that have a mottled brownish gray and white rind with a covering of bluish gray *Penicillium* mold. The paste is bone white, fairly dense, semisoft, and chalky.

SIMILAR CHEESES: Harbourne Blue, Montsec.

WINE PAIRINGS: Monte Enebro marries best with various expressions of the Muscat grape, but also quite well with many dessert wines and fruity reds.
WHITE: Tokay Pinot Gris (Alsace).

RED: Beaujolais cru (Gamay); Ribera del Duero (Tempranillo blend).
DESSERT/FORTIFIED: Dulce de Monastrell (from Jumilla, southeastern Spain); Muscat de Rivesaltes (from the Languedoc); Sherry (Moscatel); Hungarian Tokaji; Sauternes (late-harvest Sémillon).

RATINGS

QUALITY

95

STRENGTH

6

MONTEREY DRY JACK

An American original produced by the Vella Family since 1931. Ignazio (Ig) Vella is the current head of the operation, having learned at the feet of his father, Tom, the founder who passed away in 1998. Dry Jack has the advantange of a consistent source of very high quality cow's milk, typical of the Sonoma area. It has a distinct flavor, sweet and nutty, persistent but not overpowering, reminiscent of Swiss cheeses from the Emmentaler zone. It's a versatile cheese—sturdy, simple, and direct—equally good eaten on its own or for grating and blending into pasta dishes. A bit of local cheese history: Jack cheese was created in the days of the California Gold Rush by a Scotsman named David Jacks. At the dawn of World War I, an Italian American purveyor in San Francisco by the name of D. F. DiBernardi developed Dry Jack—an aged version of Monterey Jack—to replace the imported Italian cheeses (mostly Parmesan and Grana) that were blocked during wartime. It had a flavor and texture similar to medium-aged Parmesan. In the early 1930s, Tom Vella of the Sonoma Mission Creamery formed his own company and perfected his own version of Dry Jack, which hasn't changed much since.

TYPE: Cow's milk.

PROVENANCE: Sonoma, California.

PRODUCER: Vella Cheese Company.

PRODUCTION: The milk comes from a nearby farm's herd of cows (a hybrid of two-thirds Holstein and one-third Gurnsey). The milk is pasteurized. Granular curds are tied in muslin sacks, shaped, and pressed, thus the "belly button" and radiating marks on the cheese. The cheeses are dried, soaked in brine for 3 days, then aged on racks for a minimum of 7 months. The natural rind is preserved with a coating of oil, pepper, and cocoa. The "Special Select" version of Dry Jack is aged at least 1 year. At 2 years, Dry Jack has a dense granular texture comparable to that of 2-year-old Parmesan.

APPEARANCE: Comes in wheels 11 to 12 inches in diameter, weighing approximately 8 pounds. The rind is dark reddish brown and the paste is off-white, slightly uneven, and somewhat crumbly.

RATINGS

QUALITY

78

STRENGTH

3

SIMILAR CHEESES: Parmigiano-Reggiano, Piave. Rumiano Cheese Co., Humboldt Country, extreme Northern California.

(continued)

WINE PAIRINGS: Look to pair Monterey Jack primarily with medium to full-bodied fruity reds.

WHITE: Riesling (Alsatian or German Spätlese).

RED: Amarone della Valpolicella; Nebbiolo (Barbaresco or Barolo); Madiran (tannic, traditionally rustic wine from southwestern France, made primarily from the Tannat grape); California Merlot; Super Tuscan blend (Sangiovese and Merlot); California Zinfandel.

SPARKLING: Champagne.

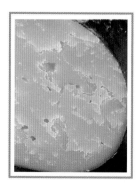

MORBIER

(more-bee-AY) A good raw-milk Morbier, between 2 and 4 months old, can be a real joy. The fact that the layer of ash in the center is now only a decoration seems to detract from the very good reputation the cheese rightly deserves. (The original purpose of the ash was to protect the first layer of milk from pests until the second layer was added later from the next milking.) A bigger problem for the reputation of the Morbier is the slackening of standards and the use of lifeless pasteurized milk. This yields a dull, pasty bore; the good raw-milk Morbiers I've tasted are full, plump, and gorgeous.

TYPE: Raw cow's milk (a pasteurized version is also made).

PROVENANCE: The Franche-Comté region of France, east of Burgundy and on the western border of Switzerland.

PRODUCERS: Roughly twenty local dairies and a handful of co-ops. Recommended producers of genuine raw-milk A.O.C. Morbier are the following. *Laitiers:* Coopérative fromagère d'Arbois; ENIL Poligny; Ets Rivoire & Jacquemin; Fromagerie Badoz; Claude Philippe; Fromagerie de Frasne; Fromagerie des Monts de Joux; Fromagerie Seignemartin; Juraflore-Societé Arnaud Frères.

PRODUCTION: Originally, curds that were left over from the production of the region's most famous cheese, Comté, were used to produce Morbier, which was consumed locally. Its exact origins are unknown but nowadays there is sufficient demand that it is made on its own account. Morbier curds in the vats are cut fairly large—about 1 inch square—to yield the semihard texture desired. The layer of ash is still included both for decoration and to distinguish the cheese—although it is now usually made from vegetable dye. The cheeses are cut in half horizontally after initial molding to add this layer. It is then remolded and given two surface saltings, then rubbed twice a week with water for 2 months. As with most cheeses, the slightly smaller formats ripen more quickly than the larger ones.

APPEARANCE: Large disks or flattened drums 12 to 15 inches in diameter and $2^{1}/_{2}$ to $3^{1}/_{2}$ inches high, weighing from 11 to 20 pounds. The edges are rounded and the rind is dark golden colored with splotches of white. The paste is creamy white with a scattering of small holes.

SIMILAR CHEESES: Fontina d'Aosta, Tomme de Savoie, St. Nectaire.

SEASONAL NOTE: Best in late winter through early summer but available year-round.

WINE PAIRINGS: Morbier pairs nicely with soft, round red wines.
RED: Burgundy (Pinot Noir); Priorat (Garnacha blend).

DESSERT/FORTIFIED: LBV Port.

RATINGS

QUALITY

75

STRENGTH

2

MOTHAIS-SUR-FEUILLE

(OR MOTHAIS À LA FEUILLE) (moh-TAY soor FOY) This delicate young goat cheese, also known as La Mothe-Saint-Heray (lah MOAT sant-eh-RAY), comes in an attractive package: resting on a chestnut leaf with a base of velvety white candidum mold covering its exterior. The leaf—no mere decoration—is what distinguishes it from the rest of the Loire Valley goat's milk cheeses made nearby. It helps preserve the moisture of the paste during its short ripening period and also helps protect the cheese from excessive drying after it has ripened. The beneficial molds on the rinds of the Mothais are slower to develop as compared with other similar chèvres; it is delightful and delicately flavored even before they start to show.

TYPE: Raw goat's milk.

PROVENANCE: Mellois Plateau in the Deux-Sevres, the old province of Poitou, west-central France.

PRODUCERS: *Fermier:* Nadine Marboeuf. *Laitiers:* Fromagerie de Fontenille; SARL La Bonde de Gâtine; SARL le villageois. *Affineur:* EURL Paul Georgelet—SCEA Le Petit Boisselage.

PRODUCTION: A cheese traditionally ripened on brown chestnut leaves, which help moderate and control its level of humidity during the maturing process, allowing it to dry gradually in well-ventilated but humid caves and also to retain enough humidity as it enters its ripening period of 3 to 4 weeks. During this stage, the cheeses are turned about once a week.

APPEARANCE: A small round $3^{1}/_{2}$ to 4 inches in diameter and $^{3}/_{4}$ inch high resting on a leaf. The rind is slightly rough and bumpy, straw colored, and dusted with white and grayish green mold. The paste is chalky white, somewhat dry in the center with a striation of darker, creamier paste just inside the rind.

SIMILAR CHEESES: Bougon and Chabichou de Poitou, which is from the same area and is somewhat similar in flavor.

SEASONAL NOTE: Available from spring through autumn.

WINE PAIRINGS: Mothais marries well with dry crisp white wines and softer fruity reds.
WHITE: Sancerre, Bordeaux Blanc (Sauvignon Blanc); Vouvray sec (Chenin Blanc).
RED: Chianti Classico (Sangiovese); southern French Syrah (Languedoc).

RATINGS
QUALITY
81
STRENGTH
2

LE MOULIS

(luh moo-LEE) From the center of the Pyrénées, just north of the Spanish border. Compared with other cheeses from the area, Le Moulis is less restrained in its aromas and flavors, even when very young. It's been one of the more reliable cheeses I've encountered; it's rarely disappointing. It is quite friendly but not overly loud or obnoxious. It seems fairly innocent at first, but it leaves a lovely, long, lingering finish—exuding enough charm and complexity to overcome its simple, rustic initial impression. When young, the cow's milk version is a fairly simple, buttery, and somewhat rubbery-textured cheese; with extra aging, the paste turns darker, and the finish lengthens and becomes pleasantly earthy. The goat's milk version has a similar rustic, earthy flavor but is far better when fairly young. The sheep's milk version has the smoothest flavor profile of the three, but, like the goat's milk version, is best consumed when younger.

TYPE: Raw cow's milk (there are also sheep and goat variations).

PROVENANCE: The region around Arriège in the French Pyrénées and the province of Comté de Foix.

PRODUCERS: Local artisanal dairies, including SARL Le Moulis.

PRODUCTION: Uncooked, washed in brine every other day for the first 2 weeks only, and turned for up to 3 months of its ripening period. No other fuss is made over these young cheeses from old mountains.

APPEARANCE: Comes in drums with bulging sides, 8½ to 9½ inches in diameter, about 3 inches high and weighing 7½ to 8½ pounds. The natural rind is light brown and matted with a dusting of white mold. The paste is off-white in the cow's milk version, firm textured and with many small, irregularly shaped holes. The sheep's milk version is more straw colored with fewer and smaller holes. The goat's milk one is white with a few small holes scattered throughout the paste.

SIMILAR CHEESE: Bethmale (cow).

WINE PAIRINGS:
FOR THE COW'S MILK VERSION: Favors red wines, especially Cabernet Sauvignon–based ones.
RED: Amarone della Valpolicella; Barbaresco (Nebbiolo); Beaujolais cru (Gamay); Cabernet Sauvignon (Bordeaux or California); Burgundy

(continued)

(Pinot Noir); California Merlot; Ribera del Duero (Tempranillo blend); Zinfandel (California).

FOR THE GOAT'S MILK VERSION: Pair this version mostly with dry to off-dry white wines.

 WHITE: Burgundy (Chardonnay); Pouilly-Fumé (Sauvignon Blanc); Vouvray sec (Chenin Blanc).

RED: Barbera d'Asti; Beaujolais cru (Gamay).

SPARKLING: Moscato d'Asti.

DESSERT/FORTIFIED: Tawny Port.

FOR THE SHEEP'S MILK VERSION: Generally mixes best with softer red wines.

 WHITE: Sancerre (Sauvignon Blanc).

RED: Barolo (Nebbiolo); Barbera d'Asti; Australian Shiraz; Super Tuscan (Sangiovese-Merlot blend).

 DESSERT/FORTIFIED: Sauternes (late-harvest Sémillon).

RATINGS

COW'S MILK
QUALITY

95

STRENGTH

4

SHEEP'S MILK
QUALITY

89

STRENGTH

3

GOAT'S MILK
QUALITY

89

STRENGTH

3

MUNSTER

(MUHN-ster) Like Cheddar, Parmesan, Brie, and other iconic cheeses, the reputation of Munster has been clouded by the appearance of many bland commercial imitations. It is an ancient monastic cheese with roots in the early Middle Ages. (The name itself is derived from the word *monastery* in the local dialect.) Munster originally had a bloomy rind; the modern washed-rind format evolved about 800 years ago. A perfectly ripe Munster is exquisite and is the equal of a fine Époisses; in fact, connoisseurs have been known to confound the two. Typical of any top-flight washed-rind cheese, Munster's paste goes from semisoft when young to soft and runny at peak; it gives off a strong, barnyardy aroma and has an assertive, deep, rich, tangy flavor. A genuine ripe Munster is as good as any representative of the stinky washed-rind category. Among my favorites are Haxaire's organic version and the Petit Munster/Gerome called La Fleur Vosgienne, which is made in 200-gram (7-ounce) rounds by Maison Fischer.

TYPE: Cow's milk.

PROVENANCE: The mountains of the Vosges region, in Alsace, northeastern France.

PRODUCERS: There are unpasteurized and pasteurized versions of Munster, the former made by *fermier* (farmhouse) producers and the latter generally by *laitier* (dairy or creamery) producers. Recommended brands are as follows. *Laitiers:* Fromagerie de l'Ermitage; Valdeweiss; Ets Bernard Louis; Marcillat. *Fermiers:* Ferme Claudepierre; Ferme des Pensées Sauvages; Fromagerie Haag.

PRODUCTION: Munster has been A.O.C. protected since 1969. (Munster's sister cheese, Géromé, a nearly identical but larger cheese that comes from the area around the town of Gérardmer just to the west, is covered under the same A.O.C., referred to as "Munster Géromé." The merger of these two types has meant that the Geromé name has been almost completely overshadowed by Munster.) The cheeses are made from mountain pasture milk in the summer and farm milk in the winter. They are aged 2 to 3 months in cellars at high humidity. Standard-size Munsters are aged for a minimum of 3 weeks with regular washings of the rind to promote development of the reddish external bacteria. (Fresh, unripened Munster, which is a fairly bland cheese, is sold and consumed mostly within its zone of production.)

APPEARANCE: Comes in two basic sizes of flattened cylinder: regular (7½ inches in diameter and 1 to 3 inches high) and small (3 to 5 inches in diameter and

RATINGS

QUALITY

79

STRENGTH

3

(continued)

about 2 inches high). The rind is a beautiful sight, with its bright pinkish orange color that turns progressively darker and more reddish/orangish with age. As with all washed-rind cheeses, its exterior should be moist but not slimy or cracked.

SIMILAR CHEESES: Époisses, Livarot, Maroilles.

SEASONAL NOTE: June through October.

WINE PAIRINGS: Munster strongly favors crisp, spicy whites and dessert wines; it also highlights the classic regional pairing with Alsatian white wines.

WHITE: Alsatian Gewurztraminer; Grüner Veltliner; Alsatian Pinot blanc; Alsatian Riesling; German Riesling (Kabinett or Auslese);

RED: Australian Shiraz.

SPARKLING: Moscato d'Asti.

DESSERT/FORTIFIED: Sherry (Oloroso).

N I S A

(NEE-sah) This is a Portuguese artisanal cheese, similar to Evora, that is eaten semihard and hard. Its flavor is quite pronounced and somewhere between walnuts and Brazil nuts. Nisa is best consumed between 3 and 5 months of age when its flavors and textures are still fairly mellow, buttery, and nutty. I think of it as a very satisfying snacking cheese as opposed to a dessert cheese to be served at the end of the meal on a cheese plate—that is, unless you happen to be finishing the meal with a fairly round, easygoing red wine, in which case the pairing makes for a lovely finale and excellent *digestif*.

TYPE: Raw sheep's milk.

PROVENANCE: The Alentejo region, east-central Portugal.

PRODUCERS: Local artisanal creameries and farmhouses.

PRODUCTION: Similar to that of Evora. The milk comes mainly from the Saloio breed of sheep, which are related to the renowned Spanish merinos. The curds are coagulated with thistle flower. The cheeses are aged 60 days.

APPEARANCE: Small wheels 5 inches in diameter and 1 inch high, weighing 10 to 14 ounces, with a light orangish brown somewhat irregular and moist rind. The paste should be firm but not rock hard and off-white to ivory in color with some cavities of varying shapes and sizes.

SIMILAR CHEESES: Queijo Amarelo da Beira Baixa, Queijo Evora.

SEASONAL NOTE: Best in spring and summer.

WINE PAIRINGS: Nisa pairs especially well with softer, more mellow red wines.
WHITE: Alsatian Muscat; German Muskateller Kabinett.

RED: Barbera d'Alba; Dolcetto d'Alba; Australian Grenache-Mourvèdre-Syrah blend (where Mourvèdre is also known as Mataro); Argentinian Malbec; Morgon (Gamay/Beaujolais cru); California Pinot Noir.

RATINGS

QUALITY

82

STRENGTH

3

ORB WEAVER VERMONT FARMHOUSE CHEESE

Marjorie Susman and Marian Pollack have been making this excellent farm-house cheese since they settled in Vermont's Champlain Valley more than two decades ago. They named their farm after the type of spider that weaves its web in an orb shape, representing their ideal of diligent artistry. Orb Weaver is a rich, creamy, Colby-style cheese, more moist than Cheddar, with a slightly tangy buttery flavor and springy texture.

TYPE: Raw cow's milk.

PROVENANCE: New Haven, Vermont.

PRODUCER: Orb Weaver Farm.

PRODUCTION: The cheeses are made seasonally from November to May entirely by hand by ancient traditional methods. Marjorie and Marian built their own cheese cave in 2000 and are now aging all their own cheeses for about 1 year with brushings and turnings twice a week. Their outstanding component is the farm's award-winning milk, which comes from its small herd of magnificent pure-bred Jersey cows. Since happy cows make the best milk, the Orb Weaver herd grazes on their 30 acres of clover pastures, is fed sweet-smelling and tasting grains when they're in the barn, and is serenaded with classical music when they're at rest.

APPEARANCE: Comes in wheels about 10½ inches in diameter and 3½ inches high, weighing approximately 10 pounds with a concave ridge around the outside edge and a somewhat rustic appearance. The natural rind is beige to light brown while the paste ranges from straw or golden in color to a mustardlike yellow-orange, depending on the season. The paste is semihard, moist yet firm, with some holes and fissures. There is also a 2-pound wheel that is 6 inches in diameter and 2 inches high.

SIMILAR CHEESES: Bethmale, Le Moulis (cow), Morbier.

WINE PAIRINGS: Orb Weaver generally finds its best pairings with milder red wines.
WHITE: California Chardonnay.

RED: Barbera d'Alba; Beaujolais (Gamay); Bourgueil (Cabernet Franc from the Loire Valley); Syrah-Mourvèdre-Grenache blends from the Rhône Valley.
SPARKLING: Champagne (Blanc de Blancs).

RATINGS

QUALITY

76

STRENGTH

1

OSSAU–IRATY BRÉBIS

(oh-sow ee-RAH-tee bray-BEE) Ossau-Iraty Brébis is a large family of cheeses that includes Abbaye de Belloc, Vallée d'Aspe, Istara, and many others—all worth a try at least for comparison and to determine your personal favorite(s). Records of this venerable artifact go back to at least the first century B.C. in the Roman market town of Toulouse. It has been known throughout history by various names, mostly depending on which section of its cheesemaking region it came from: Laruns, Esbareich-Tardets, Oloron, Iraty, and Amou Landais to name a few. Abbaye de Belloc (see page 69) was an early and particularly well-regarded version created in the seventeenth century and still sold under that name. It is a classic hard ewe's milk cheese with all the wonderful digestive and nutritive properties of that miraculous raw material. As is the case with many large families—or generic categories —of mountain cheeses, there are variations in appearance and flavor from one valley to the next as the complex, variegated, and rugged *terroir* unfolds and expresses itself. In general, the Ossau-Iraty cheeses have a fine granularity to their texture and a nuttiness to their flavor with an underlying balance of sweet and savory. Many people feel they're reminiscent of Parmigiano-Reggiano or of a mountain-style cow's milk cheese. This said, the Ossau-Iratys tend to have a sweeter, gentler finish than those other cheeses. The family also features a mouthwatering quality that is more attributable to its unadorned simplicity than to excess salt. (This is one of my criteria for the finest cheeses: less reliance on saltiness and more emphasis on the pure flavors of the milk.)

TYPE: Sheep's milk.

PROVENANCE: The Basque country, where it is traditionally called Iraty, and the nearby Béarn region, where it is called Ossau, in the Pyrénées of extreme southwestern France. Purists argue that these two regional delicacies should be treated separately but they come under the same A.O.C. largely for administrative purposes.

PRODUCERS: Eight major dairies or cooperatives (including Les Fromages Onetik and Fromagerie Agour) are supplied by more than 2,000 small farms and dairies; there are also about 100 farmhouse producers. Genuine farmhouse raw-milk versions are produced by Fromagerie Unhaldia, Fromages Agour, and Jean-Pierre Urrizaga among others. Les Fermiers Basco-Béarnais, an artisanal dairy, produces both pure sheep and mixed-milk versions of Vallée d'Aspe.

(continued)

PRODUCTION: From the milk of the Manech and Basco-Bearnaise breeds of sheep. The cheese received A.O.C. status in 1980 and is made using traditional methods in stone huts up in the mountains during the spring and summer *transhumance* (migration to higher pastures), on rustic farms down in the valleys, and also in certain dairies. The curds are heated, molded, lightly pressed, salted, and aged in cool caves for a minimum of 120 days for larger cheeses ($8^{1}/_{2}$ to 11 pounds) and 80 days for smaller ones ($4^{1}/_{2}$ to $6^{1}/_{2}$ pounds).

APPEARANCE: Medium-sized drums about 10 inches in diameter and 6 inches high, weighing between 11 and 16 pounds. The natural rinds are dry, relatively thick, and smooth, ranging in color from orangish yellow to dark brownish gray. The pastes are firm and smooth, tending toward flaky with age, and ivory to pale straw colored with occasional irregular holes, small cavities, and striations.

DESCRIPTION OF ISTARA: Millstones (with rounded edges) $3^{1}/_{2}$ inches high and 9 inches in diameter, weighing from $7^{1}/_{2}$ to $9^{1}/_{2}$ pounds. The rind is light brown to caramel colored with dustings of white mold and the pattern of the drainage shelves pressed into the top and bottom.

SIMILAR CHEESES: Roncal, Spenwood, Vermont Shepherd.

SEASONAL NOTE: Mountain cheeses are made during the migration of the flocks to the higher pastures (June to September) while the rest of the year they are made on the farms or in the dairies.

WINE PAIRINGS: Ossau-Iraty cheeses tend to pair best with dry white wines.
WHITE: Chardonnay (Burgundy and California); California Pinot blanc; Pouilly-Fumé (Sauvignon Blanc); California Sémillon.
RED: Australian Cabernet Sauvignon; Barbera d'Alba; Dolcetto d'Alba; Gamay (Beaujolais).

RATINGS

QUALITY

87

STRENGTH

3

PARMIGIANO-REGGIANO

(par-mee-JEE-ah-noh reh-JEE-ah-noh) Many experts consider this the greatest cheese on the planet, and I would certainly place it in my top ten— of course, only if we're discussing the genuine article and not one of the many cheeses that casually usurp the name. Parmigiano-Reggiano, often referred to as simply "Parmesan" in English, is, on the one hand, a straight-forward, unpretentious cheese that fits snugly into the category of simple comfort food; on the other hand, it is a magnificent artifact and Italian national treasure worthy of the loftiest accolades. A well-aged authentic Parmigiano-Reggiano has a hard, granular, crumbly, flaky paste; it is ideal for grating yet it melts in the mouth. Incredibly delicious and subtle, it offers a complex, mouth-tingling matrix of fragrant, vegetal, and savory flavors that linger luxuriously on the palate. True Parmesan is sweeter, more moist, and lower in salt than its many inferior imitators.

TYPE: Raw cow's milk.

PROVENANCE: The areas around the cities of Parma, Modena, and Mantua in the province of Emilia-Romagna, north-central Italy.

PRODUCERS: There are between 700 and 800 active production sites, including many dairies and small factories known as *caselli*. They are regulated by a consortium, the Consorzio del Formaggio Parmigiano-Reggiano, that upholds D.O.C. standards, grades cheeses, and handles worldwide advertising and marketing. The Consorzio has relatively high standards but not necessarily artisanal-quality ones. There are three levels of producers: farmers, who make cheese from the milk of their own herds; and *latterie* (dairies) and *caseifici* (cheese factories), which make cheese from sourced milk. There is also a tier of businesses (*negociants*) that per-form selection, aging, and export.

PRODUCTION: Real Parmesan is made only from milk produced by cows feasting on fresh grass or hay within the D.O.C. zone according to strict regulations. Although the name-controlled version is just about 700 years old, the recipe dates back to the Roman Empire. Parmesan's stages of maturity are *giovane* or young (1 year), *vecchio* or old (2 years), *stravecchio* or "extra-old" (3 years), and *stravecchione* or "super extra-old" (4 years). Received D.O.C. status in 1955 and D.O.P. in 1996.

RATINGS

QUALITY

97

STRENGTH

6

APPEARANCE: Comes in large drums 14 to 16 inches across and 7 to 9½ inches high with convex sides; they weigh 66 to 88 pounds. (The legal minimum is 24 kilos or approximately 53 pounds.) The natural, brushed, oiled rind is straw colored to dark yellow and has the words *Parmigiano-Reggiano* stamped on its sides in distinctive stenciled dot

(continued)

lettering. (It also has the official logo of the Parmesan Consortium, the year and month of its production, and its producer's identification number stamped on each cheese.) The paste is light ivory to straw yellow in color and contains small white crystals of denatured protein when properly aged. The cheese is at its peak when small drops of moisture are visible on a cut surface.

SIMILAR CHEESES: *Grana,* meaning "granular," is the generic term for similar hard cheeses from outside the D.O.C. zone or not made according to as strict standards. Grana Padano, a D.O.C. cheese aged around 6 months, is essentially a poor man's Parmesan with a wider zone of production.

SEASONAL NOTE: Parmesans produced in the warmer months of the year—May through September—and aged 2½ to 3½ years are ideal but can be hard to obtain outside of Italy these days.

WINE PAIRINGS: Parmigiano marries well with round, fruity reds and also the less dry sparklers.
WHITE: Italian Pinot Grigio.

RED: Barolo (Nebbiolo); Barbaresco (Nebbiolo); California Merlot.

SPARKLING: Brut Champagne.

FOOD PAIRING: Ninety-nine percent of the Western world is familiar with the delight of grated Parmesan on pasta. Always grate it fresh; avoid pregrated.

P A U

(pow) The generic name for this cheese is actually San Mateo (san mah-TAY-ooh). The brand I acquire, Picos de España, is named Pau (for "Paul" in Catalan, after the cheesemaker's son), and that is the name by which it's popularly known and acknowledged. Pau is a washed-rind goat's milk cheese that ripens from the outside in to a delicious, creamy smooth consistency and complex flavor profiles. At the same time, it possesses a quality seldom found in goat's milk cheeses—a semisoft, pliant, almost rubbery texture.

TYPE: Pasteurized goat's milk.

PROVENANCE: Catalonia, Spain, in the mountainous region around Vilassar de Dalt, a village north of Barcelona.

PRODUCER: Josep Quixart.

PRODUCTION: Made by artisanal methods in a controlled, modern small factory environment. The goats roam the hills just a few miles inland from the Mediterranean and benefit from rugged, clean *terroir*. The curds are cooked and pressed; the cheeses are aged from 5 weeks to 2 months.

APPEARANCE: A drum 5 inches in diameter and 2 1/2 inches high, weighing just over 2 pounds, with convex sides. The washed rind is light brown to dark orange with a smattering of white mold splotches. The paste is off-white to straw colored with a grayish tint, compact, and semisoft with relatively small, irregularly shaped and sized holes throughout.

SIMILAR CHEESES: Chevrotin des Aravis, Garrotxa, Mont St. Francis.

WINE PAIRINGS: Pau requires a lot of fruit from its white partners and plenty of berry flavor from its red ones.
   WHITE: South African Chenin Blanc; California Sémillon; Vouvray sec (Chenin Blanc).
   RED: Barbera d'Asti; Super Tuscan (Sangiovese-Merlot blend); California Merlot; California Zinfandel.
   DESSERT/FORTIFIED: Tawny Port.

RATINGS

QUALITY

72

STRENGTH

1

PAVÉ D'AUGE

(OR PAVÉ DU PLESSIS) (pah-vay DOHJ) Pavé d'Auge is an ancient Norman cheese, originally a product of the medieval monasteries in the area, and essentially a larger, more rustic version of the more famous Pont l'Évêque. The word *pavé* means paving stone or slab—as in "pavement"—and if you take a look at the shape of this cheese whole you'll immediately see why. Its paste is semisoft to soft, rich and flavorful, with a strong, woodsy flavor. Compared with Pont l'Évêque, the format of the Pavé d'Auge (and Pavé du Plessis) yields a more successful cheese in many ways. Less of the cheese is rind; more of it is meaty, buttery paste. The effects of the *B. linens* bacteria on the rind and ultimately the paste are mitigated, allowing the exceptional quality of the milk to shine through. You should skip eating the rind, especially if you're hoping to pair this cheese successfully with wines.

TYPE: Cow's milk.

PROVENANCE: The Pays d'Auge at the northern base of the Normandy peninsula to the west of the town of Pont l'Évêque. Local *pavé* cheeses are often known by more specific place-names such as Pavé du Plessis and Pavé de Moyaux.

PRODUCERS: Local farmhouses and creameries, including La Moissonnière (*fermier*) and Fromagerie Eugene Graindorge (*laitier*). A good genuine Pavé du Plessis is produced by the artisanal dairy Domaine du Plessis.

PRODUCTION: The curds are cut, stirred, kneaded, and placed in square molds. The cheeses are salted on the fifth day and then aged $2^{1}/_{2}$ to 4 months with regular washings to develop the rind.

APPEARANCE: Square-shaped bricks with rounded edges, $4^{1}/_{2}$ inches at the base and up to $2^{1}/_{2}$ inches high, weighing $1^{1}/_{2}$ to $1^{3}/_{4}$ pounds. The rind is straw colored or yellowish beige and is scored with a basket pattern; in humid ripening environments, the rind becomes more orange with age. The paste is light yellow, smooth, and has air pockets distributed throughout.

SIMILAR CHEESES: A genuine Pont l'Évêque would be a viable substitute. Graindorge makes an excellent one in two sizes: standard (14 ounces) and small ($8^{1}/_{2}$ ounces). Pavé d'Auge also recalls, for many, its other famous cousin, Camembert.

SEASONAL NOTE: Available year-round but best May through December.

RATINGS

QUALITY

88

STRENGTH

3

WINE PAIRINGS: This is a good cheese partner for the Claret-type wines.

WHITE: California Chardonnay; Alsatian Gewurztraminer; German Riesling Kabinett.

RED: Cabernet Sauvignon blend (Bordeaux or California); Cahors (made from the Malbec grape in southwestern France); Chianti Classico (Sangiovese); California Merlot.

SPARKLING: Champagne (Blanc de Blancs).

ADDITIONAL BEVERAGE PAIRING: Hard cider.

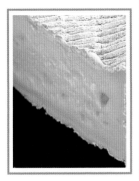

PECORINO FOGLIE NOCE

(OR "FOJA DE NOCE") (peh-koh-REE-noh FOH-leeay NO-cheh)

This is a farmhouse version of the famous central Italian sheep's milk cheese that comes wrapped in walnut leaves to give it particular aromas and flavors. It's definitely a "looker," but the wrapping of walnut leaves adds more than simple visual appeal: it helps tone down and balance some of the cheese's sheepier flavors. Pecorino Foglie Noce has an agreeable flavor, highlighted by hints of fresh-mowed grass and black walnut, and is tremendously satisfying in small portions. That feeling of satisfaction has surely been experienced by thousands upon thousands of cheeselovers over the past two millennia.

TYPE: Raw sheep's milk.

PROVENANCE: Originally from the town of Montefeltro in the northern part of Le Marche, on the central Adriatic Coast of Italy; now produced in much of the surrounding area, including nearby Emilia-Romagna.

PRODUCERS: The farmhouse producer Paolo Ferabegoli in Emilia-Romagna makes the Pecorino Foglie Noce that is sold under the Mitica brand name; the Luigi Guffanti firm also sells a good one.

PRODUCTION: Pressed curds. Aged for a total of 40 days, the first few weeks rubbed daily with a mix of olive oil and vinegar and placed in small barrels with layers of walnut leaves in between. The aging period is completed in ventilated caves.

APPEARANCE: Round-edged drums or millstones 4½ to 6½ inches in diameter and 2½ to 3½ inches tall, weighing from 2½ to 4½ pounds. The rind is natural, grayish, and covered with walnut leaves. The paste is off-white to ivory in color and becomes dry and crumbly with age.

SIMILAR CHEESE: Pecorino Toscano.

WINE PAIRINGS: The Foglie Noce version of Pecorino pairs nicely with crisp, dry whites and softer reds.

WHITE: California Sauvignon Blanc; southern French Sauvignon Blanc (Languedoc).

RED: Periquita blend (Portuguese red with Tempranillo, Syrah, and Merlot).

DESSERT/FORTIFIED: Late-harvest Tuscan Muscat (Moscato Bianco).

RATINGS

QUALITY

81

STRENGTH

3

PECORINO TOSCANO

(peh-koh-REE-noh tohs-KAH-noh) The word for "sheep" in Italian is *pecora*; the adjective is *pecorino*, which becomes the name for the cheese as well. There are hundreds of local types of Pecorino all over central and southern Italy. They can be roughly divided into major regional categories: Toscano; Romano (from the countryside surrounding Rome; often referred to as simply "Romano," although the proper D.O.P. name is Pecorino Romano); Sardo (from Sardinia); and Siciliano (from Sicily). Pecorino Toscano is the one that tops my list. Its paste is hard with an intense sheepy flavor and a mildly peppery finish. Like all great sheep's milk cheeses, its flavors can become intense and savory with age, but they retain an essential underlying sweetness and mellowness—as long as they don't become too dry and aged. Pecorino Toscano received D.O.C. status in 1986 and D.O.P. in 1996, uniting many local cheeses of similar production and appearance under one umbrella for quality control and marketing purposes. Look for brands labeled *pura pecora* ("pure sheep") from the area around the town of Pienza in south-central Tuscany. These cheeses, which form a semiofficial subcategory under the rubric Pecorino di Pienza, are the best representations of a truly class act.

RATINGS

QUALITY

81

STRENGTH

3

TYPE: Sheep's milk.

PROVENANCE: A D.O.C. cheese from Tuscany, where the cheese industry dates back to Etruscan times—long before the rise and fall of the Roman Empire.

PRODUCERS: Made in small factories and dairies; Luigi Guffanti, the major cheese *stagionatore*, supplies a reliable Pecorino di Pienza.

PRODUCTION: Made from pasteurized or nonpasteurized milk; pressed, with a natural rind. Aged from 1 month to up to 1 year. Some versions are rubbed with olive oil and/or tomato paste to encourage rind development as well as to inhibit the growth of undesirable molds and bacteria, and keep away any pests during ripening.

APPEARANCE: Pecorino Toscano comes in small to medium-sized drums of varying sizes from 6 to 9 inches across and 2½ to 4 inches tall with convex sides, like a miniature Parmesan shape, weighing from about 2½ to nearly 8 pounds. The rind colors also vary. Some mature versions of Tuscan Pecorino, which are aged at least 4 months, have dark brown rinds and a dry, hard, nearly brittle paste. I prefer a cheese that has been aged 6 months and has either tomato paste or olive oil

(continued)

rubbed into the rind to give it a special patina. I'm also partial to the "extra aged" (*stravecchio*) that is at least 12 months old and comes wrapped in walnut leaves. The paste is straw colored and semihard, aging to a mouthwatering dry crumbliness with age. Guffanti sells a limited quantity of a larger Pecorino di Pienza Gran Riserva that weighs 10 to 12 kilos.

SIMILAR CHEESES: Berkswell, Spenwood, Trade Lake Cedar.

SEASONAL NOTE: Made from September to June.

WINE PAIRINGS: Pecorino Toscano pairs well with the more focused, acidic reds.

RED: Barbera d'Alba; California Merlot; Sangiovese-based wines (Chianti Classico, Brunello di Montalcino, or California).

PEÑAMELLERA

(peh-nyah-meh-YER-ah) Asturias is really the most interesting and fertile ground for cheesemaking among Spain's various regions. Here is an intriguing and not so well-known cheese from that province. Peñamellera's paste has a smooth, satisfying slightly chewy consistency and a subtle milky aroma. Its flavor is equally smooth, mildly tangy, and slightly salty with an underlying hint of pleasant bitterness and a delightful buttery aftertaste.

TYPE: Cow's, sheep's, and goat's milk (principally cow's).

PROVENANCE: The township of Peñamellera in eastern Asturias, northern Spain.

PRODUCER: Sociedad Cooperativa Limitada "Queso de Peñamellera."

PRODUCTION: Made from the pasteurized milk of local mountain herds by ancient artisanal methods. The curds are cut large, uncooked, unpressed, formed in draining molds, salted, and gradually dried for 2 weeks. During the aging process of 1 to 4 months, the natural rind develops a coating of some beneficial molds. The cheeses are sold either "soft" (after about a month of aging) or "semihard" (after 3 to 4 months of aging).

APPEARANCE: A small disk-shaped cheese 1¼ to 1½ inches high and about 4 to 5 inches in diameter weighing 300 to 400 grams—less than a pound. Its rind is sticky, bumpy, and off-white to grayish with some orange. It has dustings of white mold and exhibits the ridged basketlike pattern of its draining shelves. The paste is white, semisoft, fairly dense, and almost chalky.

SEASONAL NOTE: Best May through December.

SIMILAR CHEESE: Queso de los Beyos.

WINE PAIRINGS: Pairs well with light, dry white wines and berry-flavored reds.
WHITE: Bordeaux (Sauvignon Blanc-Sémillon blend); California Chardonnay; Spanish Sauvignon Blanc.
RED: Chilean Cabernet Sauvignon; southern Rhône Syrah-Grenache-Mourvèdre blend; Tempranillo-Garnacha blend (Almendralejo from the Extremadura); California Zinfandel.
DESSERT/FORTIFIED: Sherry (Amontillado).

RATINGS

QUALITY

75

STRENGTH

1

PÉRAIL

(peh-RYE) From the relatively rare category of bloomy-rind sheep's milk cheeses, Pérail looks like a miniature Brie or Camembert. It provides an excellent introduction to the richness and subtlety of sheep's milk cheeses and, while it doesn't knock my socks off, it's a very pleasant little cheese. For a meal, it's ideal for consumption by one person in one sitting: why eat a filet mignon when you could have a whole Pérail instead?! It gives off fairly pronounced barnyardy surface odors but has a soft, smooth, creamy paste that is aromatic and mild.

TYPE: Raw sheep's milk (a pasteurized-milk version is also available).

PROVENANCE: From the Causses du Larzac in Rouergue, in the center of southern France, near Roquefort country. The Causses is a high, rugged plateau, made of chalky soil and calcareous rock, the perfect natural habitat for sheep.

PRODUCERS: Approximately one dozen local artisanal farmhouses and dairies. Recommended producers: Lou Pérac; Communauté de l'Arche; Coopérative des Bergers du Larzac; EURL Les Paulinettoises; S.A. Les Aliziers.

PRODUCTION: Soft-ripened sheep's milk cheeses are relatively rare in France and were made for local consumption only. Pérail, being a good modern example of a worthy old cheesemaking tradition, is uncooked, unpressed, handmade, and aged for a minimum of 1 week.

APPEARANCE: Medium-small disks no more than 1 inch high and 3½ to 4 inches across. It has a natural rind, beige with dustings of white mold all over, and imprints of the basket in which the curds were drained. The paste is smooth, supple, and ivory colored.

SEASONAL NOTE: Best March through September.

SIMILAR CHEESES: Cabecou de Rocamadour, Pavé D'Affinois, Saint-Marcellin.

WINE PAIRINGS: Marries well with Claret-type wines.
- **WHITE:** Condrieu (Viognier); Saint-Véran (Chardonnay/white Burgundy).
- **RED:** Cabernet Sauvignon (Bordeaux or California); Chilean Cabernet; Carignan (medium-bodied, fruity, spicy red from the Languedoc-Roussillon); Chilean Carmenère-Merlot blend (spicy, ripe red); Morgon (Gamay/Beaujolais cru); northern Rhône red (Syrah).
- **DESSERT/FORTIFIED:** Ruby Port.

RATINGS

QUALITY

77

STRENGTH

1

PERAL, QUESO DE LA

(peh-RAHL, KAY-soh day lah) Of all the world's great blue cheeses, this is one of my sentimental favorites. The product of three generations of dedicated Asturian cheese artisans, it has relatively high pH (low acidity) and delivers strong, distinct flavors on a smooth, creamy, buttery, rich platform without resorting to excessive bite or harshness. It features a firm yet unctuous paste with fairly sharp lactic flavors and somewhat granular mouthfeel. With age, Peral can become fairly intense (nothing wrong with that!) and is sometimes jokingly referred to as "Queso de la *Peril*." The Peral can be inconsistent, particularly in texture, but that is part of its charm. Even the strongest Peral does not disappoint.

TYPE: Pasteurized cow's milk with blue veining.

PROVENANCE: Originally from San Jorge de la Peral in the township of Illas, central coastal area of Asturias, northern Spain, near Oviedo.

PRODUCER: Leon family (descendants of Antonio Leon, who founded the dairy at the beginning of the twentieth century).

PRODUCTION: Inoculated with *Penicillium* mold and matured in natural caves for between 2 and 5 months. A small amount of sheep's milk cream is the secret ingredient that gives it its signature rich profile and mildly sheepy aftertaste.

APPEARANCE: It comes in foil-wrapped cylinders weighing 1, 2, or 3 kilos (2.2, 3.3, and 6.6 pounds, respectively). Its moist natural rind is golden to light brown in color; the interior is yellowish cream colored with some cracks, cavities, and holes, plus slashing veins of deep bluish green.

SIMILAR CHEESE: Valdeón.

WINE PAIRINGS: Peral works best with fruitier wines.
WHITE: Condrieu (Viognier); German Riesling Kabinett.

RED: California Cabernet Sauvignon; Madiran (tannic, traditionally rustic wine from southwestern France, made primarily from the Tannat grape); Ribera del Duero (Tempranillo blend).
DESSERT/FORTIFIED: Jurançon Petit Mensang (from southwestern France); Sherry (Oloroso).

RATINGS

QUALITY

89

STRENGTH

4

PERSILLÉ DE TIGNES

(pehr-see-LAY duh TEE-nyuh) A naturally bluing goat cheese from the French Alps, Persillé acquires quite a lot of character even in its youth. As with many authentic mountain cheeses, what you see is what you get: a rustic, straightforward, and unpretentious reflection of *terroir.* In many ways, it represents a typical format for aged goat cheeses—fine-textured and slightly crumbly, with pleasantly musty aromas and flavors, not unlike a Garrotxa (see page 145). In its prime—between 4 and 7 months of age—the Persillé is an intriguing, mouthwatering, and delicious mouthful. As it ages, the blue penetrates gradually and at times almost imperceptibly to the core. At about 6 months, it offers a little dryness and puckering effect that lingers on the palate, giving the overall impression of a cheese that's been aged much longer. At this point, it should still be white in the center but grayer toward the rind. The problem with extra aging of this cheese is that although the development of the blue is delightful, the cheese can lose most of its moisture, giving it a chalkier mouthfeel that may not appeal to everyone. Really, it depends on how you like it.

TYPE: Goat's milk.

PROVENANCE: Haute-Savoie, the mountains east of Lyons, France, and west of Lake Geneva.

PRODUCERS: My favorites are the ones purveyed by Denis Provent, who also sells very fine Tommes de Savoie.

PRODUCTION: Produced artisanally in mountain farmhouses. Pressed, brushed, and aged up to 3 months. Eight to 12 liters of milk are used to make each cheese. The curds are cut to hazelnut size and placed by hand in molds where they drain for 3 to 4 days. After unmolding for 4 to 5 days, they receive surface salt and are turned several times. They are then ripened in cold, humid cellars for 3 to 6 months. While ripening, the paste acquires natural blue veining. As the cheeses dry, the paste can flake or break off.

APPEARANCE: A small cylinder or drum, 3½ to 4½ inches in diameter and about 5 inches tall, weighing 1½ to 2 pounds, with a rough, bumpy light brown to gray rind that develops splotches of yellow, beige, and white molds. The paste is off-white and slightly graying toward the center and darker yellowish gray toward the rind. Irregular, naturally moldy sections can occur within the paste; often, the mold is virtually invisible but it is there to flavor the cheese. With age, the blue streaks begin to spread gradually from the rind into the body of the cheese.

SIMILAR CHEESES: Persillé des Aravis, Persillé de la Haut Tarentaise.

WINE PAIRING:
 RED: Beaujolais cru (Gamay).

RATINGS

QUALITY

72

STRENGTH

3

P I A V E

(pee-AH-veh) This is like a lighter, younger version of Parmigiano-Reggiano. It has some of the same compelling depth of flavor and memorable full, rounded taste as well as the beginnings of crystallization. A fine Piave is perhaps not as hard or crumbly as a fully aged Parmesan. Its flavors are nutty and concentrated with sweet, mildly fruity, floral undertones. If one can idolize genuine Parmesan, one can certainly show a milder form of worship for this cheese.

TYPE: Pasteurized cow's milk.

PROVENANCE: The Veneto, the province encompassing but mostly to the north of Venice, northeastern Italy; named for the river Piave, which originates in the picturesque Dolomites as a mountain stream and flows down to empty out in the Gulf of Venice.

PRODUCER: Luigi Guffanti.

PRODUCTION: Cooked, pressed paste. Piave is sold in three categories of aging: fresh (*fresco*) at 1 to 2 months; medium (*mezzano*) at 3 to 4 months; and aged (*stagionato*) at 6 to 12 months, which is my preferred version.

APPEARANCE: Flat drums 11 to 12 inches in diameter and 3 inches high, weighing from 11 up to 15 pounds. A beige, somewhat rough natural rind with the name of the cheese stenciled on its sides. The paste is hard and straw colored.

SIMILAR CHEESES: Asiago, Montasio.

WINE PAIRINGS: Piave is generally well suited for the darker, more raisiny red wines.
WHITE: Château-Grillet (northern Rhône Viognier); German Riesling Spätlese.
RED: Amarone della Valpolicella; California Merlot; Madiran (tannic, traditionally rustic wine from southwestern France, made primarily from the Tannat grape); Super Tuscan (Sangiovese-Merlot blend); California Zinfandel.
DESSERT/FORTIFIED: Sauternes (late-harvest Sémillon).

RATINGS

QUALITY

89

STRENGTH

5

PLEASANT RIDGE RESERVE

Pleasant Ridge Reserve was born of a quest begun in 1994 by Mike Gingrich (along with his wife, Carol, and their partners, Dan and Jeanne Patenaude) to create a dairy operation modeled after traditional ones in the French Alps. They incorporated rotational grazing, as exemplified by the *transhumance* or migrating herds in the Alps, by carving out twenty separate pastures on their 300-acre farm. They also cross-bred Holsteins with other fine milk-producing breeds to develop their own strong herd of hybrids. The ultimate result is this prizewinning artisanal farmhouse cheese, made in the style of Beaufort but earning its designation as an American Original. Among other awards, Pleasant Ridge received the Best in Show at the 2001 American Cheese Society conference as well as the U.S. Grand Champion at the 2001 U.S. Championship Cheese Contest, the only cheese to win both awards. Pleasant Ridge is superb, delivering pleasing nutty flavor with a little sweetness offset by a dash of salt and a bit of sour. The aged variety is excellent; it holds up well and doesn't fade to blue as quickly as others of its kind.

TYPE: Raw cow's milk.

PROVENANCE: Dodgeville, Wisconsin, USA.

PRODUCER: Uplands Cheese, Mike Gingrich.

PRODUCTION: Cooked and pressed, then washed with brine and *B. linens* for a minimum of 4 months. Sold at a variety of ages: "new" (4 to 7 months); "aged" (8 to 12 months); "extra aged" (12 to 18 months).

APPEARANCE: Wheels approximately 10½ inches in diameter and 3½ inches high weighing 10 pounds. The rind is reddish beige, and the paste is firm and straw colored with irregularly spaced holes and small fissures.

SIMILAR CHEESES: Beaufort, Comté.

SEASONAL NOTE: The cows graze in high pastures from early spring through fall. They calve in spring and are dry in the winter. The cheese is made only from milk produced when they are grazing on fresh pasture grasses, forbs (broadleafed flowering plants), herbs, and wildflowers.

WINE PAIRINGS: This cheese is a good partner for the softer, younger reds.
♥ **RED**: Beaujolais cru (Gamay); California Merlot; Long Island Merlot.
♥ **DESSERT/FORTIFIED**: Tawny Port.

RATINGS

QUALITY

89

STRENGTH

3

PONT L'ÉVÊQUE

(pon lay-VECK) Legend has it that this cheese was introduced by monks in the Pays d'Auge during the Middle Ages. In early references it's called Augelot ("from the Auge area") or Angelot (a corruption, which also means "cherub"); by the seventeenth century it also became known by its place-name. Today, it is one of the most famous gastronomic products of Normandy and a pride of the region. The Pont l'Évêque has warm, buttery, and savory flavors and mouthfeel with tangy, fruity undercurrents. The texture at room temperature should be soft and supple, but not runny.

TYPE: Cow's milk.

PROVENANCE: The Pays d'Auge, Normandy, northwestern France, specifically the area around the town of Pont l'Évêque in the *département* of Calvados.

PRODUCERS: A handful of farmhouses and approximately a dozen artisanal dairies. Recommended producers are as follows. *Fermiers:* Grand Plain; Fromagerie Martin; Fromagerie Spruyette; UNOG La Moissonnière. *Laitiers:* Domaine du Plessis; Fromagerie Eugene Graindorge; Fromagerie de la Perelle; Societé nouvelle de l'atelier laitier; and the coopérative Isigny Sainte-Mère.

PRODUCTION: The curds are heated, stirred, cut, kneaded, and molded. The cheeses are salted, washed, brushed, and aged from 2 to 6 weeks. A.O.C. status was granted in 1970, and production is strictly monitored in each of the twelve factories throughout Normandy that have license to produce it.

APPEARANCE: Standard-size Pont l'Évêque comes in a 4-inch square that is about 1 inch high and weighs approximately 12 ounces. There is also a larger size, 8 inches square, and a smaller 2-inch one. The rind goes from yellowish gold and somewhat slimy to pinkish orange and quite sticky with age. The paste is light yellow to cream colored, semisoft, smooth, and open textured with varying sizes of airholes; it will ooze or melt somewhat at room temperature when ripe. The rind should not be cracked or too dry.

SIMILAR CHEESES: Durrus, Livarot, Munster, Pavé d'Auge (Pavé du Plessis).

SEASONAL NOTE: Available year-round but best in summer and fall.

WINE PAIRINGS: Pont l'Évêque is an amiable cheese partner for fruity, light to medium-bodied red and white wines.

WHITE: Savennières (Loire Valley Chenin Blanc).

RED: Beaujolais (Gamay).

SPARKLING: Champagne (Blanc de Blancs).

RATINGS

QUALITY

86

STRENGTH

3

POULIGNY-SAINT-PIERRE

(poo-leen-yee san pee-YEHR) Of the handful of classic world-famous Loire Valley chèvres, this one is instantly recognizable for its distinctive four-sided pyramid shape, thus its nicknames, the Pyramid or the Eiffel Tower. Its paste is a very pure white, moist, and semisoft, with a well-balanced, full flavor that offers complex sweet, sour, and salty notes. The sweetness of a fresh Pouligny gives way to a sharper, saltier, more intense flavor as the cheese ages. Its flavor peak occurs when the exterior of the cheese is well covered with blue-gray mold.

TYPE: Goat's milk.

PROVENANCE: Pouligny in the Brenne Valley of the Loire, south of Paris and Orléans.

PRODUCERS: Various farms and local dairies. Recommended producers as follows: *Fermiers:* CFPA La Ferme des Ages; GAEC de Villiers. *Laitiers:* Eurial Poitouraine; Fromagerie d'Anjouin; Fromagerie de Fontenille; Laiterie de la Cloche d'Or. *Affineurs/negociants:* Hardy; Jacquin.

PRODUCTION: A.O.C. protected and handmade by an artisanal recipe. Aged 4 to 6 weeks. The A.O.C. minimum is 2 weeks; among the better cheeses, 4 or 5 weeks is common.

APPEARANCE: Like Valençay, Pouligny comes in a truncated four-sided pyramid about 3 inches square at the base, about 4 inches tall, and weighing 7 to 9 ounces. Its rind has an intriguing, somewhat rough surface; as the cheese ages, it deepens in color to reddish brown with grayish blue tinges of mold due to the application of *P. glaucum.*

SIMILAR CHEESES: Crottin de Chavignol, Sainte-Maure de Touraine, Selles-sur-Cher, Valençay.

SEASONAL NOTE: Best May through November.

WINE PAIRINGS: This lovely chèvre is best paired with crisp white wines.
WHITE: Albariño; white Beaujolais (Chardonnay); Sancerre (Sauvignon Blanc).
SPARKLING: Chenin Blanc-Chardonnay blend (*méthode champenoise* from the Loire).

RATINGS

QUALITY

90

STRENGTH

2

PRÄTTIGAUER

(prah-tee-GOW-er) This is a classic *alpage*-style cheese and a very good example of what Swiss artisan cheeses are all about. It has a firm, dense paste, thick rind, and a stout, slightly sharp, salty flavor. An aged Prättigauer is not subtle—it tends to become quite intense, even obstreperous. It would be the penultimate cheese in an all-Swiss lineup, with only a fully aged Sbrinz to follow.

TYPE: Raw cow's milk.

PROVENANCE: From the Prättigau zone of the Graubunden region in northeastern Switzerland, between the world-famous ski resorts of Davos and Klosters.

PRODUCERS: Most of the Prättigauer I get comes from the high hills at the end of the valley in one little village called Fanas, where three independent farm producers make it from a very traditional recipe.

PRODUCTION: The farmhouse artisans use wood fires and copper cauldrons, lending the cheese a hint of smokiness. Prättigauer is aged for at least 7 months in a cellar with regular brine washings.

APPEARANCE: Relatively small rounds (considering its category—hard Swiss alpage cheeses), 10 to 12 pounds and $2\frac{1}{2}$ to 3 inches high. The rind is light reddish brown; the paste is light yellow and dense with occasional air pockets.

SIMILAR CHEESES: Appenzeller, Bundner Alpkäse, Urner Bergkäse.

WINE PAIRINGS: The Prättigauer finds its top pairings with inkier reds and fruitier whites.
WHITE: Alsatian Riesling; German Riesling Spätlese.

RED: Aglianico del Vulture (smoky, spicy, rich red from southern Italy); Bordeaux (Merlot-based); Madiran (tannic, traditionally rustic wine from southwestern France, made primarily from the Tannat grape).
DESSERT/FORTIFIED: Late-harvest Muscat-based wines (such as Muscat de Rivesaltes); Sherry (Pedro Ximenez).

RATINGS

QUALITY

97

STRENGTH

5

REBLOCHON

(reh-bloh-SHOHN) I count a genuine Reblochon among the world's greatest mountain cheeses. Apparently, I'm not the only one since it is also among the most-requested cheeses I serve to cheese-loving diners. Its paste is very smooth and creamy with a soft, pliant consistency that can range from somewhat rubbery to slightly sticky or gluey. It offers mild, fruity flavors without sacrificing substance. I sometimes describe it as the "bacon and eggs" of cheese; there is an unmistakably eggy hint to its milk flavors, and it also features a savory baconlike saltiness. (A bit of cheese history: unlike most cheeses, Reblochon's name doesn't derive from a place-name but rather from a verb, *reblocher*, which is the local word for "second milking." Legend has it that the herders and dairy workers—serfs and vassals in medieval terms—would milk the cows, stop and give the proprietor or overlord his mandated share of the milk, then surreptitiously finish the milking later. They'd use that thicker, richer milk from the second milking to make delicious cheeses for themselves.)

TYPE: Cow's milk.

PROVENANCE: Haute-Savoie, east-central France, near Geneva, Switzerland, primarily around the Chaine des Aravis mountain range and its surrounding valleys, near the towns of Megeve and Chamonix. (See also Chevrotin des Aravis, essentially a goat's milk version of Reblochon.)

PRODUCERS: Recommended producers: Albert Thabius; Edelmont; Fromagerie Joseph Paccard; Lactalis; L'Alpage; Les Producteurs de Reblochon de Thônes; Société Laitière des Hauts de Savoie.

PRODUCTION: Farmhouse, artisanal, and creamery production; there are approximately 20 small factories (*ateliers*) and 180 farmhouse producers (*fermiers*). Made from the milk of the venerable Abondance breed of cow (along with Montbéliarde and Tarine), which also yields Beaufort and Abondance cheeses as well as Vacherin d'Abondance. The curds are uncooked, lightly pressed. The cheeses are aged 4 to 5 weeks with regular washings of the rind. Reblochon is A.O.C. protected.

APPEARANCE: Flattish rounds or disks about 5 inches in diameter and 1 inch high weighing about 1 pound. (I recommend these over the smaller half-pound versions.) Its washed rind is smooth and beige or gold in color with a reddish orange or pink tint and a natural dusting of white

RATINGS

QUALITY

84

STRENGTH

2

mold. The paste is yellowish ivory and shiny, with some holes. The farmhouse (*fermier*) cheeses have a green oval casein label in their rinds while the creamery (*laitier*) versions have a similar red label.

SIMILAR CHEESES: Durrus, Innerschweizer Weicher (aka Stanser Röteli), Taleggio.

SEASONAL NOTE: Best June through January; look for the summer *fermier* and *chalet* versions, which peak in the early fall

WINE PAIRINGS: Finds its best matches in soft reds and spicy, crisp whites.

WHITE: Alsatian Gewurztraminer; Tokay Pinot Gris (Alsace); Beaujolais (Gamay); German Riesling Kabinett.

RED: Pinot Noir (California or Oregon); California Zinfandel.

SPARKLING: Moscato d'Asti.

RED HAWK

This is a fine American soft-ripened artisanal cheese, made in the style of the French triple crèmes. It's brought to us by Sue Conley and Peggy Smith, founders of Tomales Bay Foods and the affiliated Cowgirl Creamery. Kudos to the cheesemakers; so far, they've been able to keep up the quality while still satisfying the mushrooming demand for this award-winning cheese. (It won the Grand Prize at the American Cheese Society's annual convention in 2003.) Red Hawk is a well-balanced and complex cheese in several respects. Its aromas contain notes of chalk and hay; its taste is full-flavored, savory, and almost beefy with a long creamy finish; its texture can be very soft and yielding, yet it retains enough heft so it doesn't get too runny. Likewise, the salt is held in check by a tang just sufficient to titillate but not overwhelm the taste buds.

TYPE: Cow's milk.

PROVENANCE: Point Reyes Station, Marin County, Northern California, USA.

PRODUCER: Cowgirl Creamery (Sue Conley and Peggy Smith, owners; Maureen Cunnie, cheesemaker).

PRODUCTION: Made from organic milk produced by the Strauss Family Creamery in Marshall, California, on Tomales Bay. The milk is coagulated with vegetarian rennet, and the cheese is actually a triple crème in the sense that it's made with additional cream. The rinds are washed and the cheeses are aged 30 days.

APPEARANCE: An attractive cheese, it comes in a somewhat irregularly shaped flat drum or cylinder with a Munster-style washed rind—orangish to light brown and bumpy with dustings of white mold. Red Hawk is 4 inches in diameter and 1³/₄ to 2 inches high and weighs 12 to 14 ounces. If its rind is in the reddish color spectrum, the paste is more toward yellowish.

SIMILAR CHEESES: Époisses, Munster.

SEASONAL NOTE: The cheese is especially rich and complex when the cows are grazing on early spring pastures —February to March.

WINE PAIRINGS: Red Hawk is best suited for acidic reds and crisp, aromatic whites.
WHITE: Alsatian Gewurztraminer; Grüner Veltliner; New Zealand Sauvignon Blanc.
RED: Aglianico del Vulture (smoky, spicy, rich red from southern Italy); Barbera d'Asti; Madiran (tannic, traditionally rustic wine from southwestern France, made primarily from the Tannat grape); Syrah (from the Languedoc, southern France).

RATINGS
QUALITY
89
STRENGTH
3

ROARING FORTIES BLUE

This notable blue cheese, created in 1994 out of a century-old dairying tradition on the opposite side of the globe, first appeared on the radar screens here in New York when it captured top honors at our Fancy Food Convention in the year 2000. It's a full-flavored blue with smooth, creamy texture that will turn slightly sandy with age; it offers sweet, slightly nutty flavors, intensifying with age, and a pleasant aftertaste. Roaring Forties is quite assertive; its blue flavor is dominant, and it has fairly light salt. It's best enjoyed when fresh cut because it does fade relatively quickly once cut. It comes from the idyllic setting of King Island, near Tasmania, where the microclimate is characterized by mild weather with the occasional clearing storm borne by the famous winds called the Roaring Forties. In Aussie food lore, the sweetest milk in the land is said to come from King Island.

TYPE: Cow's milk.

PROVENANCE: King Island, south of Melbourne, off the coast of Tasmania, Australia.

PRODUCER: King Island Dairy (Ueli Berger, cheesemaker).

PRODUCTION: Roquefort-style. King Island Dairy has been in operation for over 100 years and, while it is a factory owned by a large conglomerate, its production values remain traditional and artisanal. The milk comes from the herds of twenty-five dairy farms on the island, which benefit from a pristine environment, rich soils, lush pastures, and a year-round growing season.

APPEARANCE: Wheels covered in midnight blue-colored wax about 2 inches high and 7½ to 8 inches in diameter, weighing just under 3 pounds. The paste is yellowish or cream colored (the cows are strictly grass-fed so there is an abundance of natural carotene in their milk) with greenish blue mold throughout that darkens to a deeper shade of blue as the cheese matures.

SIMILAR CHEESES: Valdeón, Bleu des Causses.

WINE PAIRING:
WHITE: California Chardonnay.

RATINGS

QUALITY

74

STRENGTH

5

ROBIOLA

(roh-bee-OH-lah) Of the northern Italian cheeses that bear the name Robiola, there is a wider range and broader variation than, say, among the members of the Cheddar or triple crème families—that is, a *lot* of variation. Yet they are certainly a family, with many significant similarities beyond just the name. The Robiolas are all small, soft cheeses with relatively short maturation periods, many made from mixed milk. They are graceful, subtle, and very approachable—in the sense that they don't challenge the palate with excessive flavors. This is not to say they aren't delicious or even thrilling. In fact, this is precisely the success of the family. I characterize them as classic "dessert" or "luxury" cheeses. They highlight the superior quality of Piedmontese (and some Lombardian) milk. They require no accompaniments and can stand proudly on their own, if need be without joining a composed plate. Another attractive trait of the Robiolas is they marry well with a broad range of wine types. They simply don't challenge their wine partners; there are few "marriages-made-in-heaven," but also few disagreements. Robiolas with some surface mold development (*Geotrichum candidum* and related growths) are only slightly more challenging, regardless of milk types. The washed-rind Taleggio-style Robiolas are another story; they have limited pairing possibilities.

I'm partial to the Robiolas sold by two very fine creameries that serve primarily as *affineurs* (or *stagionatori* in Italian): Gianni Cora and Luigi Guffanti. These cheeses comprise a series of variations on Robiola di Roccaverano, a D.O.P. cheese. Among my current favorites are Guffanti's unwrapped three-milk version; Cora's three-milk versions, which are wrapped in chestnut and Savoy cabbage leaves, respectively; and Guffanti's all-goat Robiola di Roccaverano. Historians believe the generic name Robiola comes from the Latin *rubium* ("red"), which refers to the shade attained by the rinds of these cheeses when they're allowed to age. Many Robiolas are eaten relatively fresh—matured from as few as 3 to 10 days—but most are aged about 3 weeks and up to 3 months. The longer-aged versions begin to ripen from the outside in and take on creamy, smooth, melded, and delicious textures and flavors. The principal impressions are of fresh, untainted milk and a slight, pleasant sourness balanced by saltiness.

TYPE: Generally mixed milk.

PROVENANCE: Lombardy, north-central Italy, and Piedmont, northwestern Italy (primarily the hill country around the towns of Asti, Alessandria, and Cuneo, known as the Langhe).

PRODUCERS: Gianni Cora; Luigi Guffanti; Caseificio dell'Alta Langa—all creameries and *affineurs*, which means they are capable of collecting the milk from local farmhouses and manufacturing the cheese, or collecting the artisanally made cheeses to ripen and distribute them.

PRODUCTION: Robiolas can be made from all cow's milk, all goat's milk, or a combination of the two; occasionally, there is also a sheep's milk component. They are hand-ladled, drained gently by gravity alone (not pressed), and their curds are cut quite large—if at all. Therefore, the cheeses are less dense, less compact, quite soft, sometimes even wet and runny—and definitely lighter on the palate. They have natural rinds, although some of the more interesting varieties are leaf wrapped, and some are allowed to develop a thin coating of molds. Robiolas are aged from just a few days up to 3 months.

APPEARANCE: The Robiolas from Piedmont generally come in the shape of small wheels or disks 4 to 5 inches in diameter and 1 to 2 inches high. They are often somewhat irregularly shaped, undulating and rustic in appearance with the imprint of draining slats on top and bottom. Their rinds are generally beige to light yellow and covered in white surface mold. The pastes are soft to semisoft and will turn delectably smooth and creamy when they ripen and begin to melt at room temperature. The Lombardian Robiolas come in bricks 4 to 5 inches square, weighing from 6 ounces to 1½ pounds, and resemble smaller versions of Brescianella Stagionata or Taleggio, which is 8 inches square. Their rinds are dark orange to brownish with some ridges; their paste is off-white to light straw or yellow colored.

SIMILAR CHEESES: Brunet, Cimonino, Rochetta.

ROBIOLA DI ROCCAVERANO

(roh-bee-OH-lah dee roh-cah-veh-RAH-noh) This is the only cheese in the Robiola category with D.O.C. (1979) and D.O.P. (1996) status. The rules state that the cheese must be produced in the proscribed zone (in the vicinity of the town of the same name and also the town of Asti in southeastern Piedmont) from the milk of animals fed only fresh grasses or hay. The cheeses come in discs 4 to 6 inches in diameter and $1^{1}/_{2}$ to 2 inches high, weighing 9 to 14 ounces. Guffanti's all-goat version is one of my favorites of the category. Cora's Robiola Stagionata is its standard (non-leaf-wrapped) version of this cheese and is made with all three milks—cow, sheep, and goat. (See related leaf-wrapped versions below.) The small wheels are 4 to $4^{1}/_{2}$ inches in diameter and $1^{1}/_{2}$ to 2 inches high weighing about 7 ounces. They are aged a minimum of 3 weeks. The paste offers a very smooth, almost silky mouthfeel and good balance between bitter and sweet elements; there are also many pleasant vegetal, herbal, and even nutty tones to its flavors.

WINE PAIRINGS: The all-goat Robiola di Roccaverano pairs well with fruity, light to medium-bodied whites.

WHITE: Chardonnay (California or northern Italian); Sauvignon Blanc (California or New Zealand); Vouvray demi-sec (Chenin Blanc).

DESSERT/FORTIFIED: Quarts de Chaume (Loire Valley dessert wine from the Chenin Blanc grape).

RATINGS

QUALITY

91

STRENGTH

ROBIOLA PINETA

(roh-bee-OH-lah pee-NEH-tah) This variation, also from Cora, more closely resembles a Lombardia or Valsassina; it's like a small Taleggio with a pine-bough adornment, a "looker" but not as highly rated in terms of taste. It is made from cow's milk, aged 40 days, and comes in a brick about 5½ inches square and 1½ inches high, weighing a bit more than 12 ounces.

WINE PAIRINGS: Better suited for medium- to full-bodied, fruity reds.
RED: Amarone della Valpolicella; Barbera d'Asti; Beaujolais (Gamay); California Merlot; Sangiovese (Brunello di Montalcino or Chianti Classico).

RATINGS

QUALITY

74

STRENGTH

2

ROBIOLA A DUE LATTI

(roh-bee-OH-lah ah DOO-eh LATT-ee) Guffanti's two-milk variation (cow and sheep) of the Robiola a Tre Latti, except that it is often made in a square "mini-Taleggio" format similar to that of Robiola di Lombardia (aka Robiola di Valsassina).

WINE PAIRINGS:
WHITE: Burgundy (Chardonnay); Pouilly-Fumé (Sauvignon Blanc).
RED: Bandol (Mourvèdre-Cinsault-Grenache blend); Bordeaux (Cabernet Sauvignon blend); California Merlot; Rioja (Tempranillo blend).
SPARKLING: Moscato d'Asti.

DESSERT/FORTIFIED: Late-harvest Muscatel (Tuscany).

RATINGS

QUALITY

86

STRENGTH

1

ROBIOLA A TRE LATTI

(roh-bee-OH-lah ah treh LATT-ee) This version of the Robiola di Rocca-verano D.O.P. cheese is made from all three milks—cow's, sheep's, and goat's milk. This can be a superb delicacy when properly ripened and cared for. This Robiola comes in somewhat irregularly shaped miniature wheels about 5 inches in diameter and 1 inch tall; the rind is light beige with abundant dustings of white mold and the ridged imprint of the cheese's draining racks. The paste is off-white, fairly dense, and very smooth. Like its fraternal cheese, the Due Latti, this mixed-milk artisanal delicacy is melting when ripe, delicious, complex yet subtle—a very approachable cheese and quite irresistible to the taste. The addition of goat's milk adds yet another exciting dimension to its exciting flavor profile.

WINE PAIRINGS:

WHITE: Vouvray sec (Chenin Blanc).

RED: Amarone della Valpolicella; Periquita blend (Portuguese red with Tempranillo, Syrah, and Merlot).

SPARKLING: California Champagne-style (Chardonnay).

DESSERT/FORTIFIED: Sauternes (late-harvest Sémillon).

RATINGS

QUALITY

90

STRENGTH

1

ROBIOLA CASTAGNA

(roh-bee-OH-lah cahs-TAH-nyah) From Cora, this is a mixed-milk cheese ripened in chestnut leaves, aged 20 to 30 days. It comes in small wheels $4^{1}/_{2}$ to $5^{1}/_{2}$ inches in diameter and $1^{1}/_{2}$ to 2 inches high, weighing about 7 ounces. The paste is white to off-white with a creamier, darker striation toward the outside or just inside the rind. It is melting toward the outside and chalky toward the center. Many of Cora's other Robiolas—Incavolata, Fia, Pineta, Vite, Noce (walnut leaves), Rosmarina (rosemary)—are essentially the same cheese with a different wrapper.

WINE PAIRINGS:

RED: Barbera d'Asti; Periquita blend (Portuguese red with Tempranillo, Syrah, and Merlot); California Pinot Noir; southern French Sauvignon Blanc (Languedoc).

RATINGS

QUALITY

88

STRENGTH

ROBIOLA INCAVOLATA

(roh-bee-OH-lah eeh-cah-voh-LAH-tah) Another version of the Robiola Castagna from Cora, this one is matured in leaves of Savoy cabbage. Each of the different wrappings lends a subtle distinction to its flavor profile of its respective cheese—not to mention the visual appeal, which can be quite stunning.

WINE PAIRING:

WHITE: Southern French Chardonnay (Pays d'Oc).

RATINGS

QUALITY

86

STRENGTH

ROBIOLA FIA

(roh-bee-OH-lah FEE-ah) Cora's Robiola variation made from a combination of cow's, goat's, and sometimes sheep's milk and wrapped in fig leaves. It is aged approximately 15 days.

WINE PAIRINGS: This version of Robiola is a fairly versatile partner that is best enjoyed with young, light-bodied wines.
WHITE: Beaujolais Blanc (Chardonnay); Vouvray demi-sec (Chenin Blanc).
RED: Sancerre Rouge (Pinot Noir); Sangiovese (Brunello di Montalcino or Chianti Classico).

RATINGS
QUALITY
84
STRENGTH

1

ROBIOLA VITE

(roh-bee-OH-lah VEE-teh) Another mixed-milk Robiola variation from Cora that comes wrapped in vine leaves and tied with thin straw bands. It has splotchy white mold covering the vine leaves, which give the cheese a subtly earthy, mildly musty accent to its flavors.

WINE PAIRINGS: Not as versatile a wine partner as some of the other Robiolas.
WHITE: Pinot Blanc (Alsace).

SPARKLING: California Champagne-style cuvée.

RATINGS
QUALITY
82
STRENGTH

1

ROGUE RIVER BLUE

I consider this the most distinctive blue cheese made in America today. It can back up its claim to being one of the best blues anywhere. The Rogue River touches on so many sensory receptors: it offers perfume of flowers, fruits, vegetables, herbs, and spices; its texture is moist, a little sticky, and pleasantly yielding to the touch. Ig Vella, known as the godfather of U.S. artisan cheeses, is still listed as master cheesemaker at the Rogue Creamery; its new owners, as of 2002, are David Gremmels and Cary Bryant. This team has certainly worked wonders, developing the recipe for Oregon Blue Vein cheese that was first created by Ig's father, Tom, in 1957 into today's superstar Rogue River Blue. Tom founded the Vella Cheese Company in Sonoma, maker of Monterey Dry Jack, in the 1930s. With backing from cheese magnate J. L. Kraft, he started the Oregon operation to supply the Allied forces with cheese during World War II. In the mid-1950s, Tom went over to France for several months to study blue cheesemaking, then returned to build Roquefort-style caves in Oregon and create the first West Coast blue cheese. Tom passed away in 1998 at the age of 100, and Ig continues the family legacy.

TYPE: Raw cow's milk.

PROVENANCE: Central Point, southern Oregon, USA.

PRODUCER: Rogue Creamery (master cheesemaker, Tom Vella; owner-cheesemakers Cary Bryant and David Gremmels).

PRODUCTION: Handmade in the style of Roquefort using milk of grass-fed Jersey and Holstein cows from the local Umpqua Dairy. The original mold strain developed by Tom Vella in 1957 is still introduced into the curds. The cheeses are dry salted, and their rinds are formed by naturally occurring molds. They are aged in the cave for 8 to 12 months. The cheeses' moisture is preserved by hand-wrapping them in grape leaves that have been macerated in pear brandy.

APPEARANCE: Comes in 5-pound drums 6$\frac{1}{2}$ inches in diameter and 3$\frac{3}{4}$ to 4 inches high that are wrapped in grape leaves and tied with raffia strips. The paste is an attractive ivory to off-white in the center and a darker beige color toward the surface with irregularly distributed splotches of blue-green veining and a number of holes and fissures.

(continued)

RATINGS

QUALITY

93

STRENGTH

5

SIMILAR CHEESES: Bleu des Causses; Valdeón; although Rogue River Blue is Rogue Creamery's top-of-the-line raw cow's milk blue, they make other similar cheeses, including Oregon Blue Vein (Roquefort-style, aged 3 to 5 months); Oregon Blue Vein Reserve (aged 12 to 18 months); Oregonzola (Gorgonzola-style, aged 4 to 12 months), and Crater Lake Blue (American-style, aged 3 to 5 months).

WINE PAIRINGS: Rogue River Blue pairs well with a fairly wide range of dessert wines as well as certain fruity reds.
RED: Beaujolais (Gamay); California Cabernet Sauvignon; California Zinfandel.
SPARKLING: Moscato d'Asti.

DESSERT/FORTIFIED: Late-harvest Muscat (Moscadello di Montalcino, from Tuscany); Sherry (Oloroso); Tawny Port.

RONCAL

(ron-KAHL) Roncal is an ancient cheese and one of Spain's most revered. There are records from medieval times detailing the local junta's rules and regulations for the *transhumancia* (migration of the herds) and related activities. The raising of sheep for wool, meat, and cheese was absolutely crucial to the subsistence economy of that era. Not surprisingly, Roncal was the first Spanish cheese to be awarded official D.O. status (1981). It takes its place right at the top of the category of great hard sheep's milk cheeses, along with Manchego, Zamorano, certain Tuscan Pecorinos, the Ossau-Iraty family, Vermont Shepherd, Spenwood, and Berkswell; every time I taste such a cheese I'm immediately reminded of the superior attributes of fermented ewe's milk. Roncal is dense in texture with a pronounced, fairly piquant nutty flavor, a mild saltiness, and no trace of bitterness. The cheese also offers a very satisfying, buttery, somewhat granular mouthfeel.

TYPE: Raw sheep's milk.

PROVENANCE: From the seven towns in the valley of Roncal (the local government has been known, picturesquely and for ages, as the "University of the Seven Roncal Valley Villages"), northeastern Navarra, northern Spain, bordering on Basque Country.

PRODUCERS: Traditionally made in farmhouses according to carefully guarded old recipes. Several traditional farmhouse makers have gradually converted to cheese dairies and factories while striving to maintain artisanal standards. The Lara family makes an excellent brand; Esca is another favorite.

PRODUCTION: Made from the milk of the free-ranging Latxa and/or Aragonesa Rasa breeds of sheep. Uncooked and pressed, it is aged a minimum 4 months.

APPEARANCE: Comes in drum-shaped cylinders with slightly convex sides that weigh 2 to 3 kilos (4 to 7 pounds). Its rind ranges from straw colored to reddish brown with frequent dustings of bluish gray mold; its paste is ivory to light yellow with small regular holes and the occasional fissure or split in its interior. Like other fine hard French or Swiss mountain cheeses or a fine Pecorino Toscano, a good Roncal will often glisten with some butterfat—so don't be alarmed if it does.

RATINGS

QUALITY

90

STRENGTH

3

(continued)

SEASONAL NOTE: Prime for consumption November to July.

SIMILAR CHEESES: Roncal is similar to the ubiquitous Manchego but much more interesting. Suggestion: try an all-Spanish hard sheep-cheese comparison, sampling Manchego, Zamorano, and Roncal in that order.

WINE PAIRINGS: Roncal is a more successful wine partner for younger, livelier reds.

WHITE: Albariño; Sauvignon Blanc (Sancerre, California, or Pouilly-Fumé).

RED: Chianti Classico (Sangiovese); California Merlot; Rioja (Tempranillo blend); Zinfandel (California).

DESSERT/FORTIFIED: Jurançon Petit Mensang (from south-western France); Ruby Port.

ROOMANO

(roo-MAH-noh) Roomano, which was presumably given this name by its Dutch creators to suggest its "Italian character" (and affinity with Parmigiano-Reggiano), has a hard paste that turns a dark, caramel color and can get pretty strong and spicy while still retaining its sweet, fruity flavors. It is essentially a version of aged Gouda. Two of its more prominent notes are caramel and butterscotch, neither of which are associated with Parmesan (see note on production below). This is among my favorite hard aged cheeses—not the world's most famous but a stimulating, delightful mouthful nonetheless. Customers of mine who've tried it once come back and ask for it by name.

TYPE: Cow's milk.

PROVENANCE: Southern Holland.

PRODUCERS: Local dairies; Pradera is an excellent producer.

PRODUCTION: A cooked-curd cheese made in the style of Parmigiano-Reggiano. Some versions of Roomano are aged for as long as 6 years. To call it the Dutch version of Parmesan is not be entirely accurate, however, because it does deviate from its Italian cousin in several key aspects.

APPEARANCE: Wheels weighing 10 to 15 pounds, 3 to 5 inches high and 12 to 16 inches in diameter. Has a golden orange rind that is waxed, but not until after its long aging period. The paste is light caramel colored.

SIMILAR CHEESES: Aged Gouda (Goudse Boerenkaas), Parmigiano-Reggiano.

WINE PAIRINGS: Works best with spicy reds.
RED: Bordeaux (Cabernet Sauvignon); Carignan (medium-bodied, fruity, spicy red from the Languedoc-Roussillon); Syrah blends from the Rhône Valley (Châteauneuf-du-Pape or Cornas); California Merlot; California Zinfandel.

RATINGS

QUALITY

96

STRENGTH

5

ROQUEFORT

(rohk-FOR) The zenith of blues and one of France's national treasures. The Romans sang its praises during their conquest of Gaul in the first century B.C. and it has been a favorite among connoisseurs of exquisite moldy cheeses ever since. Among the many historical personages who were Roquefort aficionados are Caesar, Charlemagne, the popes of Avignon, and King Louis XV. Cheese-loving scribes from Pliny the Elder to Rabelais and Casanova, Brillat-Savarin and Collette have all recommended it. Roquefort received the first A.O.C. designation in 1925, but its production specifications were enacted as laws more than 300 years ago. Roquefort has an ivory-colored paste that is soft, spicy, and tart. It is known for its rich, mild creaminess. Its flavors should not be dominated by saltiness, acidity, or bitterness; its best producers achieve a balance of strong impressions supported by underlying moderation. After Roquefort, the only thing left is . . . nirvana. In a tasting, if you go back to any other cheese after the Roquefort, you'll be hard-pressed to appreciate its subtleties and nuances.

TYPE: Raw sheep's milk.

PROVENANCE: Roquefort-sur-Soulzon in the southern portion of the Rouergue region, central southern France.

PRODUCERS: There are twelve producers of authentic Roquefort. Societé des Caves et des Producteurs Reunis de Roquefort (Societé, for short) was founded in 1842 and makes the majority of the Roqueforts today. Other recommended brands are Gabriel Coulet, Le Papillon, Le Vieux Berger, and Carles—my favorite and one of the least salty of the Roqueforts, from one of its smaller producers.

PRODUCTION: A.O.C. rules state that the cheeses must be ripened in the caves of Mount Combalou for at least 3 months and as many as 9. The milk used is now primarily from the local breed of Lacaune sheep, organically raised on the limestone plateau of Larzac in the Rouergue. Roquefort was once made only from ambient molds, but now there is *P. roquefortii* added to the curds. The mold still must come from the caves of Combalou, however. In addition, pasteurization, homogenization, and *thermisation* (heat treatment) of the milk are prohibited.

RATINGS

QUALITY

98

STRENGTH

6

APPEARANCE: Smallish drums approximately 8 inches in diameter and 4 inches high that weigh approximately 5½ pounds and are wrapped in light foil. As it ages, the pale green mold evolves to a blue-gray, and holes and fissures appear in the cheese.

SIMILAR CHEESES: Beenleigh Blue, Bleu des Basques, Bleu des Causses.

SEASONAL NOTE: October through March.

WINE PAIRINGS: Roquefort is an appropriate partner for sweeter dessert wines. The Alsatian Pinot Gris is an interesting exception to this rule; Sauternes, on the other hand, is the classic pairing.

WHITE: Tokay Pinot Gris (Alsace).

RED: Zinfandel (California).

DESSERT/FORTIFIED: Banyuls (from southern France); Madeira; Muscat de Rivesaltes; California late-harvest Sémillon; Sauternes (late-harvest Sémillon); Sherry (Pedro Ximenez).

ROUCOULONS

(roo-coo-LOHN) Here is a cheese that might be denigrated by exacting connoisseurs of European cheeses—and I count myself in the American wing of that party—but I submit that it's pleasing, versatile, and very well made. I call it a successful pasteurized "industrial"–style cheese; when it's good, it's very good. Roucoulons' paste is soft and melting at room temperature and features a remarkably smooth, satiny consistency. The flavor is milky, mild, and moderately salty with a hint of wild mushrooms. I recommend it as a good starting point for any cheese plate, particularly for anyone who prefers subtler tastes.

TYPE: Pasteurized cow's milk.

PROVENANCE: Charcenne, in the Franche-Comté region, east of Burgundy and on the western border of Switzerland.

PRODUCER: Fromagerie Milleret.

PRODUCTION: Factory or *industriel* production. Aged 3¹/₂ weeks.

APPEARANCE: Roucoulons comes in rounds 8¹/₄ inches by 1³/₈ inches high, weighing just under 3 pounds. (There is also a smaller version, 4 inches in diameter, weighing about 250 grams or close to 9 ounces; I recommend buying the smaller size.) It has a light beige and orange-tinted bloomy rind with a white coating of *P. candidum* and a basket mold imprint. The paste is ivory to cream colored with fissures and a smooth, shiny texture.

SIMILAR CHEESES: Camembert, L'Edel de Cleron.

WINE PAIRINGS: Roucoulons is an easy cheese for blending with Claret-type wines but can also pair successfully with fruity, full-bodied white wines.
- **WHITE**: Grüner Veltliner; German Riesling Kabinett.
- **RED**: Bordeaux; Garnacha-Cabernet Sauvignon blend (from Tarragona, Spain).
- **SPARKLING**: Moscato d'Asti.

RATINGS

QUALITY

72

STRENGTH

1

SAINT-FÉLICIEN

(san feh-lee-see-en) I call this soft delicacy the big sister of Saint-Marcellin. Saint-Félicien is an endearing, attractive cheese renowned for its rich, creamy mouthfeel and taste, although it is by no means a high-fat cheese. Its aromas are of cream and milk. It is light in texture, rich in flavor, and shows finesse and grace in its simplicity. At its best, which is between 21 and 30 days' ripening, Saint-Félicien should be soft but not runny. Pressing the top to judge its ripeness, you should feel a slight give. It comes in a small ceramic crock to hold its shape; once it warms to room temperature, it will easily collapse and disintegrate into a delicious, spoonable ooze. There are both pasteurized and unpasteurized versions of this cheese; I strongly recommend you buy only the unpasteurized one.

TYPE: Cow's milk (also occasionally made with goat's milk or a combination of the two).

PROVENANCE: Vercors, in the Rhône-Alpes region of France, southeast of Lyons.

PRODUCERS: Local farmhouses and artisanal dairies. Recommended: *Fermier:* GAEC du Levant. *Laitiers:* L'Étoile de Vercors; Fromagerie Le Chartrousin.

PRODUCTION: Generally made with cow's milk, although at one time, like its sister cheese Saint-Marcellin, it was made with goat's milk. Ripened for 21 to 30 days.

APPEARANCE: Disks approximately 4½ inches in diameter and ½ inch high, weighing between 4 and 5½ ounces and set in a shallow crock. The rind is bloomy, white, and ridged on top; the paste is a light golden yellow.

SIMILAR CHEESE: Saint-Marcellin.

SEASONAL NOTE: Best spring through fall.

WINE PAIRINGS: While St. Félicien is a good partner for a broad range of wines, it demonstrates a special affinity for the Chenin Blanc grape.
WHITE: Burgundy (Chardonnay); California Sauvignon Blanc; Vouvray sec and demi-sec (Chenin Blanc).
RED: Amarone della Valpolicella; Burgundy (Pinot Noir); Chilean Cabernet; California Merlot.
DESSERT/FORTIFIED: Late-harvest Muscat from Tuscany (made from the Moscato Bianco grape).

RATINGS

QUALITY

90

STRENGTH

SAINT-MARCELLIN

(san mahr-se-LAHN) Saint-Marcellin is a small artisanal gem and one of France's great historical, gastronomic treasures. King Louis XI popularized this lovely little cheese in the fifteenth century because of a chance encounter in his youth. When he was still Dauphin (prince-in-waiting and lord of the Dauphiné region where the incident took place), he became separated from his hunting party (he may have fallen off his horse, according to one version of the story), was confronted by a hungry bear, and had to be rescued by some local woodsmen. They gave him a snack of peasant bread and their local cheese, which became one of his favorites. Saint-Marcellin's paste is soft, smooth, and fairly mild-tasting but rich. There's not a lot of fuss in this cheese; it's gentle and features the flavor of enriched, slightly soured milk and/or clotted cream, which is why I sometimes refer to it as "just barely cheese." It easily turns melting and spoonable when ripe at room temperature. The little sister of Saint-Félicien, Saint-Marcellin can be more challenging to the *affineur* because its smaller size makes its window of peak ripeness (*à point*) smaller. Since it's encased in a crock, it has less exposed surface area and thus successful drying can be difficult. And, as with Saint-Félicien, the Saint-Marcellin made from pasteurized milk invites trepidation.

TYPE: Cow's milk (once made with goat's milk, now rarely so).

PROVENANCE: From the Isère *département* of the mountainous Dauphiné Province, an area just west of the city of Grenoble, southeastern France.

PRODUCERS: Local farmhouses and creameries, at least one dozen of each. Recommended producers of authentic raw-milk versions are as follows. *Fermiers:* Albert and Danielle Mourrat; GAEC du Levant. *Laitiers:* Fromagerie Le Chartrousin; Fromagerie Cholet; L'Étoile de Vercors.

PRODUCTION: Artisanal, handmade production; unpressed, uncooked, and traditionally (but no longer) leaf wrapped.

APPEARANCE: Small rounds up to 3½ inches in diameter and 1 inch thick, weighing about 3 ounces and protected by a small ceramic crock. The natural rind is light yellow to straw colored—it can turn darker and brownish as it ages—with a slat pattern from the draining racks and a dusting of white mold. The paste is ivory to light straw colored, shiny, and satiny smooth.

RATINGS

QUALITY

88

STRENGTH

1

SIMILAR CHEESE: Banon.

SEASONAL NOTE: Late spring through late fall.

WINE PAIRINGS: Saint-Marcellin pairs well with light-bodied reds and spicier or floral light-bodied whites.

WHITE: Albariño; Condrieu (Viognier); Côtes-du-Rhône (Grenache); Tokay Pinot Gris (Alsace).

RED: Bandol (Mourvèdre); Burgundy (Pinot Noir); Syrah-based wines (e.g., Rhone reds); Minervois (Syrah-Grenache blend from the Languedoc-Roussillon region of southernmost France).

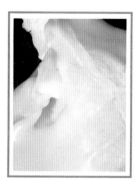

SAINTE-MAURE DE TOURAINE

(sant-MOHR duh too-REHN) An ancient type of goat's milk cheese that has been made the same way for over a thousand years. Of the classic Loire Valley chèvres, I find this one to be the most "goaty"—particularly when it reaches peak ripeness. The paste goes from semisoft and moist when fresh to soft and creamy with a full nutty flavor. Older cheeses are smaller, drier, saltier, and more acidic but nonetheless smooth and delicious. The window of peak ripeness for this cheese is between 4 and 6 weeks. Of the broader family of phenomenal Loire Valley goat's milk cheeses, the Sainte-Maure seems to deliver the biggest punch for the smallest serving. In general, as delicious as these *chèvres* may be, a little bit goes a long way. I try to avoid overusing the adjective "rich," but if someone asks me for a goat's milk cheese of this description, Sainte-Maure would be the first to come to mind.

TYPE: Goat's milk.

PROVENANCE: From the areas around Sainte-Maure in the Touraine and Poitou regions of the central Loire Valley, west-southwest of Paris.

PRODUCERS: Approximately 50 local farmhouses along with a handful of dairies and co-ops. Recommended producers are as follows. *Fermier:* Ferme de Bellevue. *Laitiers:* Eurial Poituraine; Laiterie de la Cloche D'Or; Fromagerie de Fontenille. *Affineurs:* Fromagerie Hardy; Fromagerie Jacquin.

PRODUCTION: The *laitier* (dairy or creamery) cheeses come encased in paper; if possible, stick to the unwrapped farmhouse ones, which are made from raw milk, if possible. Approximately 2 to 3 liters of milk are required to make each log of Sainte-Maure. The curd formation and draining of the whey both occur slowly, over periods of up to 24 hours. After dry-salting, the ripening takes 3 to 4 weeks, during which the surface mold starts to form.

APPEARANCE: Sainte-Maure has an unmistakable appearance. It comes in logs measuring $5\frac{1}{2}$ to 6 inches long and $1\frac{1}{2}$ inches wide, weighing about 9 ounces, with a light exterior dusting of ash that helps promote the development of beneficial grayish-white mold. (The mold will develop naturally, however, especially if the cheese is made with unpasteurized milk.) The logs are pierced down their center by a narrow straw, which helps the cheese keep its shape, particularly when fresh and moist, and also allows for aeration to encourage the ripening process.

SIMILAR CHEESES: Pouligny-Saint-Pierre, Selles-sur-Cher, Valençay.

RATINGS

QUALITY

88

STRENGTH

2

SEASONAL NOTE: May through November.

WINE PAIRINGS: Sainte-Maure de Touraine is a good partner for dry, crisp whites.

WHITE: Albariño; California Chardonnay; Sauvignon Blanc–based wines (e.g., Pouilly-Fumé, Sancerre, or California); Savennières (Loire Valley Chenin Blanc).

SPARKLING: Moscato d'Asti.

DESSERT/FORTIFIED: Ruby Port.

SAINT-NECTAIRE

(san nect-TAIR) A *tomme*-style cheese with many enthusiastic fans and a reputation as one of France's greatest regional delicacies. Saint-Nectaire's origins are obscured in the mists of history; its popularity originated in the seventeenth century when it was introduced to King Louis XIV. Be sure to purchase a good raw-milk example; otherwise, you will be disappointed. Saint-Nectaire is at its best when young. The paste should be soft and unctuous with occasional small holes. Saint-Nectaire has an aroma of mushrooms with fresh, buttery, fruity, nutty, and not overly salty flavors—all reflective of its *terroir*, which comprises the rugged volcanic plateaus of the Dore Mountains region of the Auvergne with its rich soil and fragrant flora.

TYPE: Cow's milk.

PROVENANCE: The town of the same name in the northern Auvergne, Massif Central, south-central France; also the roughly seventy surrounding communes in the northwest zone of the Puy-de-Dôme and the northern zone of the Cantal *départements*. (Although the two cheeses are very different, the Saint-Nectaire zone largely overlaps that of Cantal.)

PRODUCERS: Farmhouses (the best), small dairies (some acceptable versions), and factories (mostly inferior). There are approximately 300 farmhouse sources for the cheese and 900 for the milk, making it the largest farmhouse production by volume of any French cheese, and one of the largest industries in the Auvergne. Recommended producers/*affineurs* of genuine raw-milk Saint-Nectaire: Bernard Charbonnier; Ferme Bellonte; Fromagerie Soron; Fromagerie Saint Mary; Philippe Jaubert.

PRODUCTION: Made from the milk of the Salers breed of cows in the prescribed zone. Uncooked, pressed, brushed rind; mold ripened for a period of 3 to 5 weeks. A.O.C. protection granted in 1955. The summer high-mountain cheeses, which peak in fall, are superior. Avoid the pasteurized-milk version.

APPEARANCE: Comes in disks 1½ to 2 inches thick and 8 inches in diameter, weighing approximately 3¾ pounds, with an ivory to straw-yellow interior. (There is also a smaller version, Petit Saint-Nectaire, which is 5 inches in diameter, 1½ high, and weighs about 1¼ pounds.) Genuine Saint-Nectaire sports a green casein label—rectangular for the dairy-made versions, oval for the farmhouse ones.

SIMILAR CHEESES: Durrus, Tomme de Savoie.

SEASONAL NOTE: Best from early autumn through early winter.

WINE PAIRINGS: Saint-Nectaire's best matches are with light-bodied, softer reds.

 WHITE: White Burgundy (Chardonnay).

RED: Beaujolais cru (Gamay); red Burgundy (Pinot Noir); California Pinot Noir.

RATINGS

QUALITY

84	

STRENGTH

3

SBRINZ

This is Switzerland's *ur*-cheese, the granddaddy of them all and understandably a great source of pride in a country that constitutes the landlocked heart of European cheese artistry. Like a perfectly well-aged mound of butter, strong and profound yet possessing of divine subtlety. When I first tasted Sbrinz, it was an overwhelming experience. Like first beholding the Grand Canyon, it can cause sensory overload so that you need some time to fully appreciate its majesty. Sbrinz is believed to be the cheese Roman food writer Pliny the Elder referred to as *Caseus helveticus* (Swiss cheese). Its fans often claim that the Roman Legions brought the recipe back to Italy with them, making it the precursor to Parmigiano-Reggiano. In the Middle Ages it was prescribed to cure ills, and it is strong medicine indeed. Sbrinz features a dense texture and hard paste that begs to be grated. Its flavors are strong, spicy, and nutty; nevertheless, Sbrinz lovers maintain that it's creamier with less salt on the aftertaste than Parmesan. When I think of true showstoppers, Sbrinz comes to mind along with strong mature blues such as Roquefort and Cabrales. In fact, a well-aged Sbrinz might actually be able to outdo those two flavor-mongers. (An aged Sbrinz is so dense and hard that you can cook with it and it will never completely melt. In Switzerland, they put it in risotto, and pieces of it survive the cooking process. For effect, the risotto is often served in the hollowed-out rind of a full drum of cheese.)

RATINGS

QUALITY

99

STRENGTH

6

TYPE: Raw cow's milk.

PROVENANCE: The cantons of Lucerne, Schwyz, Uri, and Unterwald in the foothills of the Berner Oberlander Alps near Lucerne, central Switzerland. Sbrinz is named after the village of Brienz where there was a huge central produce market beginning in Renaissance times.

PRODUCERS: Thirty small local dairies.

PRODUCTION: Pressed and cooked with a washed, brushed, oiled rind. Aged at least 2 and up to 4 1/2 years. The whole cheeses are stored vertically, rather than horizontally.

APPEARANCE: Drums about 2 feet across and 6 1/2 inches high, weighing about 88 pounds. (There is also a 44-pound version.) The interior is more yellow or golden in color than Parmesan. Drops of oil (butterfat) seem to ooze endlessly out of the paste—and that's a good sign.

SIMILAR CHEESES: Grana Padano, Parmigiano-Reggiano.

(continued)

WINE PAIRINGS: As though it has nothing to prove, Sbrinz is one of the most versatile cheeses for pairing with wines; it melds especially well with Champagne.

WHITE: Chardonnay (Burgundy or California); Pouilly-Fumé (Sauvignon Blanc); German Riesling Kabinett.

RED: Barbera d'Alba; Cabernet Sauvignon-Merlot blend (Bordeaux or California); Nebbiolo-based wines (Barolo or Barbaresco).

SPARKLING: Champagne (Blanc de Noirs brut or vintage).

SELLES-SUR-CHER

(sell-soor-CHER) One of the Loire Valley chèvres that carry the banner worldwide for French soft-ripened goat cheeses. The Selles is a lovely little goat's milk item that makes for one of the finest opening acts to a cheese course, when it's in season and top form. At its best, a good Selles is as pleasing a goat's milk cheese as I've ever tasted. The primary differences between the Selles and other similarly flavored cheeses of the Loire are due to its smaller size: the higher rind-to-paste ratio yields a set cheese that is enjoyed a bit younger and therefore is more gentle and delicate. This said, a Selles should not be too wet. It should feel firm and full and should exude a faint goat smell.

TYPE: Goat's milk.

PROVENANCE: Loire Valley, central France.

PRODUCERS: At least twenty local farmhouses and a handful of dairies and co-ops. They are produced by Hardy and Jacquin, and the *fermier* producer Ferme de Bellevue and the *laitier* producers Coop. Agricole producteurs de fromage chèvre vallée du Cher and Fromagerie d'Anjouin.

PRODUCTION: A.O.C. protected. It takes about 1¼ liters, or a third of a gallon, to make each cheese. The curds are formed with slow coagulation and then drained for 24 hours. After demolding, they are covered with a mixture of ash and salt and placed in the drying room (*hâloir*) for at least 8 days at 54 to 59 degrees Fahrenheit and about 75 percent humidity.

APPEARANCE: Round, slightly truncated small drums 3 to 3½ inches in diameter (slightly larger at the base than at the top) and ¾ to 1 inch tall, weighing 5½ to 7 ounces, depending on their age. The rinds are bluish gray with a dusting of white mold; the paste is a lovely, pure bone white.

SIMILAR CHEESES: Pouligny-Saint-Pierre, Valençay.

WINE PAIRINGS: Selles-sur-Cher is a fitting partner for dry, crisp whites.
- **WHITE:** Albariño; Burgundy (Chardonnay); Sicilian Chardonnay; German Riesling Kabinett; Sauvignon Blanc–based wines (Pouilly-Fumé, Sancerre, white Bordeaux, or California).
- **RED:** Minervois (Syrah-Grenache blend from the Languedoc-Roussillon region of southernmost France).
- **DESSERT/FORTIFIED:** Sauternes (late-harvest Sémillon).

RATINGS

QUALITY

89

STRENGTH

I

SERENA, QUESO DE LA

(seh-REHN-ah, KEH-soh deh lah) This is one of Spain's wonderful "torta-style" cheeses, along with its nearby cousin Torta del Casar, and clearly among the world's greatest soft sheep's milk cheeses. (I like to think of these as the ultimate in "party cheeses" particularly because of the way they're served when ripe—by cutting off the top and scooping out the unctuous and irresistibly delicious paste. They're great for sharing with a group, and they're far better when fresh cut, so you need more than a few guests to finish one cheese.) At its peak, Serena is soft, spreadable, and ultimately liquefying. It is rich, buttery, and creamy in consistency with emphatic, fairly pungent flavors, featuring concentrated grassy notes and a sweet fruitiness — truly a superb and highly desirable delicacy. When I meditate on the greatness of sheep's milk cheeses, this is one of the first that comes to mind.

TYPE: Sheep's milk.

PROVENANCE: The community of La Serena and surrounding areas in the eastern part of the province of Badajoz, Extremadura, western Spain.

PRODUCERS: A favorite brand is Mitica El Porfiao, which also labels its tortas "Torta de Castuera" after the town of Castuera, where its factory is located.

PRODUCTION: Dairy-made, traditionally with raw milk, but there are also pasteurized versions from larger producers. Made from the milk of the esteemed merino sheep—a hardy breed, very much at home in the rugged conditions of the area, producing a relatively small amount of rich milk. The cheese is made twice daily and traditionally only during the grazing season, January through May, when the climate is moderate and quite rainy; nowadays, with staggered lactation, cheeses are available for a longer period than just spring and summer. The milk is coagulated with rennet from the *Cynara cardunculus* (cardoon thistle) plant, imparting subtle bitter and sour hints to the cheese. The cheeses are aged a minimum of 60 days. Serena has been D.O.P. protected since 1992.

APPEARANCE: Flattened cylinder or disk with rounded sides, somewhat irregularly shaped, about 6½ inches in diameter and 3 inches tall; weighing from about 1 kilo or just over 2 pounds up to 2 kilos or 4.4 pounds. The rind is rough, bumpy, dry, and beige to light orangish brown in color with some white, grayish green or blue molds. It may exhibit marks of the *pleita* or straw draining mold. The paste is satiny smooth and ivory colored; it turns more straw yellow with age. It is semisoft to soft with small irregularly spaced airholes.

RATINGS

QUALITY

91

STRENGTH

3

SIMILAR CHEESE: Torta del Casar, which is slightly more acidic and saltier. The Casar is smaller and has more of a kick. The Serena is the more mellow and manageable of the two.

SEASONAL NOTE: Available year-round; best April to November.

WINE PAIRINGS: Like many of the finer sheep's milk cheeses, the Serena is a very versatile wine partner, matching well with a wide variety of delicious wines; in general, it pairs best with fruity reds and sweeter, spicier whites.

WHITE: Albariño; Alsatian Gewurztraminer; German Riesling Kabinett; Savennières (Chenin Blanc).

RED: Cabernet Sauvignon–Merlot–Cabernet Franc blend (Bordeaux or California); Ribera del Duero (Tempranillo blend); Sangiovese (Chianti, Brunello di Montalcino, or California).

DESSERT/FORTIFIED: Late-harvest Pinot Gris; Tawny Port.

SERPA

(SEHR-pah) Serpa is an excellent mountain "*torta*-style" cheese from southeast Portugal; it is similar to Serra da Estrela (see page 242) and yet, although it's produced on a larger scale, it isn't as well known outside of its native land. There is no mistaking a Serpa for anything but a raw sheep's milk cheese if for no other reason than its characteristic sheepy aromas. Its flavors are complex and well integrated with pronounced sour and bitter notes and sweet, fruity undertones that, despite its eye-opening attack, allow it to remain balanced and elegant on the finish. A Serpa will ooze unctuously and threaten to break through its skin when ripe at room temperature. (Be sure to take it out of the fridge at the very least an hour before serving; when it's ready, carve a circular "lid" out of the top of its rind, remove the lid, and scoop out the creamy paste.) In comparison to the other Iberian soft-ripened vegetable-renneted sheep's milk cheeses, its flavor reminds me more of olive oil. Its finish is longer than any of those similar cheeses, with the exception of Torta del Casar.

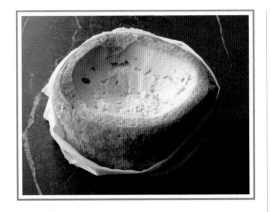

TYPE: Raw sheep's milk.

PROVENANCE: The left bank of the Guadiana River, southeastern Portugal, along the border with Spain.

PRODUCER(S): Made by farmhouse artisanal methods on big farms that own large flocks of merino sheep—up to 2,000 heads. Two good brands I've encountered come from Queijaria Artesanal Moinho de Almocreva, in the town of Beja, and Herdade da Quinta de Dom Luis, in Serpa.

PRODUCTION: Made with the milk of the merino breed of sheep. Thistle-derived rennet is added; the resulting curds are cut, molded, and hand-pressed. The cheeses are aged in cool, humid rooms for a minimum of 60 days.

APPEARANCE: A somewhat misshapen flattened drum 5$\frac{1}{2}$ to 6$\frac{1}{2}$ inches in diameter and 1$\frac{1}{2}$ to 2 inches high. (There is a fair amount of variation in size from brand to brand.) It has an orangish yellow undulating rind with cross-hatch patterns on top and bottom and dustings of white and occasional fuzzy, bluish gray mold. It comes with a cloth bandage or belt wrapped around its waist to hold its shape. The paste is semisoft, shiny, smooth, and elastic with some small to medium airholes; like all *torta*-style cheeses, it will melt deliciously at room temperature when ripe.

SIMILAR CHEESES: Azeitão, Serra da Estrela, Torta del Casar.

RATINGS

QUALITY

93

STRENGTH

3

SEASONAL NOTE: Best during spring and summer.

WINE PAIRINGS: Serpa marries well with dry whites and softer, fruitier reds.

WHITE: Bordeaux (Sauvignon Blanc); California Sauvignon Blanc.

RED: Chilean Merlot; Rhône red (Grenache–Syrah blend); Rioja (Tempranillo blend).

SPARKLING: Brut Champagne (Chardonnay–Pinot Noir blend).

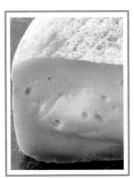

SERRA DA ESTRELA, QUEIJO

(SEHrah dah ess-TREH-lah, KAY-zho) The term *unctuous* might as well have been invented to describe Serra da Estrela, a quintessential handmade mountain cheese and the ultimate expression of Portuguese artisanal genius for the past 800 years or so. Serra's consistency is soft, and it offers a full, round, pleasantly oily flavor reminiscent of melted butter. When it is ripe and ready, it is deliciously intoxicating with salty, tangy, musty, delightfully "sheepy" flavors—pronounced yet never sharp or biting—and a lingering aftertaste. (You'll find this is true of many sheep cheeses; even at their most flavorful, they remain rounded and mellow, in part due to the richness and underlying sweetness of the ewe's milk.) Don't forget to take a whiff: between its flavors and aromas, Serra delivers a phenomenal one-two punch. In Portugal, they also eat Serra at a more mature stage where it has become firm and pungent.

SPECIAL SERVING NOTE: Like Spain's torta cheeses (Torta del Casar and La Serena), Serra is a "party cheese" because the best way to enjoy it is to let it come to room temperature, carefully slice off the top of the rind, snag a generous helping by dipping into the paste with your serving spoon or a chunk of crusty bread, then pass it around.

TYPE: Raw sheep's milk.

PROVENANCE: Serra da Estrela plateau, north-central Portugal near the Spanish border.

PRODUCERS: Traditionally were made by the shepherds' wives in stone cottages high on the plateau. Recommended farmhouse brands: Quinta Chão de Galizes and Casa Matias.

PRODUCTION: Made from the excellent milk of Bordaleira sheep that is coagulated with thistle extract, genuine Serra is strictly a handmade cheese as it has been for at least the past 800 years. D.O.P. protected. Each cheese takes an artisan about 3 hours to make; that's two, maybe three cheeses in a day. . . . Blessed are the cheesemakers!

APPEARANCE: Rounds about 10 inches in diameter and 3 inches high with a beige rind that can be tinged with a pinkish hue. The paste is smooth, thick, satiny, and off-white to light yellowish in color.

SIMILAR CHEESES: Azeitão, Queso de la Serena, Torta del Casar.

RATINGS

QUALITY

93

STRENGTH

3

SEASONAL NOTE: Best December through April, but available year-round.

WINE PAIRINGS: Serra da Estrela is a highly versatile wine partner; it works best with fruitier reds.

WHITE: Vouvray sec (Chenin Blanc).

RED: Barbera d'Alba; Beaujolais cru (Gamay); Cabernet Sauvignon blend (Bordeaux or California); California Pinot Noir; Rioja-style reds (Tempranillo blends); Australian Shiraz.

DESSERT/FORTIFIED: Vintage Port.

SHROPSHIRE BLUE

(SHRAHP-sher) In a phrase, Shropshire Blue is orange Stilton. The idea and inspiration for Shropshire Blue originally came from Dennis Biggins, a cheese wholesaler in Shropshire. (Shropshire, by the way, is the area south of Cheshire running along the Welsh border; two virtually identical cheeses, called Cheshire and Shropshire, have traditionally been made there.) Biggins contacted Ernie Wagstaff of the Colston Bassett Dairy, distinguished maker of Stilton, in the early 1980s with a suggestion for a Stilton tinted orange with annatto to be called Shropshire Blue. The new cheese was a success, and a number of other Stilton makers also began producing an orange-colored cheese. In comparison with Stilton, Shropshire Blue is closer textured, more fudgy and moist, warm flavored, less meaty, and slightly more tangy. It is very attractive as well as delicious. Fortunately, the pasteurization does not destroy its mineral content. Oh, that an unpasteurized version might be available today! A real show-stopper it would certainly be—as it must have been before 1980.

TYPE: Pasteurized cow's milk blue.

PROVENANCE: Nottinghamshire.

PRODUCERS: Richard Rowlett and Billy Kevan, Colston Bassett Dairy, makers of the standard-bearer of Stiltons.

PRODUCTION: Sold at about 3 months, slightly younger than Stilton.

APPEARANCE: Cylinders about 7 inches in diameter and 10 inches tall, weighing about 18 pounds. Very similar to Colston Bassett Stilton. Its internal blueing is more greenish than Stilton's. The yellow-orange color of the nonblued paste comes from the natural coloring agent annatto, which is derived from the seeds of *Bixa orellana*, a small tree native to South and Central America.

SIMILAR CHEESES: Colston Bassett Stilton, Cashel Blue.

SEASONAL NOTE: Available year-round.

WINE PAIRINGS: Shropshire Blue pairs best with sweeter and/or more full-bodied wines.
WHITE: California Chardonnay; northern Italian Chardonnay.
RED: California Cabernet Sauvignon.
DESSERT/FORTIFIED: Banyuls; LBV Port.

RATINGS

QUALITY

88

STRENGTH

3

SINGLE GLOUCESTER

(GLOSS-ter) Single Gloucester is a superb "anytime cheese," one of those types that can be enjoyed repeatedly and in many different circumstances—for breakfast, lunch, on an after-dinner cheese plate, at a picnic, as a quick snack. A fine example of British farmhouse artistry, it is the milder, lower-fat cousin of Double Gloucester. It has a firm paste that features a sublime, smooth, slightly crumbly texture and gentle, pleasantly tangy, smart, clean flavors with grassy undertones. It's very much like Gorwydd Caerphilly but more stable and less challenging.

TYPE: Cow's milk.

PROVENANCE: Vale of Gloucester, Gloucester-shire, west of London.

PRODUCER: Diana Smart, Old Ley Farm.

PRODUCTION: Farmhouse, artisanal. It is one of the few remaining traditional handmade skimmed milk cheeses (actually it's made from skimmed milk mixed with the previous day's whole milk). The curds are scalded, cut, salted, milled, and pressed; the cheeses are aged for 3 to 4 months. Mrs. Smart makes virtually no concessions to modern technology.

APPEARANCE: 7-pound millstones (known locally as "truckes") with a natural cream-colored rind that may develop some green mold. The paste is straw-colored, semihard, and somewhat crumbly with occasional fissures or holes.

SIMILAR CHEESE: Caerphilly.

WINE PAIRINGS: This is a cheese well suited for light-bodied, berry-flavored reds.
WHITE: Burgundy (Chardonnay); German Muskateller (dry).
RED: Pinot Noir (Burgundy, California, or Oregon); Madiran (tannic, traditionally rustic wine from southwestern France; made primarily from the Tannat grape); California Zinfandel.

RATINGS

QUALITY

89

STRENGTH

3

SOUMAINTRAIN

(soo-mahn-TREHN) There are actually two versions of this cheese: one, a bloomy-rind cheese similar to a double crème (at close to 45% fat in dry matter, it almost attains the minimum 50% fat content of that category) that bears some resemblance to a milder version of a genuine Camembert; the other, a washed-rind cheese, which is essentially a version of Époisses and made by Berthaut, a maker of Époisses. Nothing against the Berthaut version, but the former is more authentic and individualistic. (After all, an Époisses by any other name is . . . an Époisses, though I feel compelled to add that the pasteurized version is a little salty and dull.) At peak the bloomy-rind variety should feel supple, with a very soft, buttery interior. Its flavor is reminiscent of heavy cream with a delightful hint of the tang of high-quality fermented milk. It should not be too salty at all; it should offer a fresh, persistent aroma and lingering, pleasantly acidic finish.

TYPE: Cow's milk (both raw and pasteurized versions available).

PROVENANCE: Soumaintrain (province of Yonne), Burgundy, France, northwest of Dijon.

PRODUCERS: Farmhouse, creamery, and industrial versions are available. Berthaut; Fromagerie Leroux, and Laiterie de la Côte all make Soumaintrain.

PRODUCTION: The bloomy-rind version is made from a recipe similar to that of Camembert; it can be consumed when young as well as aged up to 2 months. The Époisses-style cheese is aged for 6 to 8 weeks in humid cellars with frequent washings in salt water.

APPEARANCE: The bloomy-rind version comes in a disk $5^{1}/_{2}$ inches in diameter and $1^{3}/_{4}$ inches tall, weighing between 12 and 20 ounces, with a bumpy, wavy, irregular rind that is orangish beige underneath and coated with a Camembert-like white mold. The paste, like a double or triple crème, is smooth, ivory colored, semisoft, rich, and creamy. A washed-rind Soumaintrain is like a small Époisses.

SIMILAR CHEESES: Brillat-Savarin, Coulommiers, Époisses, Langres, Munster.

SEASONAL NOTE: Best from end of spring through autumn.

WINE PAIRINGS: This cheese finds its best pairings with full, fruit-flavored whites.

 WHITE: Albariño; Burgundy (Chardonnay); Grüner Veltliner; Vouvray demi-sec (Chenin Blanc).

RATINGS

QUALITY

80

STRENGTH

2

SPENWOOD

I love this cheese! When I frequently intone the mantra, *"Sheep's milk makes the best cheese,"* it is Spenwood and a very few other cheeses of its ilk about which I'm rhapsodizing. Its maker, Anne Wigmore, is a true cheese whiz (as in technical wizard), and this glorious artifact of hers offers an incredibly satisfying depth of flavor. Its paste is firm, and, with age, it develops a dense, dryish flaky texture. It reveals a clean flavor that is deep, rich, caramelly, seductively sweet, nutty, and savory. How's that for complexity? In the spectrum of great sheep's milk cheeses, I rate Spenwood very high. Its flavors are mellower, rounder, and sweeter than an aged Tuscan Pecorino; it doesn't fall back on saltiness to uphold its character. Spenwood also compares favorably to its Spanish cousin, Zamorano.

TYPE: Raw sheep's milk.

PROVENANCE: Risely, near Reading in Buckinghamshire, west of London (named after the village of Spencers Wood in Berkshire).

PRODUCER: Anne and Andy Wigmore.

PRODUCTION: Pyrenees style; aged 6 to 7 months. Made from March to October; coagulated with vegetable rennet, like many sheep's milk cheeses.

APPEARANCE: Comes in 5-pound millstones. The natural rind is grayish beige to light brown with some gray and white powdery molds and a hint of *B. linens*. The paste is off-white to bone colored, firm and somewhat crumbly.

SIMILAR CHEESES: Pecorino Toscano, Vermont Shepherd, Zamorano.

WINE PAIRINGS: Like many fine sheep's milk cheeses, Spenwood seems to be compatible with many of the world's most beloved reds—Chianti, Rioja, and the Rhône wines in particular—and a few exceptional whites.
WHITE: German Gewürztraminer Spätlese; Tokay Pinot gris (Alsace); Vouvray demi-sec (Chenin Blanc).
RED: Bordeaux (Cabernet Sauvignon); Chianti Classico (Sangiovese); northern Rhône reds (Cornas, Gigondas, Côte-Rôtie, Hermitage, Saint-Joseph); Pinot Noir (California or Burgundy); Rioja-style Tempranillo blends.

RATINGS

QUALITY

99

STRENGTH

3

STANSER CHUA FLADÄ

(STAN-ser hoo-ah FLAH-dah) Stanser Fladä, a Vacherin-style washed-rind cheese from the heart of Switzerland, is smooth, creamy, and collapsing when ripe, in which case it begs to be spooned or scooped with a crusty piece of bread. (The *chua* part of the name, by the way, is somewhat optional and is Swiss German for "cow.") The Fladä's aroma is pronounced and barn-yardy but not arresting; its flavor is big and sweet, with hints of mountain grasses, but no excessive saltiness or sharpness. It is somewhat firm and very mild in its early days but becomes nearly soupy in texture and exquisitely complex and harmonic at peak. If well cared for, it can achieve a longer peak than other soft-ripened types; past its peak, it may overwhelm you with a near-putrid spoiled-milk flavor. (I believe this is primarily due to the excep-tionally high quality of the milk used.) Although it certainly has the appear-ance of an ancient, traditional cheese, in fact it was invented in the late 1990s by Josef Barmettler to fill the gap created by a temporary ban on Vacherin Mont d'Or.

TYPE: Raw cow's milk.

PROVENANCE: The small town of Stans, close to Lucerne, in central Switzerland.

PRODUCER: Josef Barmettler created and developed this cheese.

PRODUCTION: The milk comes from carefully selected small farms around and above Stans. It is an uncooked, unpressed cheese made to the same recipe as Vacherin Mont d'Or (with the exception of the spruce bark band encircling the Vacherin's wheel) and aged 4 weeks.

APPEARANCE: Small drums weighing about 10 ounces with a moist reddish brown rind and bumpy sur-face that may harbor some white mold. The paste is cream colored to light yellow; the cheese comes encased in a box to retain its shape when ripe.

SIMILAR CHEESES: Innerschweizer Weicher (aka Stanser Röteli), Vacherin Mont d'Or.

SEASONAL NOTE: Made year-round, but summer cheeses (available in fall) are best.

RATINGS

QUALITY

92

STRENGTH

3

WINE PAIRINGS: Stanser Fladä forms a strong part-nership with light-bodied, dry white wines.
 WHITE: Condrieu (Viognier); Alsatian Gewurz-traminer; Pouilly-Fumé (Sauvignon Blanc); Tokay Pinot Gris (Alsace); California Sauvignon Blanc; Vouvray sec and demi-sec (Chenin Blanc).
RED: Priorat (Garnacha-Cariñena blend); California Zinfandel.

STANSER RÖTELI

(AKA INNERSCHWEIZER WEICHER) (STAN-ser RO-teh-lee) A first encounter with the Röteli is, as my *fromagère* friend Michelle put it, like being downwind of a ripe-smelling cow barn on a hot summer day. It can be somewhat off-putting, but don't let that fool you: this is an approachable cheese with a restrained, balanced flavor profile that is delicious from its youngest stage to its oldest. If I had to characterize the Röteli in a phrase, it might be "Époisses in the extreme" or even "Reblochon on steroids"—it's essentially a bulked-up version of Swiss Reblochon. One of its dominant flavor components is real milk—imagine the closest thing to milk right out of a happy, healthy mountain-dwelling cow after it's rested in the milking pail for a while so the cream has begun to rise to the top; dip into that and down just a little deeper into the milk. (It was first introduced to me several years ago as Innerschweizer Weicher but the name was changed to Stanser Röteli —meaning "little red from Stans"—in part, I believe, to make it easier for us to pronounce.) Whether it's soft and runny or firmer and somewhat elastic, this cheese offers full milk that has undergone just enough breakdown (lipolysis and glycolisis) to be easily digested yet still retain its splendid seductive raw-milk flavors and textures. The pride of this cheese is in its restraint; it offers uncompromised satisfaction and persistent, insistent flavors without overwhelming the palate.

RATINGS

QUALITY

93

STRENGTH

3

TYPE: Raw cow's milk.

PROVENANCE: Stans, Canton Schwyz, central Switzerland.

PRODUCER: Josef Barmettler.

PRODUCTION: Stanser Röteli is a washed-rind, soft-ripened cow's milk cheese in the style of Reblochon made from the milk of local Simmental cows. The extreme high quality of the milk—and the lack of compromising treatments—renders the cheese especially delicious. The washings are not excessive so it doesn't develop the overly pungent character of similar types, and the rind remains thin. This seems to allow the cheese to develop gracefully with good air exchange. Soft-ripened raw-milk cheeses like this one often have a small window of ripeness; Stanser Röteli/Innerschweizer Weicher can be enjoyed at Stages 2 through 6 on a 7-point scale where 4 is peak ripeness.

APPEARANCE: A somewhat irregularly shaped flattened drum 5½ to 6½ inches in diameter and 1½ inches high, weighing nearly 20 ounces. It has a moist pinkish orangish, light

(continued)

brown to beige-colored bumpy rind with dustings of white mold and some pinkish spots as well. There is a characteristic ridge or indentation around the edge of the top and bottom faces of the cheese. The paste is smooth, shiny, and cream colored to light yellow with holes and fissures throughout.

SIMILAR CHEESES: Innerschweizer Schafkäse, Durrus, Reblochon, Stanser Fladä.

WINE PAIRINGS: Pairs well with a fairly wide and interesting range of (full-bodied) reds and (aromatic) whites, particularly those from Alsace.

WHITE: Condrieu (Viognier); Alsatian Gewurztraminer; Alsatian Pinot Blanc; Alsatian Riesling.

RED: Amarone della Valpolicella; Barbaresco (Nebbiolo); California Merlot.

SPARKLING: Moscato d'Asti.

STANSER SCHAFKÄSE

(STAN-ser SHAF-keh-seh) Here is an up-front, in-your-face mountain cheese of great character. For connoisseurs of sheep's milk cheese and anyone attracted to strong aromas and flavors, it is positively captivating. Stanser Schafkäse is of a type that combines three highly desirable elements of classic traditional cheeses from ancient times right up to the modern era—sheep's milk, washed-rind, medium-aged. It has a pedigree that, no matter whether it is to your liking or not, will make a strong and lasting impression on your senses. Stanser Schafkäses paste is smooth and compact with the consistency of firm butter. Its flavors are sheepish, grassy, and herbal and get progressively stronger from 2 months on. By 5 to 6 months, Stanser has developed a daunting aroma as well as provocative, persistent flavors—full, spicy, and pungent. At this point, it can be a challenge; its rounded, more mellow finish comes as something of a relief. Pairing wines with such a cheese might seem difficult; however, the cheese has a balance in and of itself. So although it can be uncompromising, its potential for synergies with high-quality wines is actually fairly broad.

TYPE: Raw sheep's milk.

PROVENANCE: Canton Schwyz, east-central Switzerland (the same area where they produce Hoch Ybrig, Stanser Fladä, and Innerschweizer Weicher).

PRODUCER: Joseph Barmettler (see also Stanser Fladä).

PRODUCTION: Stanser Schafkäse qualifies as simply a "mountain" cheese—not an *alpage* one (the more stringent and specific category), but it is nonetheless superb. Its curds are cut coarsely, uncooked and unpressed. The cheeses are aged a minimum of 2 months with regular washings and turnings. The milk comes from farms in the hills around the small town of Stans, and the sheep breed (Lacaune) is the same as that which produces Roquefort.

APPEARANCE: Small flattish cylinders or wheels, weighing 1 to 2 pounds, 2 to 3 inches tall, and 5 to 6 inches across. The rind is thin, moist, and light brown or beige. The paste is firm, glossy, and off-white to light yellow in color with an irregular distribution of small holes.

SIMILAR CHEESES: Flixer, Munster, Vacherin Fribourgeois.

RATINGS

QUALITY

93

STRENGTH

3

(continued)

SEASONAL NOTE: Available year-round as long as you don't mind the extra strength from the longer aging it will have received if bought in the spring.

WINE PAIRINGS: This cheese has good synergy with the more acidic reds, but it blends best with sweeter, crisper whites; it also shows an affinity with various vinifications of the Muscat grape.

WHITE: Pinot Blanc (Alsace or California); Alsatian Riesling; Sauvignon Blanc (from fairly dry to dessert-style).

RED: Beaujolais (Gamay).

SPARKLING: Champagne (Blanc de Noirs); Moscato d'Asti.

DESSERT/FORTIFIED: Sherry (Moscatel); late-harvest Muscat from the Languedoc.

STANSER SCHAF REBLOCHON

(AKA INNERSCHWEIZER SCHAFKÄSE) (STAN-ser shaf reh-blo-SHON) This delicacy gives yet more weight to the argument in favor of the supremacy of Swiss cheeses; I'd definitely call it a connoisseur's cheese. Its name invites comparisons to Reblochon and these are valid in the sense that it's an authentic mountain cheese, accentuating the high quality of real mountain-pasture milk, substantial and rich while offering delightfully fruity flavors. Yet these comparisons fall short since this is not only a sheep cheese but it's given more thorough washings to promote much fuller *B. linens* development. The daunting aroma of a Stanser Schaf Reblochon at peak ripeness belies its utterly delicious, full flavor. (If this were a pasteurized cheese with that kind of aroma, I'd stay away from it!) The paste is creamy and can become runny when really ripe; it offers rich, lush textures and a wide range of flavors, stimulating all the taste buds delightfully. Its initial impact on the palate is quite salty but it mellows out, with good balance, and lingers beautifully with pleasant grassy flavors for a charming and unusual finish. The Stanser Schaf Reblochon has a relatively small window of peak ripeness; too young and it can't give its all, too old and you'd probably rather skip it. At its best, though, it can be divine.

RATINGS

QUALITY

90

STRENGTH

4

TYPE: Raw sheep's milk.

PROVENANCE: Stans, Canton Schwyz, central Switzerland.

PRODUCER: Joseph Barmettler.

PRODUCTION: Traditional, artisanal. The milk is from several local herds of Laucaune sheep. The curds are cut coarsely and the fresh cheeses receive a salt bath, followed by about 8 weeks of maturing in a slightly humid cellar.

APPEARANCE: Somewhat unevenly shaped wheels about 4 to 6 inches in diameter and ³/4 to 1¹/2 inches high, weighing 14 to 17 ounces. The natural rind is thin, bumpy, somewhat uneven and can be sticky. It is sandy brown to reddish orange with white molds and the occasional gray streaks. The paste is bone white and glossy.

SIMILAR CHEESES: The Stanser Schaf Reblochon is essentially a sheep's milk version of the Stanser Röteli and, as such, is similar to

(continued)

the *torta* cheeses of the Spanish Extremadura (when ripe and well aged); Innerschweizer Weicher; Fladä.

SEASONAL NOTE: Produced between March and November.

WINE PAIRINGS: Pairs best with spicy, sweet wines.
🍷 **WHITE:** Alsatian Gewurztraminer; California Gewürztraminer.

🍷 **DESSERT/FORTIFIED:** Sauternes (late-harvest Sémillon).

STILTON

It would be hard to argue with the assertion that Stilton is Great Britain's number one cheese. For the past three centuries, it's been known as the "King of English cheeses" and more recently "The King of the Blues." And why not? Its style may not be as ancient as other traditional blues, but a good Stilton remains one of the most requested cheeses on the planet. It is one of the quartet of the world's most famous blues—along with Spain's Cabrales, France's Roquefort, and Italy's Gorgonzola—and the creamiest and most succulent among them. It is also the only cheese in Britain protected by legislation. Not surprisingly, Stilton's ripeness is judged by how creamy it is, not by the extent of its interior blueing. Its consistency is firm but moist and it offers a rich, minerally tang reflecting its *terroir*. Its texture is buttery and its flavor is mellow, fruity, deep, and syrupy. Stiltons are rarely oversalted, as is often the case with other blues. Its flavor is strong and full without being unpleasantly sharp or overpowering.

TYPE: Pasteurized cow's milk blue.

PROVENANCE: Central England (named after the market town in Leicestershire where it was originally sold).

PRODUCERS: Colston-Bassett & District Dairy, Nottinghamshire, is the best brand for my money. I can also recommend Cropwell-Bishop and Clawson.

PRODUCTION: Although Stilton makers are, ironically, forced by protective legislation to pasteurize the milk, Colston-Bassett retains a surprising richness and depth of flavor, due largely to the high quality of its fresh raw material, which is produced on five farms within about a two-mile radius of the dairy. Colston-Bassett is the only Stilton maker that ladles its curds by hand, which allows for less rennet in the recipe and ultimately its superior creaminess. The cheeses are matured for between 9 and 14 weeks.

APPEARANCE: Comes in a drum 8½ inches tall and 8½ inches in diameter, weighing approximately 17 pounds. (Smaller 5-pound drums or "mini-Stiltons" are produced for the holidays, but they don't offer the same depths of flavor or rich consistency as the full-sized ones.) The paste is cream colored and full of greenish blue veins, and the rind is moist and reddish brown with mold. You can see prick marks on the exterior where steel needles were inserted to help the mold spread.

SIMILAR CHEESES: Berkshire Blue, Fourme d'Ambert, Gorgonzola, Jersey Blue, Shropshire Blue.

RATINGS

QUALITY

95

STRENGTH

5

(continued)

255

SEASONAL NOTE: Stilton made from summer milk is considered superior; its paste is slightly yellower and it is best eaten in the fall and winter.

WINE PAIRINGS: Stilton is most appropriately paired with fortified red wines, especially Ports and Madeiras.

RED: Beaujolais cru (Gamay); California Zinfandel.

SPARKLING: Moscato d'Asti.

DESSERT/FORTIFIED: Jurançon (from southwestern France); Madeira; Tawny Port; vintage Port.

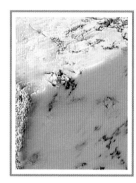

TALEGGIO

(tah-LED-joh) Although not as world famous as Parmesan, Taleggio is nearly on a par with that magnificent expression of Italian spoiled milk. Taleggio, too, was quite popular in Roman times as evidenced by references in the works of Cicero, Cato, and Pliny. Like Parmesan, it is substantial, nutritious, and—at its best—irresistibly delicious. A fine ripe Taleggio virtually shouts "Sour milk!" Paired with a hunk of crusty bread, it makes a perfect snack or picnic lunch. Until the end of the nineteenth century, all Taleggio was made in the Val Taleggio, a remote alpine area east of Milan and north of Bergamo (not far from another extremely famous gastronomic site, the source of San Pellegrino water). Commercial producers subsequently moved down to the plains of Lombardy where most of the cheeses are now aged, but the best milk production and the spirit of this wonderful cheese are still in the valley. Taleggio's paste is semisoft, creamy, and supple when fresh, generally becoming softer as it ripens. It has a sweet, mild, fruity, salty, slightly tangy taste that intensifies, becoming increasingly full-flavored, buttery, beefy, and pleasantly sour as it ages.

TYPE: Cow's milk washed rind.

PROVENANCE: Named after its place of origin, a valley north-northeast of Milan near Bergamo in Lombardy, northern Italy.

PRODUCERS: Appennino (made by Arrigoni Valtaleggio), Luigi Guffanti, Defendi, Caravaggio, and Cisera. Jean-Battista Arrigoni (see also Gorgonzola, page 146), a cousin of the producers of Valtaleggio Arrigoni, also makes an unusual and highly recommended Taleggio that is brine soaked (rather than dry salted) and aged 80 days.

PRODUCTION: Uncooked, lightly pressed, washed rind; ripens in about 40 days. Under ideal conditions, some Taleggio can mature for twice as long. D.O.C. protected as of 1988 and D.O.P. as of 1996.

APPEARANCE: A slab about 8 by 8 inches square and 2 to 2$\frac{1}{2}$ inches high, weighing 3$\frac{3}{4}$ to 4$\frac{3}{4}$ pounds, wrapped in paper. It has a rind that is pinkish orange to warm brown color and often mottled with gray and/or red-brown mold. (The industrial cheeses don't have mold; their rinds are clean, evenly colored, and spotless.) As it ripens, the cheese will flatten out, its surface will crack, and the paste will begin to ooze out at room temperature.

RATINGS

QUALITY

83

STRENGTH

3

SIMILAR CHEESES: Brescianella Stagionata, Durrus, Innerschweizer Weicher (aka Stanser Röteli), Reblochon, Robiola.

(continued)

WINE PAIRINGS: An easily paired cheese that goes well with a range of wines, including the regional (northern Italian) reds made from the Nebbiolo as well as the Barbera grapes.

WHITE: Sicilian Chardonnay; Alsatian Gewurztraminer; Pinot Grigio; Savennières (Chenin Blanc).

RED: Barbera d'Alba; Nebbiolo-based wines (Barolo or Barbaresco).

DESSERT/FORTIFIED: Malvasia delle Lipari (from Sicily); late-harvest Muscat-based wines (e.g., Muscat de Rivesaltes).

TARENTAISE

(tah-ron–TEHZ) An American version of the great French alpine cheeses Abondance and Beaufort. Tarentaise is an authentic, handcrafted farmstead cheese that reflects its classic Vermont dairy-country *terroir*. Tarentaise is comparable to the summer, high-mountain versions of Beaufort and the like, which are denser, softer, and richer in their aromas than the winter cheeses and/or commercially produced ones. Tarentaise is a dense, complex cheese, smooth and with a subtle nutty flavor that establishes a large, lingering presence on the palate without becoming obnoxious. I strongly recommend seeking out the more aged Tarentaises; they're worth waiting for.

TYPE: Raw cow's milk.

PROVENANCE: North Pomfret, Vermont.

PRODUCER: John and Janine Putnam, Thistle Hill Farm.

PRODUCTION: This is referred to as a Vermont alpine cheese and is handmade in the traditional style of Abondance and Beaufort, which hail from the Tarentaise Valley of the Savoie region of the French Alps. The curds are cooked, then pressed; the cheeses are brined, and the naturally formed rinds are washed during an aging period of 4 to 10 months. The Putnam family makes the cheese by hand using traditional methods with the certified organic milk of the farm's herd of grass-fed Jersey cows, carefully and lovingly cared for. The Putnams do not cut corners; they do not employ machinery or modern methods. They even went so far as to have a copper vat custom made for them in France.

APPEARANCE: Medium-sized wheels 14 inches in diameter and 4 inches high with concave sides. The rind is a warm butterscotch color with a dusting of white mold. The paste is smooth, dense, and ivory with occasional eyelets.

SIMILAR CHEESES: Abondance, Beaufort.

SEASONAL NOTE: The summer cheeses are pasture based.

WINE PAIRINGS: The Tarentaise is best suited for medium to full-bodied fruity red wines.

RED: Aglianico del Vulture (concentrated, complex, tannic, and fruity red of southern Italy); Madiran (tannic, traditionally rustic wine from southwestern France; made from the Tannat grape); California Merlot; Pinot Noir (California or Oregon); Australian Shiraz; Super Tuscan blend (Sangiovese and Merlot); various Syrah and Syrah-Grenache blends from southern France (northern Rhône or Languedoc); Periquita blend (Portuguese red with Tempranillo, Syrah, and Merlot).

RATINGS

QUALITY

88

STRENGTH

3

TAUPINIÈRE

(toh-peen-YEHR) A most agreeable goat cheese that at peak is milder and not as acidic or salty as some of its Loire Valley counterparts such as Selles-sur-Cher or Valençay. I like to call it "a kinder, gentler goat cheese" because of its approachable, even endearing qualities. At peak, it is entirely covered with blue-gray mold, which may be slow in coming but is worth the wait. If there ever was such as thing as a buttery-tasting, rich goat cheese, this is it; when perfectly ripened, it's a delightful variant of the classic chèvre package. Taupinière is made in the shape of a molehill, hence its name (*taupe* means mole in French). This dome shape helps promote a gradual ripening. At peak, Taupinière should give a little bit when poked or prodded. Note: Every other chèvre that comes to mind can be turned, upended, or rolled over to allow for uniform drying and moisture balance; because of its shape, the Taupinière can't. The dairy should release the cheeses with sufficient *affinage* so that, even if they rest on the same surface for a few more weeks, they don't develop what I call a "soggy bottom" (excess moisture). Check to see if a cheese has this condition and, if so, avoid that particular piece.

TYPE: Goat's milk.

PROVENANCE: The region of Angoulême in west-central France, north of Bordeaux and west of Limoges.

PRODUCER: Made at the farm of M. Jousseaume in Roullet.

PRODUCTION: Farmhouse, artisanal production in the style of traditional chèvres. Its natural rind is lightly dusted with wood ash to encourage the subtle ripening process.

APPEARANCE: A dome shape, 3½ inches in diameter at the base and 2¼ inches tall, weighing about 9½ ounces. The characteristic dome develops a bumpy surface to its rind with greenish bluish gray mold and some white fuzz. The paste is chalky white in the center, melting and off-white from the outside in.

SIMILAR CHEESES: Bonde de Gâtine, Selles-sur-Cher.

SEASONAL NOTE: Available year-round but is best from early spring to late fall.

WINE PAIRINGS: Taupinière pairs best with dry, crisp whites.

 WHITE: Beaujolais (Chardonnay); Burgundy (Chardonnay); southern French Sauvignon Blanc (Languedoc).

RED: Burgundy (Pinot Noir); Periquita blend (Portuguese red with Tempranillo, Syrah, and Merlot).

RATINGS

QUALITY

85

STRENGTH

1

TERRINCHO VELHO, QUEIJO

(teh-RINCH-oh VEL-yoh, KAY-zho) The Terrincho is a fairly assertive and most distinctive Queijo de Ovelha (Portuguese sheep's milk cheese) from a mountainous area in the far northeast of the country known as Tras-os-Montes or "behind the mountains." Its paste is hard, dry, and crumbly—like a well-aged Parmesan or Grana. The Terrincho is among the "endangered species" of Iberian cheeses: traditional, artisanal products that may or may not be able to survive in today's world of increasing industrialization and of the trend toward emigration from rural zones. Terrincho tastes toasty, salty, spicy, sharp, and assertively sheepy—as opposed to sheepish. Its flavor profile includes hints of cashew and Brazil nut, warm and a little leathery. Yet it retains the clean flavors of top-quality mountain milk. I recommend it for anyone who likes a cheese that packs some punch; it is one of those that reminds us a little bit of real cheese goes a long way.

TYPE: Raw sheep's milk.

PROVENANCE: The area surrounding the town of Vila Flor in the Terra Quente and upper Douro River Valley, northeastern Portugal.

PRODUCERS: Quinta da Veiguinha and other local artisanal, farmhouse dairies.

PRODUCTION: Made from the milk of the local version of the free-grazing Churra breed of sheep known as Churra de Terra Quente or "Terrincha" for short; traditional methods of animal husbandry are used, with no artificial insemination or staggered lactation. The cheeses are aged for a minimum of 90 days. Terrincho has D.O.P. status.

APPEARANCE: A flattened drum with a bright reddish orange rind. Two bands of straw are tied around its middle like a ribbon; there is also a wheat sheaf tied into the ribbon of straw.

SIMILAR CHEESE: Nisa.

SEASONAL NOTE: Best summer through winter.

WINE PAIRINGS: Blends well with fruity, softer young red wines and crisp, light, dry whites. **WHITE**: Chilean Sauvignon Blanc.

RED: Beaujolais (Gamay); California Cabernet Sauvignon.

RATINGS

QUALITY

78

STRENGTH

4

TESSINER GEISSKÄSE

(teh-see-ner GUYS-keh-seh) Brilliant, though it can be challenging in its own way. Due to the vicissitudes of local, specialized production, the colors, textures, and of course flavors of this *alpage* cheese can vary quite a lot. It is made in different alps (small, isolated alpine communities of just a few farmhouses—and sometimes only one) in Canton Ticino, in the area of the St. Gotthard Tunnel, known locally as "the tunnel to the rest of Switzerland." Ticino is sometimes called "the sunny patio of Switzerland" due to its relatively warm climate. The cheeses available in spring are milder and younger with a semifirm paste; later in the season, into the fall, they become firmer and more robust with further aging. Younger or older, this is a cheese for goat's milk cheese lovers only. The traditional alpine cheesemaking methods applied here extract the most flavor possible from the milk. As it ages, Tessiner's flavors evolve from creamy, fresh, and milky to full, deep, and barnyardy. I recommend trying it on the young side at first and then, as you build up an appreciation of what it has to offer, try a more aged example. But note that while cow's milk cheeses can mature beautifully for 1 to 3 years (and sometimes significantly more), most goat's and sheep's milk ones begin to fade after about 6 months.

TYPE: Raw goat's milk.

PROVENANCE: The alps around the St. Gotthard (Gottardo) Tunnel in the northern part of the Canton Ticino, central southern Switzerland.

PRODUCERS: Various artisanal alpine cheesemakers in the area.

PRODUCTION: Cheeses are made daily from spring through the end of summer. The curds are cooked over wood fires and then lightly pressed to form the wheels of cheese. The fresh cheeses are washed with brine and turned regularly during an *affinage* of at least 2 months. Cheeses made earlier in the season are consumed on the alps. Those made in the last 2 to 3 months of summer—that is August, September, and into October, are brought back down to the valleys for further aging—up to 6 months. They are the most intense and highly regarded of this type.

APPEARANCE: A small wheel 6¼ inches in diameter and 2 inches high with a brownish beige, rough rind with white mold dustings and small holes or perforations in the surface. The paste is off-white and hard with an irregular distribution of small airholes.

RATINGS

QUALITY

81

STRENGTH

3

SIMILAR CHEESES: Chevrotin des Aravis, Mont St. Francis.

SEASONAL NOTE: Spring cheeses are mild and semifirm; late summer ones are packed with more intense, rewarding flavors, and they age beautifully.

WINE PAIRINGS: Look to pair the Tessiner with crisp, light-bodied whites or a fine Sauternes-style dessert wine.

WHITE: Grüner Veltliner; Riesling (Alsatian or German Kabinett); Tokay Pinot Gris (Alsace); Vouvray demi-sec (Chenin Blanc).

DESSERT/FORTIFIED: Sauternes (late-harvest Sémillon).

TÉTOUN DE SANTA AGATA

(teh-TOON duh san-tah AH-gah-tah) A goat's milk cheese from Provence, where such cheeses are made in small sizes and thus are ready for consumption after a very short ripening phase. The Tétoun's defining characteristic—aside from its rather suggestive shape—is the peppercorn placed at the pinnacle of its cone, which imparts a slight peppery flavor to the paste during its brief maturation period. The cheese is just big enough so the peppercorn's influence is noticeable without detracting from the fresh, creamy flavor of the high-quality milk. Its size is also ideal in that it can ripen enough prior to release from the dairy to deliver satisfying taste while avoiding the notorious "soggy bottom" (a phenomenon whereby the moisture in a cheese settles to its base and renders the texture in that part muddled). The Tétoun is less goaty and also less tangy than most other better-known French chèvres. What mold these young cheeses do pick up may add a little tartness to enhance their clean goat's milk flavors.

TYPE: Raw goat's milk.

PROVENANCE: The plateau of Valensole in Haute-Provence, southeastern France.

PRODUCER: Capitelles, a small farmhouse-style creamery in Valensole (other similar, slightly smaller cheeses are made by other local artisans under the name "Tétoun").

PRODUCTION: Artisanal. The curds are formed by lactic coagulation, and the cheeses are shaped by hand then aged for about 10 days.

APPEARANCE: A small cone or pear shape, about 2½ inches tall and 2½ inches in diameter at the base, weighing about 4½ ounces, topped with a single peppercorn. The rind is off-white to cream colored, and it can acquire some blue-gray mold with age; the interior remains chalky white.

SIMILAR CHEESES: Picodon de la Drôme, Truffe de Valensole.

SEASONAL NOTE: Best from spring through fall.

WINE PAIRINGS: Recommended with light, floral whites and fruity, younger reds.
🍷 **WHITE**: Vouvray demi-sec (Chenin Blanc).

🍷 **RED**: Barbera d'Asti.

RATINGS

QUALITY

81

STRENGTH

THOMASVILLE TOMME

Here is a fine American farmstead cow's milk *tomme* from Georgia that offers a semifirm texture, mellow flavor, and very attractive melt-in-your-mouth characteristics. It features a slightly dryish yet buttery mouthfeel. The Thomasville Tomme has an even flavor that is satisfying and delicious.

TYPE: Raw cow's milk.

PROVENANCE: Thomasville, southwestern Georgia, USA.

PRODUCER: Sweet Grass Dairy (cheesemakers Jeremy Little and Desiree Wehner).

PRODUCTION: The milk is collected from the nearby Green Hill dairy farm, which rotationally grazes its cows. The curds are cut and pressed, then placed in molds when they are still quite soft, which yields a smooth, creamy cheese. The cheeses are aged in a humidity-controlled room for at least 2 months.

APPEARANCE: Comes in wheels about 10½ inches in diameter and 3½ inches high weighing approximately 10 pounds with a concave ridge around the outside edge and a somewhat rustic appearance. The natural rind is beige to light brown while the paste ranges from straw or golden in color to a mustardlike yellow-orange, depending on the season. The paste is semihard and firm yet moist with some holes and fissures.

SIMILAR CHEESE: Orb Weaver.

SEASONAL NOTE: Produced from February through December; some variations in flavor and appearance occur due to seasonal changes in the cows' grazing and feed.

WINE PAIRINGS: Thomasville Tomme sides with medium- to full-bodied red wines.
RED: Bordeaux (Cabernet Sauvignon blend); Burgundy (Pinot Noir).

RATINGS

QUALITY

78

STRENGTH

2

TICKLEMORE

This is a much milder cheese today than it was a few years back, before the milk was pasteurized. While I might have once said its tantalizing dryish texture was guaranteed to titillate your tastebuds, now I'd say it's more of a tease than a tickle. It's a difficult task for the cheesemaker to create a successful goat's milk cheese in this format, but Ticklemore has certainly succeeded. The draining and drying must be strictly monitored; otherwise, the cheese can end up a bit of a sloppy mess and/or develop some unflattering molds and bacteria. The consistency is firm but moist and pleasantly creamy; the taste is light, fresh, and clean, with a little bit of a tang. The overall flavor impression is fairly mild but with a long, satisfying finish. With age, it develops a slightly crumbly texture that nevertheless melts in your mouth.

TYPE: Pasteurized goat's milk.

PROVENANCE: South Devon, southwestern England.

PRODUCER: Robin Congdon (the cheese is named after Robin and his partner Sarie Cooper's store, the Ticklemore Cheese Shop, Ticklemore Street, Totnes).

PRODUCTION: The milk comes from a herd of about 200 goats kept 10 miles from the cheesemaking operation on the edge of Dartmoor. It is produced specifically for Ticklemore and collected by the cheesemakers six days a week. It is pasteurized and cooled down, then culture and rennet are added. When set, the curd is cut and then stirred for about 30 minutes. The whey is then run off, the curd is scooped out, mixed with salt, and hand-pressed into colanders. Cheeses are then turned (and turned twice more that day), once the next day, salted again the next, and put in the maturing room 2 days later. They are rubbed down and turned weekly and are usually sold at about 6 weeks old.

APPEARANCE: Shaped like a flattened sphere or basket with slight ridges from the draining colander. The cheeses weigh about 1¹/₂ kilos (3¹/₃ pounds) and are about 8 inches in diameter and 3 inches tall. The natural rind is dusted with mold, sometimes predominately white, sometimes gray and powdery. The paste is white, somewhat flaky, and open-textured.

SIMILAR CHEESE: (Queso de la) Garrotxa.

SEASONAL NOTE: The winter cheeses are very creamy in texture; the summer ones are drier and flakier.

WINE PAIRINGS: We find it best matches with medium-bodied, aromatic whites.
WHITE: Albariño; Italian Chardonnay; German Riesling Kabinett; California Semillon; Tokay Pinot Gris (Alsace); California Viognier.
RED: Amarone della Valpolicella; California Cabernet Sauvignon.

RATINGS

QUALITY

77

STRENGTH

TOMME DE SAVOIE

(TUM duh sah-VWAH) Tomme de Savoie is not a specific brand or place-name but rather a more general regional appellation. In fact, there may be as many as 100 or more cheeses throughout France that fall under the term *tomme;* the common thread is that they are small to medium-sized traditional alpine-style cheeses. The ones from the Savoie are among my favorites. Each valley of the Savoie—Bonneval, Val-d'Isère, Faucigny, Thônes, and so forth—has its own variations and flavors, mostly reflecting *terroir.* A genuine Tomme de Savoie features a semihard consistency that melts in your mouth when ripe, and mild, delightfully nutty flavors, in contrast to its typically funky, barnyardy, musty aromas.

TYPE: Raw cow's milk.

PROVENANCE: The mountainous Haute-Savoie region of France, on the Swiss border, south of Lake Geneva.

PRODUCERS: *Tommes* are made at many local farms and dairies, large and small, artisanal and industrial. There are variations from place to place throughout the area, some even made with goat's milk. There are also imitators from outside the region, some of which are imported for aging; they can use the name—at least until the pending A.O.C. is confirmed. Be sure to choose the ones with labels indicating they are both *fabriqués* (manufactured) and *affinés* (ripened) in Savoie. Among my favorites is the one purveyed by Denis Provent. Other *laitier* producers and/or *affineurs* of genuine raw-milk Tommes de Savoie are: Coopérative Laitière de Yonne; Lactalis; Société coopérative laitiere Ayn-Dullin; Fromagerie Chabert; Fromagerie Missillier; Fromagerie Joseph Paccard; Fromagerie Pochat & Fils; SCA Les producteurs de reblochons de Thônes; and Verdannet SA.

PRODUCTION: Genuine *tommes* are handmade with great attention and care. They are generally pressed and uncooked. Many traditional ones are made with skimmed milk and therefore have relatively low percentages of fat in dry matter—between 20 and 40 percent, as opposed to 40 to 45 percent for other similar cheeses, and greater than 50 percent for the richer double-crème cheeses. They are aged for about 2 months in cellars with regular turnings, brushings, and rubbings to encourage development of beneficial surface molds.

APPEARANCE: Somewhat irregularly shaped flattened cylinders, approximately 8 inches across and 2 to 5 inches tall, weighing 4 from 7 pounds. There are also some *tommes* that come in oversized 12-pound disks. Their rinds are hard, crusty, and cratered, gray to light brown or beige in color with frequent splotches of white, yellow, and red molds and

RATINGS

QUALITY

82

STRENGTH

3

(continued)

occasional holes. Their pastes are straw to light yellow in color, darkening somewhat with age, and have many irregularly spaced small holes.

SIMILAR CHEESES: Saint-Nectaire, Wildmannli.

WINE PAIRINGS: Tommes de Savoie pair well with soft-bodied, younger reds and fruity whites.

WHITE: Alsatian Riesling.

RED: Beaujolais (Gamay); Burgundy (Pinot Noir); California Cabernet Sauvignon; Rioja (Tempranillo blend).

SPARKLING: Moscato d'Asti.

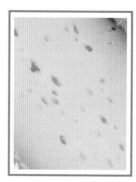

TORTA DEL CASAR

(TOR-tah del kah-SAR) One of Spain's two great "party cheeses" (see also Queso de la Serena, page 238) and among my candidates for one of the greatest cheeses in the world. "Torta" is the local designation for a cheese that undergoes thorough proteolysis and liquefies at its peak of ripeness, the shape collapsing under its own weight and the paste oozing out onto the plate. Torta is considered a deluxe cheese in Spain, relatively expensive, and much of its production is exported. It has a thick, soft, creamy, oily paste, maturing to a gooey consistency and offering provocative, rich, sour, nutty flavors with floral notes. It's generally eaten by cutting off the top and spooning delectable dollops onto a crusty piece of lightly toasted bread. For me, the Torta's flavor is a little more provocative and interesting than the more buttery Queso de la Serena. The milk of the *churra* ewes provides more complexity and a bigger flavor profile in the Tortas as opposed to the Serenas, which are made by more industrial methods. Interestingly, this makes the Tortas less versatile in wine pairings than the Serena.

TYPE: Raw sheep's milk.

PROVENANCE: From the area around the town of Casar de Caceres (just north of the capital of the region, Caceres) in the Extremadura, western Spain.

PRODUCER: The Andrade family dairy is a favorite. Producers include Quesero del Casar, S.L., Rafael Pajuelo Bautista, Queseria José Alvarez Rhocha, and Queseria San Diego, S.L.

PRODUCTION: Similar to that of its cousin, La Serena. Torta del Casar is labor intensive to produce. The local *churra* ewes each produce about half a liter of milk per day, and it takes 6 liters to make one cheese. Their milk has more protein, less fat, and less acid than the milk used for a Queso de la Serena. Its coagulation is slower, which results in a softer curd mass; Casar is also slightly saltier than La Serena. Like Serena, the Casar is coagulated with cardoon thistle extract, which adds a pleasantly bitter hint to the taste. Peak production season is at the end of winter and the beginning of spring; it is aged for 60 days and then quickly reaches peak ripeness. D.O.P. protected.

RATINGS

QUALITY

93

STRENGTH

3

APPEARANCE: Comes in flattened cylinders with rounded edges, about 2¼ inches tall and 6 inches in diameter, and weighing about 2 pounds. The rind is dark yellow or straw colored with reddish shadings, somewhat loose, and undulating; when the cheese is ripe at room temperature, the rind often detaches from the paste and cracks open. The paste is yellowish white and compact with occasional pea-sized fermentation holes.

SIMILAR CHEESE: Queso de la Serena (see comparisons above).

(continued)

SEASONAL NOTE: Spring to early winter.

WINE PAIRINGS: Like many of the world's finest sheep's milk cheeses, not only is this one superb in its own right but it pairs well with an impressive range of wines, from full-bodied and complex reds such as Bordeaux, northern and southern Rhône wines, and Rioja to a dessert wine such as Sauternes and a sophisticated, relatively light-bodied white such as Savènierres.

WHITE: Albariño; Savènnieres (Chenin Blanc).

RED: Beaujolais cru (Gamay); Burgundy (Pinot Noir); Cabernet Sauvignon-Merlot blends (Bordeaux or California); California Cabernet Sauvignon; Chianti Classico (Sangiovese); Rhône Valley (Syrah blend).

TRADE LAKE CEDAR

Mary and David Falk operate their LoveTree Farmstead in the woodsy wilds of northern Wisconsin. The property is surrounded by eight small lakes, after which its cheeses, including Trade Lake Cedar, are named and from which they derive much of their individual character. The Falks' cheeses aim to capture the indigenous flavors and aromas of their environment; when I approach this cheese, the first thing that comes to mind is a whiff of northern Wisconsin. Now that's *terroir*! The cheese is firm, robust, and aromatic with a silky smooth texture and offers grassy, fruity, spicy, and nutty flavors with a pleasant woodsy undertone.

TYPE: Raw sheep's milk.

ORIGIN AND MAKER: Grantsburg, northern Wisconsin, USA.

PRODUCERS: Mary and David Falk, LoveTree Farmstead.

PRODUCTION: A natural-rind cheese aged for a minimum of 2 months on cedar boughs in the farm's fresh-air aging caves that overlook the shores of one of its five-acre ponds.

APPEARANCE: Trade Lake Cedar comes in millstones weighing approximately 8 pounds and has a decidedly rustic appearance. The rind, which features a small cedar bough on top, is light brown to beige, mottled, and displays a basket-weave pattern. The paste is dense and a light yellowish ivory color when young (60 days), darkening to a light caramel color as it ages up to 4 months and developing a semihard, crumbly texture and irregular small fissures and holes.

SIMILAR CHEESE: Berkswell.

WINE PAIRINGS: Blends well with sparkling wines and the primary varietals that go into their vinification: Pinot Noir and Chardonnay.
WHITE: California Chardonnay.

RED: Burgundy (Pinot Noir); California Syrah; California Zinfandel.
SPARKLING: Champagne (Blanc de Noirs).

RATINGS

QUALITY

80

STRENGTH

4

TRIPLE CRÈMES

(triple KREM) This is a category of French cheeses that are—in a word—luxurious, mostly because they are made by adding more cream to the already-rich milk. The best triple crèmes are soft and moist with a rich, buttery, mild flavor—imagine a perfectly blended mixture of butter and cream cheese. Their textures are rich and creamy, very smooth and pliant; their flavors are, to summarize, salt and butter, presented in an irresistibly subtle and extremely accessible format. The triple crèmes and their double crème cousins are all given somewhat fanciful or evocative brand names; it's simply part of the tradition of this family of cheeses, a quaint sort of "marketing handle" that helps the producer-dairies distinguish them from each other. My current favorite of the group is Brillat-Savarin; I also enjoy Pierre-Robert.

TYPE: Cow's milk.

PROVENANCE: The Seine-et-Marne *département* of Île-de-France, the province surrounding Paris.

PRODUCTION: Made with the addition of extra cream to achieve the required 75 percent fat content (most are made with pasteurized milk, some with raw milk). Triple crèmes are gently introduced into their draining molds, lightly pressed, and then carefully aged for about 3 weeks with the help of some unobtrusive white, velvety surface molds.

WINE PAIRINGS: The rich pastes of the triple-crème cheeses dissolve easily into fruitier white wines; they also luxuriate in the bubbles of Champagne and melt into the complexity of a classified-growth Bordeaux.

WHITE: Chardonnay (Burgundy or California); Condrieu (Viognier); Alsatian Gewurztraminer; Alsatian Riesling; German Riesling Kabinett or Spätlese; Tokay Pinot Gris (Alsace).

RED: Beaujolais cru (Gamay); Bordeaux (Cabernet Sauvignon).

SPARKLING: Champagne (Blanc de Blancs or Blanc de Noirs).

BRILLAT-SAVARIN

(bree-YAH sah-vah-RAN) This is the original triple crème. It actually originated in Normandy in an area to the south of Rouen but is now produced in the Île-de-France. It was named after Jean Anthelme Brillat-Savarin, the great *gastronome* of the late eighteenth and early nineteenth centuries, by the cheese merchant Henri Androuët in the 1930s. Brillat-Savarin comes in a small drum or wheel up to 5 inches in diameter and $1^1/_2$ inches tall, weighing approximately 1 pound. Made by Fromagerie Fermière de Juchy; also the Societé Fromagère de la Brie and Rouzaire's Fromagerie de Pre-Fôret, both artisanal dairies.

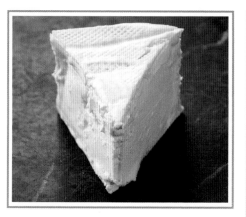

RATINGS

QUALITY

81

STRENGTH

1

EXPLORATEUR

(ex-ploh-rah-TER) Devised in the early 1960s and named in honor of the French explorer Bertrand Flornoy, a cheese lover. It has a picture of a Sputnik-type rocket ship on the label. Comes in small drums about $3^1/_4$ inches in diameter and $2^1/_2$ inches high, weighing about 9 ounces. Made by the Fromagerie du Petit Morin.

RATINGS

QUALITY

72

STRENGTH

1

PIERRE-ROBERT

(pee-YEHR roh-BEHR) One of my favorites of this genre; the Pierre-Roberts I've tasted have been outstanding (but the Brillat-Savarins have been "outstandinger"). I like to ripen it to the point where its rind turns brownish in color and its paste becomes so meltingly soft that it virtually collapses when you cut it. It comes in a miniature drum about 5 inches in diameter, 2 inches high, and weighing about 1 pound, with a Brie-like rind—white, bloomy, and slightly moldy—and a cream- to light-straw-colored paste. The rind can become fairly thick, hard, and crusty with age. Made by Fromagerie Rouzaire.

SIMILAR CHEESES: The double crème cheeses are very similar but have less fat in dry matter (60 to 75 percent fat content rather than the 75 percent of a triple crème). Rouzaire also makes the triple crèmes Aviateur, Jean Grogne, and Grand Mogol as well as Bries and Coulommiers, which are all related bloomy-rind cow's milk cheeses of the Île-de-France region. Societé Fromagère de la Brie, another prominent dairy in the region, also makes several triple crèmes: Bayard Gourmand, Jean de Brie, and Vignelait. Gratte-Paille is a worthy double-crème cousin of Pierre-Robert made by Fromagerie Rouzaire; it comes in squarish brick shapes 3½ to 4 inches long and 2½ inches high weighing up to 12 ounces. Other recommended triple and double crèmes are Brique Fleurie, Fontainbleau, Saint-Clair, and Saint-André.

RATINGS

QUALITY

79

STRENGTH

1

TRUFFE DE VALENSOLE

(troof duh vah-lohn-SOHL) This little artisanal chèvre comes from the northern part of Provence, in the region of Valensole, and is shaped like a black truffle—hence its name. With its gray matted rind, it may appear to be a fiercer, more challenging cheese than it is. Cut into it, however, and try its very white (and preferably still moist) interior; no doubt you'll conclude that there are few cheeses more gentle and agreeable. I think of it as the Ugly Duckling—fairly scary looking, even forbidding, on the outside but surprisingly beautiful and innocent on the inside. A Truffe can ripen to the point where it becomes more tart for those who prefer it that way. When properly stored—at high relative humidity (about 75%), a cool temperature (42° to 50°F), and good ventilation—uncut Truffes will keep beautifully up to 2$\frac{1}{2}$ months. They should be firm but moist in texture with just a little give when lightly prodded. The flavor is fresh, creamy, gentle, and mildly goaty.

TYPE: Raw goat's milk.

PROVENANCE: The plateau of Valensole in Haute-Provence, southeastern France.

PRODUCERS: Capitelles, a small farmhouse-style creamery in Valensole, as well as other local farmhouses.

PRODUCTION: Artisanal. The curds are formed by lactic coagulation. This is a handmade cheese in the most literal sense: its curds are molded in the hollow of the hands. During its short ripening period of 2 weeks, it receives a light dusting of ash to help promote beneficial mold growth.

APPEARANCE: A small dome shape up to 2$\frac{1}{2}$ inches in diameter and weighing 3$\frac{1}{2}$ to 4$\frac{1}{2}$ ounces. To me, it looks like a scale model of the moon with a slightly flattened bottom, a dark gray rind, and a dusting of white mold. The paste is white and slightly grainy.

SIMILAR CHEESES: Selles-sur-Cher, Tétoun de Santa Agata.

SEASONAL NOTE: Best in spring but available through the fall.

WINE PAIRINGS: This lovely little cheese is a good partner for softer reds and light-bodied whites.
WHITE: Vouvray demi-sec (Chenin Blanc).

RED: Beaujolais (Gamay); Periquita blend (Portuguese red with Tempranillo, Syrah, and Merlot).

RATINGS

QUALITY

| 81 |

STRENGTH

1

TUMALO TOMME

(TOO-muh-loh TUM) Pierre Kolisch has been making this mountain-style cheese from the milk from his herd of sixty to seventy goats since 1987. The paste is firm but creamy and smooth with a semihard texture and hints of hay and salt in the flavor. To create a goat's milk cheese in this format—where the paste remains firm and the flavor graceful—is a challenge for any cheesemaker, one that is rarely answered so well.

TYPE: Raw goat's milk.

PROVENANCE: Redmond, central Oregon, USA.

PRODUCER: Pierre Kolisch, Juniper Grove Farm.

PRODUCTION: The cheeses are aged on pine planks in a cave-type cellar for 3 to 6 months. They are hand washed with brine to encourage development of their natural rind.

APPEARANCE: Wheels 8 inches in diameter and 2 inches tall, weighing 4 pounds. The natural, coarse-textured rind is orangish beige with a dusting of white mold. The paste is ivory colored with quite a few irregularly shaped holes.

SIMILAR CHEESES: Capricious, Hilltown Wheel, Redmondo (by the same maker).

SEASONAL NOTE: Summer cheeses are fruitier and more flowery; winter cheeses are heavier and richer due to the changes in butterfat content of the goat's milk.

WINE PAIRINGS: Its most successful pairings are with light-bodied whites.
WHITE: South African Chenin Blanc; Alsatian Pinot Blanc; Vouvray demi-sec (Chenin Blanc).
RED: Beaujolais (Gamay); California Merlot; California Zinfandel.

SPARKLING: Champagne (Blanc de Blancs).

DESSERT/FORTIFIED: Tawny Port.

RATINGS

QUALITY

84

STRENGTH

2

URNER ALPKÄSE

(OOR-ner ALP-kay-seh) This chameleon of a cheese appears gentle when young and attractive when aged, yet is full of surprises at each stage. At 3 months, it has a semifirm texture that becomes firmer and drier with time. At peak, it develops an almost flaky texture and its paste begins to turn golden in color. The flavors are very reminiscent of the alpine meadows from which the milk comes—so much so you could almost imagine you'd been eating all those beautiful, lush flowers and grasses yourself.

TYPE: Raw cow's milk.

PROVENANCE: Three alpine meadows (Urnerboden, Surenen, and Oberalp) near the Klausen Pass, central eastern Switzerland.

PRODUCERS: Kurt Bauman in Urnerboden; a communal dairy supplied by five farmers in Surenen; and Gery Zurfluh in Oberalp.

PRODUCTION: Alpine, artisanal. The milk comes from local herds of Red and Simmental cows. The curds are cooked and pressed; the cheeses are salted and drained, then aged for at least 3 months and up to 6 or more in cool, slightly humid cellars.

APPEARANCE: Wheels 10 to 12 inches in diameter and about 3 inches high, weighing between 10 and 12 pounds. The rind is hard, dry, and compact, reddish light brown in color with some dustings of white mold developing over time. The paste is ivory colored and semifirm when young; it turns light yellow and eventually golden with age and develops small to medium-size holes.

SIMILAR CHEESES: Alp Drackloch, Sbrinz.

SEASONAL NOTE: Produced between June and the end of September; the best wheels are the ones made in July and August and aged at least 6 months.

WINE PAIRINGS: Champagne and dessert wines are the most successful partners for this cheese.
WHITE: Alsatian Pinot Blanc.

RED: Burgundy (Pinot Noir); Chianti Classico (Sangiovese).
SPARKLING: Champagne (Chardonnay-Pinot Noir-Pinot Meunier blend).
DESSERT/FORTIFIED: Montbazillac (Sauternes-style late-harvest Sémillon blend from west of Bordeaux); Tawny Port.

RATINGS

QUALITY

90

STRENGTH

4

VACHERIN FRIBOURGEOIS

(vash-RAN free-boor-ZHWAH) This is the original banquet cheese—mentioned in the earliest records of fondues. Now, probably 1,000 years after its invention, it is made by only a handful of local artisanal cheesemakers. This cheese is a taste of history, so get it while you can. Today's cheesemakers have a difficult time justifying the effort that goes into making a genuine Vacherin Fribourgeois and thus it has become a precious, rare, and endangered species. It is the key ingredient in Swiss fondue, lending it its silky smooth consistency and keeping the mix from turning gummy. A genuine Vacherin Fribourgeois should be very profound in its aromas and flavors—strong yet not overpowering from start to finish with full-milk character. As gnarly as the rind may appear, with its look of a muddy rhinoceros hide, the interior should remain smooth and creamy. It's a firm cheese featuring pronounced aromas and a persistent mild sourish flavor. Its lingering finish should be reminiscent of fresh, whole, uncompromised cow's milk—for those of us who've been fortunate enough to taste it.

TYPE: Cow's milk.

PROVENANCE: The mecca of this cheese is the region between the towns of Bulle (Canton Vaud) and Fribourg (Canton Fribourg) in west-central Switzerland; it is also made in other parts of western Switzerland, right up to the Jura Mountains on the border with France.

PRODUCERS: Small, old-fashioned, artisanal dairies. One of the best versions is ripened by Rolf Beeler and comes from the producers of the Vacherin Fribourgeois Co-op in Bulle.

PRODUCTION: A pressed, uncooked, washed rind that is cured 3 to 4 months. Firm, but it is relatively soft compared with other typical Swiss cheeses such as Gruyère. It is made by a painstaking ancient method, with repeated washings and turnings. Comes from the milk of the Fribourgeois breed of cows, which is the local name for Holsteins.

APPEARANCE: Comes in comparatively small wheels, about 16 inches in diameter and 3 inches thick, weighing approximately 15 pounds. It has a thick brown, undulating, wavy, rough rind—unlike almost any other cheese—with an underlying cross-hatch pattern and tinges of yellow, gray, or pink; its paste is light yellow and smooth, often with eyeholes and some slits.

RATINGS

QUALITY

95

STRENGTH

4

SIMILAR CHEESES: Fontina d'Aosta; also Morbier, which is better known but has less individualistic character.

WINE PAIRINGS: Although it's a full-flavored cheese, Vacherin Fribourgeois pairs best with red Bordeaux and other bold, full-bodied red wines.

WHITE: German Muskateller Kabinett; Alsatian Riesling.

RED: Amarone della Valpolicella; Barbaresco (Nebbiolo); Bordeaux (Cabernet Sauvignon blend); California Merlot; Syrah (Shiraz) blends (California, Australia, or Rhône Valley).

SPARKLING: Moscato d'Asti.

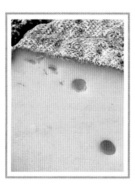

VACHERIN DU HAUT-DOUBS

(OR VACHERIN MONT D'OR) (vash-RAN do oh-DOOB) This cheese originated with *fruitières* (small rustic dairies) in the Jura Mountains of eastern France at least 500 years ago. In the time of Louis XV, it became widely popular throughout the land and from then on was shipped in wooden boxes to protect its shape. (Mont d'Or is a more specific subcategory protected under the larger Vacherin du Haut-Doubs A.O.C.) Vacherins have a characteristic satiny smooth texture, healthy shine, and subtle flavor. They are, in a word, unctuous. At peak, they melt to a gooey, slightly runny consistency and are often eaten with a spoon. They feature very creamy, moist paste with small holes. The best ones have a baconlike spicy flavor underlying their characteristic milkiness; they should also strike a delightful balance between saltiness and creaminess. For a soft-ripened cheese, the Vacherin Mont d'Ors, at their peak, can offer a big, full flavor. Even though it would be inappropriate to call a fully ripened Mont d'Or unclean, its flavors can have an outdoorsy, barnyardy character. Fans of these cheeses—or anyone with an "initiated" cheese palate—will taste the fullness of vegetation on which the cows graze as well as the influence of the band of spruce bark that holds the cheese together.

TYPE: Raw cow's milk (pasteurized for the "faux" versions).

PROVENANCE: The Doubs *département* of the mountainous Franche-Comté Province of France, near the Mont d'Or Massif, bordering on Burgundy to the west and Switzerland to the east.

PRODUCERS: Recommended producers of authentic Vacherin Mont d'Or A.O.C.: Coopérative des Jarrons; Ets Rivoire & Jacquemin; Fromagerie Badoz; Fromagerie Claude Philippe; Fromagerie de Frasne; Fromagerie du Haut Doubs; Fromagerie des Monts de Joux; Fromageries Georges Grillot SA; Fromagerie Seignemartin; Juraflore-Société Arnaud Frères; Société coopérative agricole de Fromagerie.

PRODUCTION: Traditionally made from the raw milk of the local Montbéliard or Pierouge de l'Est breeds of cows. A.O.C. protected as of 1981. Vacherins are traditionally encircled in bands of spruce bark, which help hold the cheeses together and also give them a subtle woodsy flavor and aroma. They are brine washed and aged for at least 3 weeks.

RATINGS

QUALITY

90

STRENGTH

3

APPEARANCE: Vacherins come in various sizes of flattened cylinders or small wheels, from 8 to 12 inches in diameter and 1 to 2 inches thick, weighing from 3½ to 8 pounds. A Vacherin Mont d'Or weighs from 1 to 2¼ pounds; it is 7½ to 8 inches in diameter and 1½ to 2 inches high, featuring a slightly rough, somewhat undulating rind that is light yellowish brown to pinkish or reddish gold with marks of the cheesecloth still visible on its surface. The paste is off-white to ivory and satiny smooth.

SIMILAR CHEESES: Vacherin d'Abondance, whose curds are cooked to a higher temperature giving it a firmer, more dense paste by comparison; also, L'Edel de Cleron, Krümmenswiler Försterkäse, Vacherin Haut-Rive, and Stanser Fladä.

SEASONAL NOTE: For Mont d'Or, the cheesemaking season is lare-August to mid-March; therefore, its purchasing window is October through March, and it is best consumed in the winter, though still available into early March.

WINE PAIRINGS: Vacherin Mont d'Or works well with Champagne, spicy whites, and also softer, young reds.
- **WHITE**: Alsatian Gewurztraminer; Vouvray demi-sec (Chenin Blanc).
- **RED**: Bordeaux (Cabernet Sauvignon blend); Chianti Classico (Sangiovese); California Merlot; Super Tuscan (Sangiovese-Merlot blend); southern French Syrah (Languedoc).
- **SPARKLING**: Champagne (Blanc de Blancs).

VAL BAGNER

(val BAHN-yer) In Switzerland and France, they melt this type of cheese to make *raclette*. I recommend you skip that step and just try the Val Bagner on its own. It's a magnificent firm cheese, very meaty and beefy, with a full, lactic, authentic mountain pasture flavor. It will turn harder with age, eventually becoming almost crunchy in texture and developing deliciously deep flavors. The descendants of Val Bagner—the melting cow's milk cheeses—are all very nice. But it is a special experience to savor an original-style well-aged example that is now made only by a handful of artisans in the Canton Valais in southwest Switzerland. Not to be missed, and certainly not to be melted over potatoes!

TYPE: Raw cow's milk.

PROVENANCE: From the famous ski town of Verbier in the Valais region of southwestern Switzerland.

PRODUCERS: Raclette cheeses are traditionally produced in four different valleys in the Canton Valais. The best ones are acknowledged to come from the Bagne Valley (Val Bagner) around Verbiers. Among the benchmark cheeses is the one ripened by Rolf Beeler and made by Dairy No. 98.

PRODUCTION: Apart from its *terroir*, the other key to this cheese's excellence is that it's made from the milk of two breeds: the Fribourgeois (which also produce the milk for Vacherin) and the Ehringer, an old German breed of large, sparse milk producers. Val Bagner is an uncooked, washed-rind mountain cheese that is aged for 5 to 6 months and can be eaten up to a year.

APPEARANCE: Flat wheels about 12 inches in diameter and 2 to 3 inches high, weighing about 12 pounds. They have hard, dry, light brown rinds with a possible dusting of white mold. The paste is yellowish with some small holes.

SIMILAR CHEESES: Fontina D'Aosta, Raclette Combes, young Vacherin Fribourgeois.

WINE PAIRINGS: Val Bagner marries best with wines made from the Nebbiolo or Riesling grapes.
WHITE: Burgundy (Chardonnay); Alsatian Riesling.

RED: Bandol (Mourvèdre blend from Provence); Barbaresco (Nebbiolo); Burgundy (Pinot Noir).

SPARKLING: Champagne (Blanc de Noirs); Moscato d'Asti.

RATINGS

QUALITY

91

STRENGTH

4

VALDEÓN

(vahl-day-OHN) Valdeón is a fairly powerful blue cheese, saltier than Stilton but not harsh or taxing, and always one of my favorites. The paste is semifirm and it delivers a powerful and complex ensemble of flavors with a consistent, reliable underlying sweetness. The complexity is multiplied by the inclusion of goat's milk, which seems to be more the rule than the exception of late. We're fortunate here in the United States to be able to obtain a mixed-milk, leaf-covered delicacy such as this, one that has been around for a very long time in northern Spain. There are other cheeses from that region made according to similar recipes, but Valdeón is the clear winner.

TYPE: Pasteurized cow's milk blue (may include goat's milk).

PROVENANCE: The remote valley of Valdeón, northwestern section of the province of Leon, at the beginning of the Picos de Europa Mountains.

PRODUCERS: Local dairies.

PRODUCTION: Aged a minimum of 2 months and up to 4 in caves. It is made according to virtually the same recipe as Cabrales, but with a few key differences. First, the ripening caves in this area are slightly less humid than those in the Cabrales zone, allowing for a somewhat less pronounced mold development in the cheeses. Second, traditional Valdeón is still available wrapped in *plageru* (sycamore) leaves, which allow certain bacteria to penetrate the cheese and add complexity. For this reason, I like to refer to Valdeón as "illegal Cabrales." (Cabrales was once leaf wrapped, but EEC import-export regulations now direct that it must be wrapped in plastic and/or foil.) Traditional Valdeón is also made with small amounts of goat's and sheep's milk.

APPEARANCE: Cylinders weighing roughly 4$\frac{1}{2}$ to 6$\frac{1}{2}$ pounds with a light gray natural rind. Some of them are leaf wrapped. The paste is creamy off-white with many holes and striations of grayish green mold.

SIMILAR CHEESES: Cabrales, Gamonedo, Picón, Picon-Beyes Tresviso.

WINE PAIRINGS: Valdeón favors wines made from the Gamay grape as well as various vinifications of Muscat.

WHITE: German Riesling Kabinett.

RED: Beaujolais cru (Gamay); Periquita blend (Portuguese red with Tempranillo, Syrah, and Merlot).

DESSERT/FORTIFIED: Late-harvest California Chardonnay; Dulce de Monastrell (from Jumilla, southeastern Spain); Muscat de Rivesaltes (from the Languedoc); Sauternes (late-harvest Sémillon).

RATINGS

QUALITY

92

STRENGTH

6

VALENÇAY

(vah-lohn-SAY) Like many other French cheeses, this one is said to have received the nod of approval from the Emperor Napoleon. He visited the statesman Talleyrand at his Château de Valençay, where they sampled this local delicacy. Legend has it the cheese was originally made in the shape of a four-sided pyramid. The top of the pyramid was chopped off—some say by the emperor himself—in deference to the Imperial Army's travails in Egypt. Valençay is a classic mold-ripened chèvre: smooth, creamy, and rich in texture, with a somewhat dense mouthfeel, and mild in flavor. Like other chèvres, I find it somewhat variable from one "vintage" to the next. When made according to the most exacting standards and given proper *affinage* and care, however, it can be especially lovely. Look for Valençays that are blanketed with surface mold in shades of gray, blue, green, and purple; their edges should be fairly straight, and they should have a little bit of give to the touch. Close to the rind, it should display some moisture and a slight ooze.

TYPE: Goat's milk.

PROVENANCE: The village of Valençay and surrounding areas in the Berry and Touraine regions of the Loire Valley.

PRODUCERS: Made by at least twenty local farmhouses as well as several co-ops and dairies. The best farmhouse examples are ripened and sold by the *affineurs* Jacquin and Hardy. Other recommended producers: the *fermier* EARL Les Piverts; the *laitiers* Co-op. Agricole producteurs de fromage chèvre vallée du Cher; Fromagerie d'Anjouin; and Laiterie Segre Fromagers de traditions—Triballat.

PRODUCTION: Ripened for a minimum of 8 days and usually up to 4 weeks in humid, well-ventilated cellars. It should be made from uncompromised milk and given just a dusting of lightly salted ash.

APPEARANCE: Truncated pyramids about 3 inches square at their base, 3 inches high, and weighing about 9 ounces. They have a dusting of charcoal ash on their surface, which attracts various shades of whitish and bluish gray molds. The paste is bright white.

SIMILAR CHEESES: Sainte-Maure de Touraine, Selles-sur-Cher, Pouligny-Saint-Pierre.

SEASONAL NOTE: May through November.

WINE PAIRINGS: Valençay marries well with light-bodied, dry whites.
 WHITE: Albariño; Grüner Veltliner; Alsatian Riesling; Sauvignon Blanc (Sancerre, Bordeaux, or California); Savennières (Chenin Blanc); Tokay Pinot Gris (Alsace).
 SPARKLING: California Champagne-style (Chardonnay).

RATINGS

QUALITY

91

STRENGTH

1

VERMONT SHEPHERD

The Vermont Shepherd, one of my favorites since I first tasted it, is rustic, uncomplicated, elegantly simple, hearty, and incredibly delicious. It has a smooth, creamy paste that is simultaneously soft and dense. It is aromatic and herbaceous, pleasingly full-flavored, and profound, but not overwhelming, revealing subtle layers of complexity with sweet, rich, earthy, nutty tones and hints of clover, wild mint, and thyme as they melt in your mouth. When I began pairing it with wines, my appreciation and respect for this top American artisanal cheese increased; not only is it delicious on its own, but it's a versatile partner for many completely different wine types, an admirable trait in any cheese.

TYPE: Raw ewe's milk.

PROVENANCE: Putney, southern Vermont, USA.

PRODUCERS: Cynthia and David Major, Major Farm.

PRODUCTION: Made in the style of the French Pyrenees. Aged 4 to 8 months. The Majors operate their own cave, which is built into the side of a small hill at their farm.

APPEARANCE: Drums weighing 5½ to 10 pounds with bulging sides—a kind of flying-saucer shape—that have golden brown brushed rinds and a smooth ivory-colored paste.

SIMILAR CHEESES: Berkswell, Ossau-Iraty Brebis, Spenwood.

SEASONAL NOTE: The Majors do not employ artificial insemination so the cheese is only available 7 to 8 eight months a year, September till April or May.

WINE PAIRINGS: Vermont Shepherd is wonderful with many wine types—reds, whites, sparkling, and dessert—but the cheese is particularly successful with the fruitier ones.

WHITE: Chardonnay (Burgundy or California); Riesling (Alsatian or German Kabinett).

RED: Beaujolais cru (Gamay); Chianti Classico (Sangiovese); Pinot Noir (Burgundy, California, or Oregon); Syrah blends (Rhône Valley or California); California Zinfandel.

SPARKLING: Champagne (Blanc de Noirs).

DESSERT/FORTIFIED: Vintage Port.

RATINGS

QUALITY

98

STRENGTH

3

WABASH CANNONBALL

Master cheesemaker Judy Schad, a shining light of the cheese world, named this one after the famous train and eponymous song of southern Indiana. She also recalled a visit to France where similar small ball-shaped cheeses are called *boulets*, which translates to "cannonball." Wabash Cannonball features a semisoft paste with a gentle, creamy, slightly acidic flavor. Its rind, originally a fluffy, mushroomy covering of *P. candidum* mold, which gave the cheese a snowball-like appearance, has been altered to a more wrinkly surface of *G. candidum* which has a musky, slightly sweet and more delicate flavor. This is a relatively minor adjustment—it doesn't affect the paste much—but nevertheless an improvement.

TYPE: Pasteurized goat's milk.

PROVENANCE: Greenville, Indiana, USA.

PRODUCER: Judy Schad, Capriole, Inc.

PRODUCTION: Made from the milk of the farm's own goat herd in the style of chèvre. Aged 10 days to 3 weeks.

APPEARANCE: 3-ounce balls with bluish gray, somewhat wrinkly rinds covered in bloomy white mold; the paste is smooth, white, and chalky.

SIMILAR CHEESES: Crottin de Chavignol, Humboldt Fog, Truffe de Valensole.

WINE PAIRINGS: The Cannonball mixes well with light-bodied, dry whites.
WHITE: Bordeaux (Sauvignon Blanc); Grüner Veltliner; California Sauvignon Blanc.
RED: California Zinfandel.

SPARKLING: Champagne (Blanc de Noirs).

RATINGS

QUALITY

76

STRENGTH

1

WENSLEYDALE

Wensleydale used to be made by farmhouse artisans in and around the dales of northern Yorkshire throughout the nineteenth century. Manufactured from May to October when the cows enjoyed their summer pastures, it was somewhat moister than today's version. Modern Wensleydale comes from a relatively large dairy, but thankfully it is still a traditional cheese, reliably cared for and ripened at Neal's Yard Dairy. In 1992, Dairy Crest, which began as the commercial arm of the Milk Marketing Board and is now among the United Kingdom's largest milk processors, announced plans to close the Wensleydale Creamery in Hawes. Local opposition saved it, however, and the workforce has actually expanded. The cheese is a hugely satisfying one, comparable at times to Caerphilly. Hawes Wensleydale is close textured and fairly dry; the flavor is gently mellow with grassy, herbal, and lactic components.

TYPE: Pasteurized cow's milk.

PROVENANCE: Hawes, rural Yorkshire (in the Dales), northern England.

PRODUCER: Wensleydale Creamery.

PRODUCTION: The milk is bought from surrounding farms and the cheese made by traditional methods, including the cloth binding. The Neal's Yard cheeses are made at lower acidity (the key factor) and then matured at warmer temperatures than the rest of the creamery's production, allowing them to develop an extra dimension of flavor.

APPEARANCE: Clothbound upright cylinders weighing about 11 pounds each.

SIMILAR CHEESES: Gorwydd Caerphilly, Single Gloucester.

WINE PAIRINGS: Wensleydale is recommended with a variety of whites but also with medium-bodied fruity reds.
WHITE: Burgundy (Chardonnay); Alsatian Gewurztraminer; Grüner Veltliner; Alsatian Riesling; Vouvray demi-sec (Chenin Blanc).
RED: Pinot Noir (California, Oregon, or Sancerre); northern Rhône Syrah.
SPARKLING: Moscato d'Asti.

RATINGS

QUALITY

79

STRENGTH

2

WILDMANNLI

(vild-MAHN-lee) Wildmannli is like a ramped-up, more substantial version of the classic Tomme de Savoie cheeses from the French Alps. Like the *tommes*, a Wildmannli is firm and moist but has more of the wonderful mushroomy flavors. It is also beautifully balanced, buttery, sweet, gently acidic, and ever-so-slightly salty with a finish that proves surprisingly complex. Its texture is somewhat toothsome though yielding. In a word, it is smooth, smooth, smooth. A cheese of somewhat reserved character, Wildmannli might risk being ignored in comparison to some of its louder compatriots. That isn't such as bad thing, though, because the second, third, or fourth time you try it, you'll always recall why you loved it so much to begin with. Wildmannli is one of those cheeses that requires a little bit of effort—you've got to chew it—but the pleasures it affords when it settles across the tongue are exquisite.

TYPE: Raw cow's milk.

PROVENANCE: The village of Krümmenswil in the flatlands of Canton Thurgau, northern Switzerland.

PRODUCER: Diriwaechter & Schmid, a dairy known for its innovative yet traditional cheesemaking (they also make Krümmenswiler Försterkäse).

PRODUCTION: Made from the milk of local Simmental cows. The curds are cooked and lightly pressed. The cheeses are aged between 2 and 3 months; they develop gray and blue molds on the rind that affect their texture and flavor like few other cheeses. The cheeses are brushed roughly to help spread the mold—if it doesn't happen on its own.

APPEARANCE: A disk or flattened drum 6 inches in diameter and 1½ inches high. It has a grayish blue and brown rind with some white mold. The paste is elastic, somewhat moist but firm; its color turns from light yellow when younger to deep golden with age.

SIMILAR CHEESES: Single Gloucester, Tomme de Savoie.

SEASONAL NOTE: Although it's produced year-round, the summer wheels are clearly the best.

WINE PAIRINGS: Wildmannli is a fine partner for full-bodied whites as well as the fruitier reds.
WHITE: Chardonnay (Burgundy or California); Alsatian Riesling; Tokay Pinot Gris (Alsace).
RED: Beaujolais cru (Gamay); Madiran (tannic, traditionally rustic wine from southwestern France, made primarily from the Tannat grape); California Pinot Noir; Rioja (Tempranillo blend).
SPARKLING: Brut Champagne (Chardonnay-Pinot Noir blend).

RATINGS
QUALITY
94
STRENGTH

3

WINCHESTER AGED GOUDA

Cheesemaker Valerie Thomas's dad, Jules Wesselink, was born and raised in Haarlem, Holland, but he's owned and operated dairies in California since the 1950s. The Winchester Cheese Company has 500 Holstein cows to provide milk for its cheeses. The aged Gouda is based on the classic Dutch Boeren Kaas or farmhouse-style cheese, and it offers a stimulating and complex array of flavors, featuring the caramelized, nutty tones so alluring in its European forebears. With proper aging, its texture is initially similar to Parmesan but it has a stronger, mustier basis; it is stout, crumbly, and fairly sharp in flavor.

TYPE: Raw cow's milk.

PROVENANCE: Winchester, California.

PRODUCERS: Valerie and David Thomas, Winchester Cheese Company.

PRODUCTION: Traditional methods that have been practiced by the family for generations in Holland. In America, they no longer use wooden vats and utensils but rather stainless steel ones; otherwise, the basic cheesemaking process is unchanged. Boeren Kaas Sharp Aged Gouda is aged a minimum of 6 months. The Super Aged Gouda is aged over a year.

APPEARANCE: 10- to 12-pound wheels with a yellowish waxy exterior and a straw- to light caramel-colored interior whose texture is hard, dry, crumbly, and flaking in the manner of a long-aged Parmesan or Gouda.

SIMILAR CHEESES: Coolea, Doddington, Aged Gouda (Goudse Boerenkaas, which is Dutch aged farmhouse Gouda), Parmesan.

WINE PAIRINGS: Winchester pairs better with darker, raisiny red wines.
🍷 **RED:** Amarone della Valpolicella; Rhône Valley Syrah; Australian Shiraz; California Zinfandel.
🍷 **DESSERT/FORTIFIED:** Muscat de Beaumes-de-Venise (from the Côtes du Rhône area).

RATINGS

QUALITY

74

STRENGTH

4

ZAMORANO

(sah-moh-RAHN-oh) This is a noble, ancient, and majestic cheese, a true Spanish regional treasure, reflecting centuries of tradition: the migrating herds and their shepherds on the Castilian plateau, as well as the itinerant artisanal cheesemakers who offered their services to the ranchers and shepherds. In the mid–twentieth century, this ancient system was transformed into a more modern cheese industry, but D.O.P. laws ensure that many of the artisanal standards still apply. A good Zamorano has the same dignified bearing as Beaufort or Parmesan; it often reminds tasters of a sheep's milk version of those wonderful hard cow cheeses. The paste is very firm, yet creamy in taste and consistency with a full, round, nutty flavor and hints of tartness and saltiness. With age, it can turn lumpy, flaky, and crystalline like a genuine aged Parmesan. In the more mature cheeses, it also typically develops a subtle bite that gradually suffuses the palate and makes way for a persistent, lingering aftertaste. Zamorano has the underlying sweetness of a classic sheep's milk cheese and a balance of lactic acidity with buttery milkfats. Proud Zamorano is a cheese that can be placed in any number of places in a progression, from relatively mild to relatively strong. How many other cheeses hold that distinction? Zamorano offers many attractive qualities, including balance, digestibility, keeping potential, and versatility. The milk of the Churra and Castilian breeds of sheep is resplendent.

RATINGS

QUALITY

90

STRENGTH

3

TYPE: Raw sheep's milk.

PROVENANCE: The province of Zamora, northwestern Spain, near the northeastern corner of Portugal.

PRODUCERS: Fourteen small to medium-sized producers.

PRODUCTION: Similar to that of Manchego, but the local breeds of sheep—the Churra and the Castilian, both bred for excellent milk production—have a higher fat content in their milk, giving the cheese an added heft and richness. Pressed, uncooked, and aged a minimum of 100 days in cool caves, which were also used traditionally for barrel aging of wines. Peak production is from late winter to late summer.

APPEARANCE: Comes in drums weighing from about 1 to 4 kilos (2.2 to 8.8 pounds). Its hardened natural rind has the distinctive cross-hatch or zigzag pattern of the molds made from mats of the *esparto* grass that are used to form and drain the cheese. It also has a wheat-ear pattern on top and bottom from the presses. The rind is cleaned and oil rubbed, and it develops a light dusting of mold and a dark beige or slightly ruddy brown exterior with age. The paste is straw colored and dense but open textured, with many very small eyeholes spread throughout.

SIMILAR CHEESES: Berkswell; also comparable but more interesting than its more famous cousin Manchego (see also Roncal).

SEASONAL NOTE: Made from the end of winter to the end of summer.

WINE PAIRINGS: Zamorano finds its best matches in berry-flavored, medium-bodied reds.

WHITE: Albariño; German Riesling Kabinett.

RED: Periquita (soft, low-tannin, light-bodied Portuguese red); Pinot Noir (Burgundy or Oregon); Beaujolais cru (Gamay); Ribera del Duero (Tempranillo blend); Syrah blends (Rhône Valley and other regions of southern France); California Zinfandel.

ACKNOWLEDGMENTS

In addition to the cheesemakers themselves, there are many individuals who have contributed to the production of this book. I want to especially thank the cheese teams at Picholine, Artisanal Brasserie, and Fromagerie, and the Artisanal Cheese Center. The thousands of customers of these three operations who have helped determine the selection of fine cheeses over the past decade must also be recognized. There are countless other cheese people who have helped me with this book. I want to mention the following by name, with apologies to anyone who's been inadvertently left out: Lonnie Allen, Tony Amira, Serena Ball, Hank Balle, Job Bass, Bruce Beck, Gilles Berger, Richard Betts, Ric Bing, Jane Black, Roger Black, Greg Blais, Delphine Boutier, Terrance Brennan, Holly Briwa, Bob Broderick, Kelly Brown, Friedrich Bubner, Jock Busser, Vitali Bynda, Enric Canut, Alex Carvajal, Michael Casey, Jeffrey Churchill, Tom and Nancy Clark, Kevin Clarke, Myra Clement, Jessica Coffin, Kelly Coleman, Connie Collins, Sue Conley, Diane Connell, Heather Cook, Matthew Cortellesi, Denis Cottin, Mike Cohen, Chris Cox, Todd Crowley, Jeff Ben David, Sasha Davies, Gerry Dawes, Carl and Linda Del Negro, Debra Dickerson, Tony Di li Coli, Donna Doel, Jason Donnelley, Brian Driscoll, Danny Ettinger, Mary and David Falk, Lyn Farmer, Maggy Feldman, Arlene Feltman, Jay Fletcher, Nancy Fletcher, Nathan Fleury, Art Fortuna, Thomas Fryer, Ross Gagnon, Karen Galayda, Franck Galzy, Alex Garcia, Lorraine Garcia, Brian Gaskey, Dave Giambalvo, Mike and Carol Gingrich, Chantal Girerd, Aisling Glynn, Jackie Gordon, David Gremmels, Taylor Griffin, Wendy Hallgren, Diana Halton, James Hanley, Andrew Harwood, Linsey Herman, Eric Hipp, Judith Hoffman, Craig Hopson, Caroline and Daniel Hostettler, Gerald Hylla, Jessica Jaffe, Sarah Jennings, Tom and Kristi Johnson, Catherine Jones, Akiko Katayama, David Katz, Mateo Kehler, Chad Kennedy, Peter Kindel, Kelly Kingman, Pierre Kolisch, Allison Lakin, Paula Lambert, Victoria Langley, Martha Lersky, Rachelle Login, Waldemar Albrecht

Luna, Charles Mahal, David and Cynthia Major, Charles Maki, Michelle Masiello, Olivier Masmondet, Jason Miller, Jennifer Minnick, Roberto Molina, David Morrow, Marvin and Susan Numeroff, Arlene Oconitrillo, Steve Olsen, Carole Palmer, Manuel Panameno, Amanda Patterson, Mariano Sanz Pech, Jose Plaséncia, Chantal Plasse, Georgette Pogaceanu, David Pogrebin, Sarah Powers, Michael Preis, Nick Prescher, John and Janine Putnam, Hanitra Rasondiherisoa, Dick Rogers, Shirley Rosas, Lee Salas, Judy Schad, Lucy Schaeffer, Tobias Schreiber, Johanna Shipman, Richard Shipman, Shari Siegel, Andrew Sikorski, Caroline Smialek, Sarah Stern, Bernard Sun, Mark Sutherland, Terri Taffer, Dana Tanyeri, Kevin Taylor, Charlotte Thompson, Denis Toner, Lee Valentino, Xavier Villasosa, Suzanne Wade, Christopher Wainhouse, Christina Wang, Lee and JoAnn Weisel, Jennifer Weiser, Rick Weissman, Josh Wesson, Elizabeth Woessner, and Ellen Yin.

—Max McCalman

Thanks to Max and Angela for affording me the challenge and opportunity to write two good cheese books; to all the cheesemakers for their willingness and generosity; to Michelle, Ross, Daphne, and all of Terrance's staff at the ACC for putting up with my presence and our photo shoots; to Chris for all his perspicacity and backing; to Adina, Marysarah, and their Clarkson Potter colleagues for making the books happen and ensuring they look great; to my kids, Marley and Will, for humoring me; and to Serena for her love and support.

—David Gibbons

INDEX

CHEESES BY COUNTRY